Appropriating English

new literacies

AND DIGITAL EPISTEMOLOGIES

Colin Lankshear, Michele Knobel,
Chris Bigum, and Michael Peters
General Editors

Vol. 8

PETER LANG
New York • Washington, D.C./Baltimore • Bern
Frankfurt am Main • Berlin • Brussels • Vienna • Oxford

Michael Singh, Peter Kell,
& Ambigapathy Pandian

Appropriating English

Innovation in the Global Business of English Language Teaching

PETER LANG
New York • Washington, D.C./Baltimore • Bern
Frankfurt am Main • Berlin • Brussels • Vienna • Oxford

Library of Congress Cataloging-in-Publication Data

Singh, Michael.
Appropriating English: innovation in the global business of English language teaching / Michael Singh, Peter Kell, Ambigapathy Pandian.
p. cm. — (New literacies and digital epistemologies; vol. 8)
Includes bibliographical references and index.
1. English language—Study and teaching—Foreign speakers. 2. English language—Study and teaching—Foreign countries. 3. English language—Study and teaching—Technological innovations. I. Kell, Peter. II. Pandian, Ambigapathy. III. Title. IV. Series.
PE1128.A2 S58 428'.0071—dc21 2001034679
ISBN 0-8204-5658-6
ISSN 1523-9543

Die Deutsche Bibliothek-CIP-Einheitsaufnahme

Singh, Michael:
Appropriating English: innovation in the global business of English language teaching / Michael Singh, Peter Kell, Ambigapathy Pandian.
–New York; Washington, D.C./Baltimore; Bern;
Frankfurt am Main; Berlin; Brussels; Vienna; Oxford: Lang.
(New literacies and digital epistemologies; Vol. 8)
ISBN 0-8204-5658-6

Cover design by Joni Holst

Table of Contents

Figures and Tables

Editors' Foreword

The "New Literacies and Digital Epistemologies" series aims to explore two related dimensions of the massive social, institutional, economic, cultural, and technological changes that have unfolded throughout the West and, increasingly, across the globe since the 1950s. Educators continue to grapple with understanding the nature and extent of these changes and with developing principled and critically informed responses to them at the level of pedagogy and curriculum development. The purpose of the series is to develop a range of positions that will be useful to educators in responding to the changes in question.

The first dimension of change addressed by the series is the emergence of a range of distinctively new literacies—especially, but by no means solely, ones associated with new electronic information and communications technologies. The second involves new kinds of phenomena and processes to be known and understood, and new concepts of and approaches to knowing and understanding that are associated with characteristically postmodern and postindustrial forms of change.

From its inception, school-based learning has been grounded in conventional print-based literacies. Curriculum and pedagogy have assumed an epistemological model based on propositional truth. Conventional literacies and traditional epistemology have formed a powerful union that saturates educational "common sense." This "common sense" must now be evaluated and augmented to provide a sound basis for learning in the present and future. And yet, much current educational policy and practice seem committed to shoring up traditional ways and trying to accommodate new developments into the familiar.

"New Literacies and Digital Epistemologies" explores cutting-edge issues in these areas. It challenges familiar ways of thinking and acting in education and provides a forum for exploring innovative, unusual, and risky ideas and perspectives. By way of specific substantive themes, the books in the series tackle questions such as

- What *are* the so-called 'new' literacies, and what distinguishes them from the 'old'?
- How do new literacies emerge, where do they come from, and what issues do they generate?
- Where, in what ways, and with what effects are new literacies impacting on schools, homes, communities, workplaces, leisure sites, etc?
- How well are our educational institutions meeting the challenges of new literacies?
- What prevailing epistemological assumptions and 'mindsets' underlie current educational theories and practices?
- How well do these handle the nature and scope of contemporary change?
- What new theories, concepts, tools, and mindsets are emerging in fields outside education to understand social, cultural, economic and technological changes?
- How far might these be helpful for educational theory and practice?

Appropriating English is a powerful book that delivers in full measure on our editorial aspirations for the series. Written by a collaboring team of authors from Australia and Malaysia, and based on case studies undertaken in Australia and Malaysia, it tackles major issues that have arisen from English having become "big business" in our everyday face-to-face worlds and in cyberspaces alike. The case studies provide a strong empirical base from which the authros theorise and comment incisivelly upon the worldwide spread of English and explore dilemmas associated with the transnational English language teaching business. Throughout the book the authors write boldly and directly from a clearly enunciated political stance. The result is a hard-hitting but closely argued and impressively principled response to the globalisation, commodification, and technologising of English language teaching. More than just a critique, the book offers clear signposts for pursuing ethically informed innovations in the practice of teaching speakers of other languages.

The authors set out from three pressing concerns experienced by progressive English language teachers. The first of these is the sheer spread of English across the globe and, particularly, the implications of this for the death of other languages. This trend raises the important question of what English language teachers might do to help promote global linguistic diversity and to play some role in rejuvenating languages threatened by extinction. Readers concerned with the issues currently surrounding language diversity and survival will find strong arguments and clear perspectives in the pages that follow.

The second concern faced by progressive language teachers involves the ways in which English has been commodified—turned into a commercial product—and the significance of this for the current globalisation project. In response, the authors do not shy away from asking difficult questions, and within their book they address and discuss pressing issues such as: What roles might teachers want (or not want) for themselves in relation to the historical quest to create a fully integrated global economy—given that other "full integrations" are likely to ride on the back of economic integration? What should we do now in order to contribute to developments we would be happy to "own" later?

Third, there are issues concerning English as arguably the most powerful medium on the Internet, and the way English mediates racist and sexist constructions of Others. The authors note how increasingly "insult-driven flame-wars erupt on the Internet over use of..."cyber-English to [police] non-White Englishes and to advance racist assertions that equate different Englishes with inferiority." The authors ask and discuss how English language teachers might be able to turn such events into principled learning opportunities.

Within a broad frame marked out by these concerns, the authors explore the development of English as a worldwide language. This, however, is the development of English not as a singular, homogeneous global language but, rather, as a series of heterogeneous hybridisations of global/local Englishes owned by many culturally different peoples. This hybridity now means that participation in the transnational English language teaching business demands a sensitivity and responsiveness to the diverse uses that culturally different clients will make of complex global/local Englishes. What this means and how it may be pursued is explored in fascinating ways and from complementary perspectives.

The combination of conceptual, theoretical, and normative argument in the opening chapters of the book, along with a detailed case study that traces points of convergence and divergence between English language teaching in Australia and Malaysia, respectively, provides an excellent balance in the treatment of the book's defining issues. The case study grounds and illustrates in powerful ways the concept of appropriating English that is developed as a framing device in earlier chapters. As a result, the ground is well laid for the invitation extended to readers in the two concluding chapters to personally test out in their work a critical orientation toward "appropriating English." This invitation is presented very persuasively in two steps. In the first, language teachers are presented with a range of workpoints for engaging tactically with the globalising English project, its marketisation, and it's powerful presence on the Internet. In the second, the authors make practical suggestions that can be taken up by language teachers in relation to curriculum and pedagogy.

This is an invaluable book for teachers of English to speakers of other languages. It is written with conviction, respect, and the utmost integrity. These are qualities we need now more than ever before it we are in the business of English language education.

Colin Lankshear
Ballarat. October 2001

Preface
Michael Apple

It is now a truism to say that education is political. The real issue is to demonstrate how it is political, who benefits from the ways it is organized, funded, and controlled, and what struggles arise from all of this. Education has always been a contradictory assemblage of policies and practices. It can simultaneously embody forms of cultural and bodily control and forms of liberation.

Of course, since education has been and is political, it has served as an arena in which differential economic, political, and cultural power is reproduced and produced. As I have demonstrated at length elsewhere, currently neo-liberal discourses, policies, and practices increasingly dominate the terrain of education. A new common sense has been constructed in which "public" is by definition bad and "private" is by definition good. Marketized forms, combined with a new managerialism, have become ever more dominant. The constantly enterprising and entrepreneurial individual replaces collective sensibilities and commitments at both the personal and the institutional levels. And both individual and institutional actors must constantly provide evidence that they are indeed "making an enterprise of themselves" (Apple, 2001).

These dynamics have had very serious consequences on identifiable peoples and cultures nationally and internationally. This is the terrain into which *Appropriating English* enters. It provides a powerful case study of some of the most significant political, economic, and cultural dynamics and effects of the struggles over language and literacy that now play such a powerful role in education throughout the world. Singh, Kell, and

Pandian have decided to act in a way similar to what Eric Hobsbawm described as the social critic's duty. For Hobsbawm and for the authors of this book, the task is to be the "professional remem-brancers of what [our] fellow citizens wish to forget" (Hobsbawm 1994, 3). That is, they want to detail the absent presences, the there that is not there, in the policies that dominate English Language Teaching, and so much other teaching as well. How do dominant "pro-fessional" and corporate discourses work to highlight certain things as "real" problems while marginalizing others? What are the effects of the policies that have been promoted?

Nowhere are these questions more necessary than in the current status of teaching of and about language. For example, educators engaged in the teaching of English to speakers of othered languages (TESOL) are working hard to make sense of the huge socio-economic, cultural, and technological transformations that have been occurring in reaction to and as a manifestation of contemporary global restructuring and destruct-uring. So too have those who are involved in the preparation of English language teachers. As the interdependent processes of globalisation and localisation, combined with the neo-liberal ideological advocacy of globalism, have intensified since the end of the Cold War in the late 1980s, the work of developing principled educational expressions and responses has been fraught with considerable difficulties. Appropriating English addresses two interrelated features of these important changes that have major significance for those involved in English language teaching and the globalisation of education.

The first is the rise of new English language literacies, especially those made possible and necessary by the new technologies of human interaction, reflection, and knowledge production. The second is the changes wrought by the emergence of a new era of globalisation which have now generated new kinds of Englishes to be known and under-stood. The global commodification of English, the emergence of new varieties of local Englishes, and the threat the project of globalising English poses to speakers of othered languages now require innovative approaches to transnational English language teaching. These need to be different from those policies and practices that have been sustained from the days of the English empire. These innovative approaches include digital epistemologies capable of informing our productions of and responses to a world of cyber-English, the emerging knowledge economy in on-line education, and the discursive appropriation of English by "cyborgs" speaking othered languages.

Since the nineteenth century, the constitution of mass education operating at all levels from preschool to university has been based on the literacies of the printed book. Curriculum and pedagogy for the teaching of English, and teaching in English, have been grounded in an epistemological model that takes for granted the interests of constructing an avowedly monolingual nation-state operating within a global framework of Anglo-American colonial capitalism. Print-based English language literacies and colonialist epistemology have created a potent force that infuses the contemporary project of internationalising education, so much so that the commodification of English and the insistence on English-only teaching are often taken as unquestionable traditions. A very real critical sensitivity is now required to evaluate, translate, or otherwise appropriate these to provide a sound basis for innovation in English language teaching. However, contemporary market-driven policies in the education industry seem committed to exactly the opposite, to reproducing colonialist ways of English language teaching and to accommodating the development of the new technologies of human interaction, reflection, and knowledge production through creating an enterprise culture using costly auditing regimes to effect compliance.

The cultural dynamics and power relations involved in this situation are complicated and dangerous. But that is not all. In human terms, the implications for teachers' work by these kinds of transformation are profound as well. Teachers' lives and the conditions of their work become deeply problematic. Deskilling and a loss of autonomy are not the ideal circumstances for the development of pedagogic relationships that go beyond simply the distribution of disconnected technical information. Yet such technicist models of teaching increasingly dominate the terrain and threaten to make it ever more difficult for more meaningful, socially just and critical curricula and teaching to evolve.

Singh, Kell, and Pandian get at the heart of what is happening here. In so doing, they recognize that any complete analysis of the complex relationships between education and power must deal with what critical cultural theorists have called "the circuit of cultural production" (Johnson 1983). This circuit has three moments: production, circulation, and reception. The first involves issues of political economy, the material and ideological conditions both nationally and internationally that provide the context for the actual creation of a commodity or a cultural practice. The second involves the means by which it is distributed and made available. The third asks us to take very seriously the ways in which "products" are taken up, accepted, mediated, struggled over, re-sisted, and/or re-appropriated, perhaps even for counter-hegemonic purposes.

This third aim is of critical importance. Our tasks not only involve rigorously criticizing differential relations of power, but also detailing the contradictory dynamics in these relations. That is, we need to show the spaces where alternative and oppositional actions are either currently going on or are possible. Hegemonic relations are never total; they are almost always filled with contradictions and with possibilities for dis-articulating things like English from their previous relations of power and rearticulating them into new and more positive formations.

One of the most important characteristics that sets Appropriating English apart is the fact that it traces out the entire circuit of cultural production. In many ways, it is the equivalent in the field of English Language Teaching of the critical accounts that have been done on global commodities such as the "SONY Walkman" (DuGay 1997).

In accomplishing this, the book opens up to further exploration cutting edge issues in these areas. It aims to promote a global consciousness of contemporary changes in English and to inform the principled appropriation of English language teaching theory, policy, and practice. It assists all of us in addressing such questions as:

How has "global English" emerged, where did it come from, and what issues does it generate for the teaching of languages and literacies?

What is "new" about postcolonial English language and literacy education, and what distinguishes it from the colonialist and colonising English education?

What are the prevailing epistemological assumptions and colonialist "mindsets" that underlie current theories, policies and practices governing teaching of/in English?

What new conceptual tools are emerging from the cultural studies of the interdependent processes of globalisation and localisation to help educators understand and tactically engage contemporary socio-economic, cultural, and technological changes?

How are educational institutions being changed in the process of meeting the challenges of global English, global market regulation, and the new literacies required by cyber-English?

Where, in what ways, and with what effects are varieties of Englishes, the internationalisation of the curriculum, and the new technologies of human interaction, reflection, and knowledge production impacting on teachers" work?

How well do the providers of English language teaching handle the nature and scope of contemporary change?

How far might these new interpretive frameworks be helpful for informing innovations in English language teaching?

In sum, *Appropriating English* confronts taken-for-granted traditions of thinking and acting in English language teaching and explores risky perspectives on education in order to chart innovative courses of hope. I can think of few things more important internationally at the present moment.

Acknowledgments

The research for *Appropriating English* was conducted under the auspices of RMIT's Research Institute for Globalisation and Cultural Diversity with funding from the Australian Research Council and assistance from the RMIT/USM International Literacy Research Unit.

We are grateful to Helen McLean, Anne Douglas, Heather Ross, Veronica Luk, and Vasilia Tsiambazis for assistance that made it possible to bring this project to fruition.

Michael Singh is as always most appreciative to Linda and Benjamin for their valuable time that enabled his work on the research project.

In preparing Chapter's 5 to 8 Peter Kell gratefully acknowledges the valuable research assistance of Linda Singh in organising and transcribing interviews, collecting and cataloguing of relevant documentation, and undertaking the preparation of the camera-ready version of the manuscript.

Ambigapathy Pandia thanks Marilyn Robert, Jamiah Baba, Sachithanantham Tachinamoorthi, and Charles Lesslar for the research assistance in preparing Chapter 6. Appreciation is also extended to Rohani Abdul Hamid, S. Sivagnanachelvi and Mokolus Rowther (Curriculum Development Centre), and Irene Teoh (British Council, Penang) and Tony Crocker (British Council, Kuala Lumpa).

Chapter 10 extends the conceptualisation of a framework developed at RMIT University, by Bill Cope, Andrew Scown, Grace Lynch, Maria Katsabanis, Helen McLean, Sally Harris, and Stavroula Tsembas (www. ed–leaderships.eu.rmit.edu.au/process/process. html).

Acknowledgments

Introduction

English seems to be becoming *the* global language. It is now big business and for the moment it rules cyberspace. For teachers of English to speakers of other languages, and those involved in the education of such teachers, understanding these changes is a major challenge in itself. Developing principled responses to these changes is riven with significant dilemmas. English language teachers now find the worldwide spread of English a cause for concern, especially given its role in the death of other languages. Likewise these teachers are asking questions about the turning of English into a commercial product and the role it is playing in the political project of creating a fully integrated global economy. Moreover, teachers are worried not only because English has colonised virtual reality but also because even there the English language's racist constructions of Others still have yet to be decolonised. *Appropriating English* brings together a range of empirical evidence, experiential knowledge, and conceptual tools to enhance teachers' understandings of these changes and what they might do. The idea of "appropriating English" is advanced as a tactical response to and expression of the globalisation, commodification, and technologisation of English language teaching, providing a practical basis for informing and mobilising innovations in the business of teaching English to speakers of other languages.

After a preliminary critique of the project of globalising English, Chapter 1 goes on to establish the book's conceptual framework around considerations of globalisation/localisation, the knowledge economy, and the intensification of the risks posed to the sustainability of the world's linguistic diversity. It concludes with an account of the relational case study reported in *Appropriating English.*

By distinguishing the idea of appropriating English from that of colonialist and colonising English, Chapters 2, 3, and 4 provide a conceptual basis for innovation in English language teaching. Chapter 2 explores four relationships arising from the globalisation and localisation of the English language and its teaching. Issues examined include linguistic homogenisation and differentiation; the restructuring and destructuring of the nation-state; the electronic compression of time and space by means of the new digital technologies; and the rise of a global consciousness. The assumptions governing global providers of English language teaching (ELT) and their policies and practices are canvassed in Chapter 3. Specifically, it examines the diversification of ELT providers, the culure of ELT products and services, and the changing features of competition in the industry. An account of six major risks created by the project of globalising English, risks now being reproduced in cyberspace, is provided in Chapter 4. The opportunities these risks create for innovation are briefly highlighted.

Chapters 5, 6, 7, and 8 explore points of convergence and divergence between Australia, a nation-state where English is the "primary" language, and Malaysia, where English is a "second" language. These chapters include accounts of the blurring of boundaries between these nations and between their cultures. The historical structuring of the relationship between Malaysia and Australia is examined in Chapter 5. It shows that these nations are intersected by an array of complex political and economic processes. Chapters 6 and 7 provide insights into how Malaysian and Australian ELT providers are handling the challenges of globalising English, the regulation of the ELT industry by global market forces, and the new literacies required by cyber-English. The effects of these changes on the work of English language teachers are analysed in Chapter 8.

The last two chapters invite English language teachers and those who educate them to test an anticolonialist orientation to "appropriating English." This is presented as an exploratory contribution to developing a responsible ethic of globalisation, commodification, and technologisation in education. Chapter 9 provides teachers with a range of workpoints for tactically engaging with the project of globalising English, its marketisation and its domination of cyberspace. Practical illustrations of how these contestable pointers might be used in the curriculum and pedagogical work of teachers are provided in Chapter 10.

While the demand for English grows worldwide, its effects on other people and their languages are not always the positive benefit they hope or we promise. Teachers of English to speakers of other languages, and those who make a business out of this educational work, now confront the dilemma of using their power to further the project of globalising English and being agents working for the sustainability of the world's biolinguistic diversity. The complex issues involved in counteracting the global dominance of English are central to any consideration of equitable power relations among the world's speakers of diverse languages. *Appropriating English* adds to the calls for paradigmatic innovations in English language teaching, new frames of reference for reinventing the project of globalising English that situates it within a perspective of risk analysis, and makes use of multivocal Englishes to help sustain the biolinguistic diversity of humanity.

CHAPTER 1

The Challenges of Appropriating English

> If we think the English language rules, in the Chinese world across Asia, for every transaction conducted in English there must be a thousand in Chinese. (Fitzgerald 1997, 167)

Despite the need to sustain global multilingualism, English has attained the extraordinary status and prestige of *the* global language, and in doing so has outgrown England and its (former) imperial territories. Although increasingly multi-form English is setting the linguistic patterns for the way people around the world eat, drink, work, relate to each other and express affection. Terms such as OK, crash, meltdown, freeze, software, white wash, blackout, and screw have worldwide currency. Even the creative readvertising of the global slogans of corporate consumerism such as "FCK" or "Just do it? Don't believe it!" are widely understood by speakers of many other languages (www.cleansurface.org). English is spoken in such diverse settings as Nepal, Belise, Guyana, Cyprus, the Falklands, and Gibraltar. In glitzy global cities like Stockholm, Berlin, Amsterdam, Buenos Aires, Hong Kong, and Rio de Janeiro the preferred second language of communication is English. The experiences of colonisation, dispossession, diaspora and migration that characterised the expansionism and defeat of the English empire ensured that its language found expression throughout huge swathes of the world's population. Nevertheless, the normal condition of human existence is living in multilingual contexts. Half the world's population is bilingual.

The possibilities of disseminating knowledge of how speakers of other languages make English serve their own purposes remains largely untapped. The English language teaching (ELT) industry itself produces an array of marketable commodities—English language programmes for various purposes, tests, teacher education courses, language learning materials, theories of second language acquisition, and classroom pedagogies. Moreover, English is now the *lingua franca* of international commerce, science, engineering, and technology. It is also the language of the world's popular (US/American-based) culture industry—film, television, and music. English is the dominating language of the United States of America, the world's largest political-industrial-military-entertainment complex. The US dominates the cultural products and services produced, distributed, and delivered globally via online businesses. The experiences of Cold War superpower struggles and the victory of capitalism over communism have ensured American Englishes of their widespread dispersal throughout the world. Despite standardised Englishes being a part of the global knowledge economy, other knowledges of its uses are not typically part of the slate of ELT products and services.

In a multilingual world where the major political project, driven by the ideology of neo-liberal globalism, is to create a single, unified global economy, the construction of cyberspace was begun on the basis of linguistic exclusion. The American Standard Code for Information Interchange (ASCII) made the use of alphabets and characters othered by standardised English unmanageable if not impossible. In turn US/American techno-speak has brought the world words such as cyberspace, electronic mail, online, Web page, electronic bulletin boards, user networks, data streams and netisens. The transnational tongue for expressing the problems produced and revealed by the Internet is also US/American e-language, flame wars, digital divide, smog, digitised pidgin, cyber-coolies, digital geishas (Ow 2000, 51–68). Huge flames are generated through online e-mail debates. Insult-driven flame wars erupt on the Internet over the use of its command language, cyber-English, to effect the policing of non-White Englishes and to advance racist assertions that equate different Englishes with inferiority (Lockard 2000, 179). The new technologies for human interaction, reflection, and knowledge production allow for computer-mediated communication to be both asynchronous (e.g., e-mails, bulletin boards) and synchronous (e.g., chat groups). In addition these new technologies enable users to create (author/produce/consume) and access (browse/surf) an immense array of multimedia documents (text, graphics, pictures, sound, video) hyperlinked via globally distributed databases. English language teachers are now talking of screen-based literacies, electronic literacies, multiliteracies, digital literacies, computer and Internet literacies, technological literacies, metamedia literacies (Cope and Kalantzis 2000, 191–212; Warschauer 1999).

For those involved in the teaching of English to speakers of languages which have been othered through the processes of globalisation, commodification, and technologisation, understanding what these changes mean for their roles and the English language is a major challenge. While the risks of language death created by the worldwide spread of English may be appreciated (Crystal 2000; Nettle and Romaine 2000), what English language teachers might do to promote global multilingualism and rejuvenate languages facing extinction remains unclear. Likewise, turning English into commercial products for a transnational knowledge economy necessitates consideration of an ethical role for teachers in the political phenomenon globalisation. Moreover, the colonisation of cyberspace by English and the continuing racist and sexist constructions of Others in *the* language of the net raises questions about teachers' work in making innovations of the opportunities created by these risks. To better our understandings of the opportunities created by these challenges, *Appropriating English* gathers together a range of resources–field data, firsthand experiences, and key concepts. The idea of "appropriating English" is advanced as a tactical response for informing and mobilising innovations in teaching the speakers of languages othered by English.

Striking Back at the English Empire

With the expanding circle of those now learning English (and how to teach it) we can expect that the transnational ELT industry will become a focus for intensified critiques by a growing range of people. Further, those learning English as a foreign language might be expected to turn to those who have learned it as a second language for insights into ways of deconstructing the technologisation, globalisation and commodification of ELT. How the ELT industry understands these changes and the critiques made of them, as argued below, is important for developing tactical, innovative responses.

Promoting Anglo-American Cultural and Economic Interests throughout the World

English is promoted both for economic and political gains, as much as it is for achieving control over speakers of other languages. ELT has often been used as a means of subjugation and continues to be an important means through which the power of Anglo-American nations is exercised (Canagarajah 1999; Pennycook 1998; Thiong'o 1994). For instance, Gauri Viswanathan (1992) argues that the invention and development of the study of English as an educational subject in British India served the English colonialist agenda of pacification through a process of intellectual seduction. What distinguished the teaching of English were the efforts made by the English Raj to obscure its connections with religion and politics through appealing to narrow scientistic conceptions of rationality, objectivity, and truth. This created an air of impartiality around the claims that ELT offered knowledge for improving the human condition.

Viswanathan (1992, 167) argues that the humanistic functions of ELT served English imperial priorities by disciplining students' character, aesthetic sensibilities, and ethical thinking in ways consistent with these priorities. Despite resistance, this was useful to the English colonists for securing their socio-political control. The strategy of locating English colonial authority in the language and literature from England served to efface English imperial interests associated with colonialist expropriation, material exploitation, and class and racial oppression. Just how Anglo-American cultural and economic interests suffuse the contemporary ELT industry requires further investigation, as too do the frequent challenges to the reproduction of colonialist representations of speakers of other languages via ELT.

Reproducing Colonialist Constructions of Speakers of Languages Othered through English

The English language is imbued with orientalist views, words, images, about the speakers of other languages who now pay for the opportunity to learn it (Said, 1978). Those who study English to access its knowledge base find that the language has already produced racist and sexist constructions of them, and continues to do so in cyberspace. For instance, the very act of learning of English is constructed as a sign conferring civilised status, or putting an end to imaginings about "rote learning." Alistair Pennycook (1998, 19–20) argues that there is a "loud absence" about colonialist cultural constructions of the other in ELT

> showing…the strange isolation of much thinking in applied linguistics from academic and political work going on outside it…The study of the continuing effects of colonialism and postcolonial strategies to resist such effects has become a major focus of work in many disciplines. Its virtual absence from applied linguistics and TESOL becomes even stranger when one considers the centrality of English language teaching to the [neo]colonial project.

Cyberpsace reveals a global English which is fraught with colonialist overtones, tellingly revealed in popular descriptions of the Internet as a new electronic frontier over which Anglo-American nations, along with Japan, are rapidly advancing. To have fun Anglo-Americans find enjoyment in fleeing white, middle-class urbanity to exotic Asia where digital skin disguises their whiteness to become virtual, digitised Yellow-faced cyborg's engaging in colonialism, tourism, and rape (Ow 2000). Once again English is tied to the primary goals of colonialism and tourism; conquest and exploration are the grand narratives of cyberspace. Those in the tourist industry, hoteliers, and promoters are responsible for producing at least some of the Web's racist and sexist stereotypes about Others. The reinscription of the white master's narratives of racism in cyber-English is evident: "when the students ventured out into English-language Web sites to gather information for their research projects, they often came across racist stereotypes about Hawaiians" (Warschauer 2000, 164).

However, the colonialist cyborg, marching along the culturally superior highway of white imperialism, now finds itself up against a heterogeneous array of Asian consumers and businesses. The failure of ELT to address the colonising of the languages othered by English is a recurring criticism. Moreover, Japan has demonstrated its own capacity for cultural imperialism by manipulating, repackaging, and reselling aspects of Anglo-American culture (Ow 2000, 63). Sega, Sony, and Nintendo recycle US/American myths to ensure a broader distribution and consumption of their products. There are questions as to whether the highly competitive ELT industry can continue to rely on the marketing of colonialist and colonising English internationally. Crudely speaking, can the ELT industry survive with a strategy that denigrates the Asian market? Can the trivialisation of Asian cultures be peddled to Asian students interested in learning English and Asian businesses interested in investing in alliances in this field? Would ELT businesses benefit from attending to strategies for preventing a consumer backlash over inappropriate products? Minimally this means making non-stereotyped gender and ethnicity choices. However, English language teaching remains problematic as its reach expands beyond the countries colonised by Anglo-American interests to encompass nearly all the world's nations. ELT continues to be criticised, especially by those who have learned it as a second language for promoting Anglophone cultural and economic interests throughout the world.

Colonising the Languages Othered by English

There are concerns about the English language's colonisation of the space of other languages, histories, identities, and knowledges (Crystal 2000; Nettle and Romaine 2000). It is in this context that bell hooks (1994, 168) reminds us that standardised English is "the language of conquest and domination…it is the mask which hides the loss of so many tongues." For instance, like so many other languages, ka 'olelo Hawai'i was forcibly suppressed by US/American colonisers before active Hawaiian citizens succeeded in their seventy-year struggle to overturn the ban on teaching their language and it became an official language of the state of Hawaii (Warschauer 2000, 159). The project of globalising English is cause for concern among those involved in the contemporary transnational ELT industry because of its threats to the sustainability of global multilingualism. These risks are integral to the new technologies of the knowledge economy:

> the English language ASCII interfaces of the university's computers caused many obstacles in Hawaiian language computing, and forced the students to resort to complicated procedures to produce and view their work in the full Hawaiian alphabet. (Warschauer 2000, 164)

ELT is also being questioned for failing to constructively engage with the appropriation of English by speakers of othered languages.

Failing to Constructively Engage the Other's Appropriation of English

At least as far back as 1956 England's Ministry of Education (cited in Pennycook 1994, 155) acknowledged that the demand for learning English by speakers of other languages is "not necessarily connected with any desire to imitate [English] ways or to understand [English] history and culture." In Malaysia the official school curriculum emphasises the link between learning English and the complementary acquisition of knowledge required for the new technologies of human interaction, knowledge production, and reflection rather than the learning of cultural heritage English. In the United States Black Americans have made English their own linguistic possession and used it to build communities where none existed, to create political solidarity, and to resist slavery and its continuing legacies. Black Americans reinvented and remade the English language so that it spoke "beyond the boundaries of conquest and domination....English was altered, transformed, and became a different speech" (hooks 1994, 170).

Not surprisingly England did not give Africans a language for singing the virtues the imperialists claimed for colonialism, but it did give them a language with which to critique English imperialism and its racist arrogance and prejudices (Achebe 1994, 433). While English was forced on them, it is now possible for people throughout Africa to speak of their ambivalent experiences of English imperialism, and to do so in a transnational language. However, making English their language required more than imitation. To make the best uses of English they have had to produce it anew. Thus, the price English is paying to become *the* global language is its submission to many different local uses.

Recognising that postcolonial India no longer has the option of rejecting or resisting English, attitudes toward its uses have changed (Rushdie 1991, 17–18). Throughout this multilingual nation English is now regarded as but another Indian language along with Bengali, Hindi, Telugu, Marathi, Tamil, Gujarati, Malayalam, Kannada, Panjabi, Bhojpuri, Marthili, Awadhi, Assamese, Haryanui, Magahi, Chattisgarlu, and Deccan, among others. In India, the second largest English-speaking country in the world (after the US, and just before Nigeria and the UK), the English language has ceased to be the sole possession of the peoples of England. However, Indians do not just use English in the same way as those who live in England do. In India, English is not only used to access technical knowledge, to effect international communication, or to enhance transnational social mobility, but it also enables Indians from different regions of the country to talk to each other in a language which neither party rejects (Rushdie 1991, 65). However, few ELT providers from Anglo-American nations have yet to engage with the development of these multivocal Englishes.

With increasing numbers of people learning English (and how to teach it) the transnational ELT industry can anticipate that foreign language students will join with those who have learned English as a second language in order to develop the skills needed to appropriate it (Wallraff 2000). For this reason it is important to advance our knowledge of the changes the ELT industry is making as a manifestation of and as a contribution to the globalisation, commodification, and technologisation of English. In a departure from the anticipated triumph of global English (Crystal 1997), we extend the critiques developed by those who have learnt English as a second language (Canagarajah 1999). The tactical art of "appropriating English" is advanced as an idea for developing innovative responses to the challenges now facing the ELT industry and the sustainability of the world's linguistic diversity.

Globalising English, the Knowledge Economy, and the Risks to Global Multilingualism

Studying the English language teaching industry provides an important source of understanding of the cultural processes of globalisation (Appadurai 1996). To understand the problems of reworking ELT, *Appropriating English* tests a conceptual framework that foregrounds the multiple and contradictory linkages between globalising English, the emerging knowledge economy, and the risks both of these pose to global multilingualism. First, the worldwide spread of English must be understood in terms of the interrelated but disjointed processes of globalisation and localisation. Second, the transnational role the ELT industry provides insights into what it means to develop a fully integrated global knowledge economy. Third, an appreciation of the risks to the sustainability of global multilingualism caused by the project of globalising English, given its colonialist and colonising worldview, creates opportunities for developing productive innovations. Following the introductory overview provided below each of these inter-linked elements is discussed in the next three chapters of *Appropriating English.*

Multivocal Englishes: The Globalisation and Localisation of English

Given its complexity in terms of definition and processes, globalisation cannot be explained in terms of a single proposition. Rather than a totalising concept standing for a fixed and closed body of knowledge globalisation is an open-ended concept that attempts to come to terms with an ambiguous but widely contested phenomenon. Here it is useful to distinguish between the processes of globalisation and the rhetoric of globalism. Globalisation is a term used to explain the stretching of the links and the deepening of economic, socio-political, and cultural relations across the planet. Globalism, on the other hand, refers to the neo-liberal discourses used to elaborate, legitimise, and naturalise social and economic policies favourable to the needs of global capital. Globalism is the rhetoric used to justify the preferred developmental trajectories of neo-liberalism and to boost support for its selected change strategies and action programmes. A familiar, fatalistic refrain of globalism is the claim that this particular neo-liberal political orientation to globalisation is an unstoppable, inexorable force.

In the post–Cold War era the ELT industry is now engaging with the complex, overlapping, and disjunctive trajectories of globalisation and localisation. The global flows of English created through English imperialism and US/American neo-colonialism have produced as much differentiation as homogeneity in the language. The flow of English worldwide has not led to a stable standardised global language. The global spread of English has met with resistance and hybridisation as it is integrated into and merged with other languages. Rather than speaking of "global English" as promulgated by the "English-only" political movement (Macedo 2000), our preference is for the ideas of "multivocal Englishes" and the "project of globalising English" to emphasise the complexities and agency involved.

Globalisation should not be seen solely in terms of uniformity and predictability. The major constituents of changing global relations involve the fluid and irregular movements of people, technology, money, images, ideas, and risks (Appardurai 1996). English and ELT now flow around the world along differentiated and uncoordinated paths. Students are moving to study English. ELT providers are exploring the possibilities for distributed learning using the new technologies. Money is being made in the selling of ELT products and services. The colonialist images of the Other constructed using English are being challenged by these same Others. Speakers othered by English are developing new ideas for its use. Each of these flows is structurally independent and their particular effects can and do vary from time and place. While the global flows of ELT show common features in different parts of the world, they impact unevenly on global cities and marginalised rural communities, and on rich and poor people. They are not unified in any way, nor are they part of any given single relationship. The globalisation of English looks different from the different standpoints of those who see it as an opportunity for transnational migration and those who see it as the cause of the death of their own language.

Each flow is increasingly decentered from the Anglophone metropolises in complex and multidimensional ways. Australia, for instance, is hospitable to ideas from Japan about the reorganisation of mechanisms to regulate and reconstitute the work of English language teachers (e.g., just-in-time training, total quality management), more so if they have gained legitimacy in the US. On the other hand, Australia is resistant to the local ownership of ELT businesses by Taiwanese corporations. Australia accepts the importation of computers from Korea and is keen to export ELT services to Malaysian students. However, it displays hostility to the acceptance of asylum-seekers from Asia and has been reticient about the entry of qualified teachers of languages othered through English from Asia. These contradictions suggest that certain constituents of globalisation are subject to enthusiastic acceptance (e.g., finance, commodities) while others meet entrenched suspicion and resistance (e.g., workers and refugees) by differing nation-states.

Governing the Global Knowledge Economy: Trends in the Business of Teaching English

Global restructuring has created anew the governmental problem of ensuring people's social, cultural, and economic security (Beck 1999). The self-regulating power of the nation-state over its economy has been displaced within the framework of a larger neo-liberal political project of global economic rationalisation with its unstable and changing patterns of international trade and foreign investment. Since the 1980s a range of strategies have been used to reposition national economies within the international marketplace and to secure people's endorsement of and contributions to developing these new economic models, compliance regimes, and enterprise culture (Apple 1996; Williamson-Fien 2000). To avoid being a loser in the global marketplace neo-liberal strategies for effecting economically efficient competition have come to dominate governance. This has led to a reassessment of the public sector in terms of the neo-liberal commitment to reduce public resources and, more im-portantly, its value in promoting (or inhibiting) the nation's economic efficiency in a globalised marketplace. The changes in the ELT industry have been in response to and a contribution to these developments.

However, despite rhetoric to the contrary, there has been no reduction in or minimisation of governmental activity. Instead, the focus of governance has shifted to investment in strategies for producing enterprising self-management and away from providing for people's security—except under electoral pressure. Contemporary radical neo-liberal politics have demonstrated the ability to reinvent the state and to reposition it within new problematics of governing.

On the one hand neo-liberalism is a bipartisan political intervention by the parties of labor and capital which problematises the bureaucratised, distant welfare state and rejects its intergenerational reproduction of a disaffected and dependent underclass (and idealised, nostalgic reconstructions of welfarism) (Giddens 1994, 134–197). On the other hand this governmental coalition multiples the domains of human life restructured (and destructured) by market forces. The extension by neo-liberal governance of the regulatory power of market relations has induced a retreat from public provision of ELT. This has led to the creation of a market in ELT which seeks to reconstitute students from passive, dependent welfare recipients to active consumers consciously choosing to maximise their talents and opportunities (Axford 1995).

This model of the knowledge economy has given rise to the establishment and deployment of a repertoire of powerful calculative regimes that valorise and empower the expertise of performance administration that constructs, produces, and manages by "measurable" outputs. It is these technologies of audit and accountancy which for the moment have a high status in the hierarchy of organisational values and through which an increasing range of line managers, workers, and agencies, including ELT providers, are continuously monitored and evaluated. Given the uncertainties created by the market, no one is trusted by this new regime. Their operations are reduced to a series of per-formance indicators; judgments are made accordingly, and appropriate forms of conduct are induced via changes in market mechanisms. ELT providers are now held responsible to the (unquestionable) truths of these auditing criteria; any assertions to expertise by English language teachers are overridden. In other words, neo-liberal governance operates through the institutionalisation of regulatory frameworks (e.g., performance indicators, stretch targets, balanced scorecards, league tables) which promise to ensure the optimal operation of these self-disciplinary technologies. These technologies create the illusion of local or individual autonomy. However, the reconfiguring of governance into marketplace forms enhances the possibility for manipulating individuals by rendering them perpetually responsive to shifts in their economic circumstances. Competition among ELT providers is used to ensure institutional compliance with governmental objectives for internationalising the market for its products and services (Singh 1998a).

Related to this is the development of an enterprise culture and its valuing of artificially free, entrepreneurial competition (Apple 1996). The elaboration of the enterprise culture of neo-liberal governance involves the legtimisation and naturalisation of processes of marketisation, commodification, commercialisation, and the new calculative regimes. Neo-liberal governance constructs active, self-actualising consumers who optimise their quality of life by their own decisions. They reconcile the advancement of their interests with this enterprise culture, coming to regard them as equivalent. The neo-liberal vision is to institutionalise the extension of the market throughout the social fabric by structuring this culture into the whole assemblage of human life.

Risking Global Multilingualism: Whither Colonialist and Colonising English

Any political innocence that English language teaching (ELT) might have once claimed has been lost in a world where this global teaching enterprise continues to be a controversial and complex business. The challenge is to map and respond to a range of contradictory contingencies, unintended consequences, and manufactured uncertainties arising from radical projects for globalising English. The identification of these risks presupposes the need for decisions (Beck 1999, 4). Like any socially significant concept both the definition of "risk" and who has the authority to define it are contested, because its definition is a major force in the mobilisation of innovatory decisions and actions. But we know that the risks of death facing over 5,000 of humanity's languages is uniting disparate personalities and localities in the transnational language rights movement, adding to the growing array of organisations of global civil society (Nettle and Romaine 2000).

There is a growing sense of uncertainty and tension about the project of globalising English and its impact on various communities and their languages around the world. Analysis of the risks that arise from the globalisation of English is important for ELT providers operating in an increasingly competitive and diversified language teaching environment. The globalisation of English has created ever-present and increasingly worldwide risks to the sustainability of biolinguistic diversity that are of increasing concern. The multiplication of risks on a global scale also places in jeopardy the stable and long held linguistic, economic and political reference points of ELT. The combination of these alienating and destabilising features of globalisation is producing a worldwide community with a sense that English might be dangerous, and so mobilising significant opposition to the inroads of English into different languages and even resistance to learning English. The transnational features of the ELT industry ensures that the distribution of a range of risks creates the possibility that there will be side effects which can simultaneously impact on the industry itself as well as radiate from it. Some of these risks are irreversible and cause irreparable damage to the cultural and linguistic fabric of diverse and unique human communities.

Investigating Points of Convergence through a Relational Case Study

Investigators in ELT face the challenge of developing research methodologies (and teaching practices) that are not grounded in assumptions about there being absolute differences between nations having first and second language speakers of English or construct dangerous contrasts between their orientations to ELT. Research in ELT that is framed by orientalist notions of unbridgeable cultural differences tends to reinforce racialised antagonisms (Said 1978). However, the difficulty of developing an appropriate research orientation is not due to a lack of determination, but is a result of the challenges of moving beyond the sterility of unitary constructions of modern nation-states and their century long efforts to build ethnically and linguistically mono-cultural nations. Said's (1978) critique of "differentialist culturalism" suggests the possibility of framing the research process in a way which shows that nations where English is the "primary" and a "second" language (Crystal 1997, 53–63) are intersected by complex structural, organisational, and institutional realities. Framing research in these terms necessitates ex-ploring points of affinity and continuity between Anglophones and speakers of other languages so as to investigate the blurring of boundaries between nations and cultures.

One of the basic goals of postcolonial research is to explore points of significant similarity between nations and cultures rather than constructing hierarchies of racialised differences. In working against the legacy of orientalism Bryan Turner (1994, 22–46) argues that transnational research requires the investigation of sites of convergence. For the purposes of *Appropriating English* this involves the provision of accounts of actual intersections along with evidence of the hybridisation process whereby Other knowledges enter dominating discourses and estrange the basis of their authority (Singh and Greenlaw 1998). This suggests the need for a relational case study that explores similarities in frameworks and, examines shared processes and features that could unite people. By focusing on sameness rather than otherness, a relational case study investigates "how common elements or themes are handled [and] examine...areas of cultural overlap" (Turner 1994, 46). It should be noted that this methodology does not provide a guaranteed way out of the problems of Anglocentrism for which ELT and its associated research is rightly criticised (Canagarajah 1999, 57–77; Pennycook 1998). Critical reflection on the research process itself is necessary to any consideration of how this problem might be mitigated before, during, and after the research.

This relational case study of ELT providers focuses on two major cities in South East Asia which market themselves as centers of educational excellence. Melbourne (Victoria, Australia) and Penang (Pilau Pinang, Malaysia) were selected with due regard to the three key factors that have contributed to the globalisation and localisation of English. These are namely the dispersal of Anglophone peoples throughout the world; the learning of English by those people colonised by the English, and the economic pulling power of US/American English for people beyond the English empire (Crystal 1997, 53–54). It is in countries formerly colonised by the English empire, such as Sri Lanka, India and Malaysia where much of the interesting practical and conceptual developments in the appropriation of English and its teaching are continuing to occur (Canagarajah 1999; Pennycook 1998). It is anticipated that the expanding array of interests beyond the reach of the English and US/American spheres of influence will become more forthright in their efforts to make and remake English as their own.

Appropriating English looks at the responses and contributions of the ELT industry to technologisation, globalisation and commodification through a relational case study of providers in Penang (Malaysia) and Melbourne (Australia). Here it is important to characterise the relative positioning of these cities in the context of the emerging worldorder of speedy and intensified multi-religious, multiethnic, and multicultural interdependence (Beck 1999, 2–3). The location of ELT providers within Melbourne and Penang can be thought of in terms of a hierarchical positioning between the core, hinterland, and periphery within and across the global ELT industry. In Melbourne the main universities and private providers, such as the International Language Academy, are all located within a radius of two kilometers of the city center. Their location in the city's central business district, which has the highest rent and property values in Australia, is indicative of the high-yielding returns these businesses are capable of generating. There is a similar pattern in Penang, where a cluster of ELT providers are located in the prestigious areas of Jalan Burma and Gurney Drive creating a distinctive educational precinct linked to up-market tourist venues. There is not just unevenness in the location of ELT providers within these cities, but these cities themselves are unevenly positioned within the competitive transnational markets for ELT. These cities are representative of the new entreports of globalisation. They are part of newly energised international financial hubs, embedded in the growing new technology industries, possessing long-established resource industries and equally declining manufacturing sectors.

In a departure from its formerly provincial agrarian-based, England-centred economy, Melbourne now constructs its image as a city closely connected to Asia through the global industries of information technology, financial services, transport, tourism, education, and com-ponent export. Penang is a historic port city and trading center dating back to 1786 when Captain Francis Light of the British East India Company colonised the island; his brother Colonel William Light developed the town plan for Adelaide, one of Australia's best laid out cities. Malaysian government policies designed to create corridors for economic growth, including generous tax concessions and start-up allowances, have facilitated the movement of multi-national information technologoy (IT) and component manufacturers into Penang. For investors the presence of an English-speaking community proved to be an added benefit. This enhances Penang's participation in the English-dominated environment of software creation, multimedia development, computer component production, and silicon chip manufacture.

This relational case study used a range of data collection techniques to generate evidence concerning the ways in which nations where English is the "primary" and a "second" language are intersected by complex structural, organisational, and institutional realities. *Appropriating English* draws on interviews and documentary evidence from and about a slice of ELT providers in Australia and Malaysia including those in the corporatised public sector and the private commercial sector. Interviews were conducted with representatives of businesses operating in the new knowledge economy which are involved in the selling of English globally.

The case study includes data on the national flagships, the British Council, and Australia's International Development Program (IDP), as well as ELT providers which cross the boundaries between the public and private sectors. Typically, these collaborative, hybrid enterprises which are now entering the ELT market are alliances of universities, colleges, media distributors, self-funded government agencies, and private Internet companies. Newspapers and online Web sites reveal both the debates and marketing associated with the project of globalising English.

Acting and Thinking Globally for Local Viability

At this time choosing between English and one's vernacular no longer seems possible for many. The very maintenance and rejuvenation of local languages now requires increasing action on a global basis. As Roland Robertson (1992, 72) argues, "acting (and thinking) globally is increasingly necessary in order to make the very notion of locality viable." The sustainability of local languages, the preservation of the world's biolinguistic diversity, now needs to be institutionalised globally. The commodification of environmental industries such as ecotourism represent key sites for the production and consolidation of localised differences in all their material and cultural varieties. For effective intervention in local/global problems of language death it is important to recognise and analyse their embededness in larger contexts.

Likewise English must now be appropriated by the speakers of other languages and made their own. Rather than rejecting ELT out of parochial ornationalistic interests or merely seeing it as a postmodern plaything, much effort is now directed to reconstituting "it in more inclusive, ethical, and democratic terms" (Canagarajah 1999, 2). In a world of dangerous languages and endangered languages we are less concerned about having students cross the border from their vernacular to English, because of increasing awareness of the costs they have to pay in doing so (Crystal 2000; Nettle and Romaine 2000). The focus is now on teaching bilingual students how to appropriate the discourses of English on their own terms, so as to enable them to display the agency to critically negotiate the relations between languages. Speakers of other languages keen to appropriate English for their own interests need support for learning how to judge and engage with the colonialist values and colonising history of

English (Pennycook 1998). Appropriation is a process that involves understanding the discursive rules of the globally dominating language, as well as bringing the resources of one's vernacular to critically engage in the reconfiguration of English. This necessitates the creation of spaces for one's own voice within that discourse and inserting one's own language within the world's resources of knowledge, identity, and history. As Chapter 2 indicates, the globalisation of English has produced a range of multivocal, local Englishes.

CHAPTER 2

Multivocal Englishes: Globalising and Localising English

> It is unclear whether the regionalising bloc is an attempt by nation-states to collectively manage the effects of global capitalism, or whether it is an attempt by global capitalism to manage nation-states. It is a chicken in the egg question that can deflect attention away from global capitalism's effect on education, training and equality policy. (Brine 1999, 41)

Since the late 1980s the worldwide project of internationalising ELT has intensified due to the acceleration of disjointed trends toward globalisation and localisation. This project has moved rapidly in response to an exploding demand for ELT products and services from students in "second" and "foreign" language countries, with support from the new technologies promising borderless online education. The shifts in the transnational knowledge economy have caused a crisis in the legitimation of the nation-state as the neo-liberal political program has subjected public ELT providers to the totalising regulation of global market forces.

This chapter analyses the responsiveness of the ELT industry to the globalisation/localisation of English. The discussion seeks to tactically interpret and engage with the worldwide spread of English and the rise of transnational ELT businesses. The imperialist trajectory involved in the worldwide spread of English has not led to a singular homogenous global English, but the emergence of heterogeneous "multivocal Englishes" owned by many culturally different peoples. Four salient attributes of the globalisation and localisation of English have been selected to inform innovation in ELT: linguistic homogenisation and differentiation; globalisation from above and below; the knowledge economy; and the rising global consciousness.

The Ebb and Flow of Globalisation: Linguistic Homogenisation and the Differentiation of English

Suspicion over globalisation arises because it is seen as justifying and legitimating the spread of US/American English, US/American popular consumer culture, and the more exploitative and obscene injustices of international capitalism. Moreover, the rhetoric of neo-liberal globalism seems to suggest that this process of transforming the world into an Americanised globe is beyond the control of nation-states and virtually beyond human intervention. However, it is possible to oversimplify and dehumanise the process of globalisation by positioning individuals as passive and governments as submissive. While the whole world may not necessarily speak US/American English or become neo-liberal capitalists, everywhere in the world is struggling to establish a position in relation to these major phenomena. In some places globalisation is reviving regional particularisms and regressive parochialism. In opposition to the promotion of linguistic homogenisation, efforts are being made to sustain or even revive languages that differentiate particular communities. The regeneration of languages to mark group distinctiveness has been a counter tendency to that of globalisation. Language rights movements have emerged around the globe to preserve the linguistic heritage of particular communities in the face of the homogenising imperialism of English.

On one level, we see the movement toward political and economic organisation based on a continental, regional, or global scale. At another level we see the reorganisation and reassertion of linguistic and cultural identities at local levels. Thus globalisation encompasses possibilities for diversity due to the revival of language, nationalism, and religion, as well as changing structures of economic and political domination. For instance, the globalisation of US/American English via popular culture has

> paradoxical but actually consistent effects in simultaneously homogenising and differentiating. Certainly it can homogenise across the globe in that what is available in any locality can become available in all localities, but at any particular locality it increases the range of cultural opportunity. (Waters 1995, 142)

The contradictory tendencies which characterise the global spread of

English have prompted efforts to retain local languages as well as giving rise to particular expressions of localised Englishes (Newbrook 1993). Thus globalisation does not necessarily mean English language conformity, but it involves a complex interweaving of linguistic homogenisation, the differentiation of multivocal Englishes, and efforts to maintain linguistic diversity.

Linguistically diverse peoples learn English so they can use it to further their education by gaining access to the range of knowledge and skills which Anglophone nations insist on being made available exclusively in English. A combination of historical factors has given English its global force as an educational commodity including military might, colonial oppression, and restrictive mercantile practices. The status of English has been bolstered by its incorporation into the legal and judicial systems of international trade. For example, entry into Anglophone universities by international students prescribes a specified level of proficiency in English, thereby sustaining the English-testing, English teaching, and English-only pedagogy now integral to the ELT industry.

The foundation for this hegemony of colonialist and colonising English was provided through such inventions as the printing press, mass schooling, and the early entry of England into the industrial revolution. The status of English as a global language was re-enforced by the spectacular success of US/American neo-colonialism through popular culture, mass communication technologies, and the Internet (McArthur 1998; Crystal 1997). This economic imperialism produced influential technological and scientific knowledge most of which is written in English. The power of this knowledge hegemony is reinforced by a politics of English-only pedagogy which ensures that clients of linguistically diverse capabilities anxious to learn about and from new technological and scientific advances require training in English as a gateway to this new knowledge.

The knowledge economy assigns English a key role in globalisation by making it possible to integrate the material, political, social, and cultural life of so many people on the planet, while simultaneously destructuring previously established languages and forms of socio-economic organisation (Gill 1993, 6). English occupies a dual role in both of these processes. The current acceleration of globalisation, and in particular the role of the ELT industry in the rapid distribution of ideas via electronic communication and personal mobility, does not necessarily mean homogenisation around a single "global English." While at one level globalisation means heightened integration and uniformity in the use of simplified English by elites engaged in transnational business and travel, its globalisation is also leading to an increased diversity of Englishes. For instance, as globalisation weakens the nexus between the nation and language, the links of power and authority between Englishness and the English language are also undermined. The more widespread the cultural commodities from England are circulated the more the different Englishes spoken by the English themselves become noticeable. Moreover, its appropriation by second language speakers around the world involves the reconstitution of the English languages.

The imperial centre brought English to the distant colonies of the periphery. Now these postcolonial nations not only bring new Englishes to the monolingual Anglophones, but are contesting their power to authorise English and its teaching. The emergence of these new Englishes challenges long held assumptions about the values of standardised UK, US, or Australian Englishes and associated views on English teaching:

> Globalisation is uncoupling the taken-for-granted connection between language and the nation, languages and national memories, languages and national literature." The English spoken in Australia by Malaysian-Australians is not given the same legitimacy and cultural and ideological power as the Australian English spoken by Anglo-ethnics. The very concept of a national language is becoming difficult to sustain in some countries as a site for people's construction of common interests, histories and aspirations. English may be becoming the language it is not carrying with it all the weight and value of Anglophone interests. (Mignalo 1998, 42–43)

These changes in the nature and ownership of English create a number of risks that are linked to globalisation where the levels of control are dispersed and diffused.

Systematic and Uneven Linguistic Interrelationships

Globalisation signifies a significant compression and unification of planetary relationships. Everybody is inescapably linked to and affected by the political project of contemporary globalisation. Individual teachers of English are establishing new social ties across the planet—for instance, linking Malaysia with Korea and Mozambique, creating complex systematic worldwide interrelationships (Waters 1995, 62). Such relationships are confirmed by the stratification among the world's languages. Within a single global system some languages have secured dominance over others; Chinese, Hindu and Urdu, English, Spanish, and Arabic are particularly significant global languages (Crystal 2000, 11–19). This has little to do with the number or geographical spread of first language speakers but has more to do with the penetration and durability of the economic and political interests of the speakers of these dominating languages. Capitalism has given English its global predom-inance. Approximately one hundred languages are spoken by 95 percent of the world's population and 75 percent of the world's population speaks twelve languages of which six are the languages of European colonialism, which includes English, Spanish, German, Portuguese, French, and Italian. Mandarin Chinese and not English is the language spoken by the largest number of people on the planet. The claim of English to be *the* global language arises from its accompaniment of and support for English imperialism and the global interests of the United States (Mignalo 1998, 39).

Being the languages of European imperial powers, English, German and French are dominant in today's world. They dominate knowledge production, intellectual property, technological developments, and scientific applications. True, there are more Hindi speakers than German. Likewise there are more Japanese, Arabic, and Bengali speakers than there are speakers of either French or Italian. However, the languages of European colonisation have left an enduring legacy across the world. Certainly the combined number of speakers of Asian languages—Chinese (Mandarin, Wu, Cantonese), Hindi, Urdu, Japanese, Bengali, and Arabic—outweighs the number of speakers of English. However, the agency of Anglo-American colonialism ensured that English is now indeed an "Asian" language. While Portuguese is spoken in Macau, Goa, and East Timor and French is spoken in Vietnam, Laos, and Cambodia, English is widely spoken throughout Asia. It is not just that English is used in Malaysia, Singapore, and Hong Kong, but India is one of the world's largest English-speaking countries. The Philippines inherited US/American English from its colonisation by the US. Together with Myanmar (Burma), Sri Lanka, and Pakistan this bloc of Asian nations has more English speakers than a combination of the US, the UK, Australia, New Zealand, and Canada. English colonisation did more than spread the speaking of English worldwide; it led to the delinking of English from England, so now the English can no longer control what was once their language (Graddol 1999; Mignalo 1998, 40).

Distance has often been seen as the primary barrier and impediment to social and economic intercourse. However, the density of the linkages between the metropolis and colonies in terms of language, political economy, people, technology, and culture has created new forms of proximity (Waters 1995, 28). These networks identify patterns based on such factors as trade, religion, ethnicity, ideas, strategic alliances, communications, and legal conventions, and serve to challenge claims about the tyranny of distance, suggesting that it is a racialised notion, signifying the separation between White Anglophone nations. Mapping these relationships reveals the dramatic variability in any one ELT provider's changing relations with Africa, Asia, Europe, and the Americas. Current global restructuring is intensifying these changing relations. New relationships are being formed across new frontiers by the new technologies of human interaction, knowledge production, and reflection. These developments are making the transglobal networks of those working in the ELT industry more intense and robust, if also rather stretched and attenuated.

Indians enthusiastically embraced the cultural pursuits of the English as their own, sustaining them in quite distinctive ways long after English colonial administration ceased. The Indian enthusiasm for English and cricket are useful examples. Along with ELT, cricket was one of the main vehicles used by the English colonists to transform Victorian India (Baucom 1999). Prince Ranji, a noted Indian cricketer who represented England, saw cricket as the common ground for the empire's subjects, being able to generate a sympathetic association among Indians for their English colonisers. The chief value of cricket as a colonialist project was its use to perpetuate and strengthen the view of Englishness as culturally superior, to enlist compliance from the colonised, and to bolster the power of the English empire. Cricket did this through social norms that stressed English interpretations of fairness, justice, and loyalty, along with the individualism and hierarchy that saturates the values and rules of the game.

As a colonialist project cricket has proven to be yet another durable link between imperial Inglestan and its former colonies. Cricket is now a major participant sport for males in India, Pakistan, and Sri Lanka. While the global reach of cricket is evidence of the homogenisation created by the English empire, the game has been substantially modified through appropriation by different nations, corporations, and women. These appropriations have ensured the survival of a plurality of crickets and enabled these to flourish in very different socio-cultural and economic contexts. In the process cricket has been reshaped from its origins as a rural English game for wealthy White men into being a hybridised ritual celebrating multiple identities and global commodity (Appadurai 1996). Like the English language, cricket is no longer owned by the English (Kell 2000). The hybridising capacities of globalisation continue to reshape and change the colonising technologies of both English and cricket.

English is neither a pure nor a single language. Throughout its history English has taken from other languages. The medieval users of English liberally integrated form and content from Norse, Saxon, Gaelic, Norman, Latin, French, and German. During the four centuries of the global English empire this power of appropriation was extended to the languages of the colonised throughout India, Indigenous Australia, Zulu Africa, and Orang Asli Malaysia to name all too few. This reminds us, however, of how hybridised the English language of the people of Inglestan really is. Currently the world has a huge variety of Englishes. A few are included in the thesaurus for Microsoft's Word processing programmes which gives legitimacy to the Englishes of Australia, Belise, Canada, the Caribbean, Jamaica, New Zealand, Northern Ireland, the Philippines, South Africa, Trinidad, the United Kingdom, the United States of America, and Zimbabwe. It does not do the same for Hawaiian English, Singlish, Torres Strait Kriol, Ebonics, Tok Pisin, Scottish English, or many other Englishes. Paradoxically, as the status of these multivocal Englishes gains prestige via the new technologies the greater the arguments about which ones are to be legitimated as standardised Englishes and who can legitimately claim the role of arbiter.

English is a language spoken by many of the world's peoples who have adapted, modified, and influenced its vocabulary, grammar, tone, phraseology, and meaning in accordance with local interests. New localised Englishes continue to emerge, sustaining irreconcilable ideological and pragmatic debates in the ELT industry over intelligibility, stigmatism, acceptability, and appropriateness (Newbrook 1993). These Englishes combine elements of one or other versions of "standardised English" with more localised derivatives and variations incorporating Indigenous languages. This linguistic cross-fertilisation has typified the spread of English through which a range of new hybridised Englishes have been created. Analysis of the English used by Queen Elizabeth II has shown that over forty years it too has been influenced by middle-class southern English, slowly shifting away from the "received Establishment pronunciation" (Harrington, Palethorpe, and Watson 2000). If the Republican president of the US, George "Dubya" Bush, gains widespread credibility and legitimacy, then his tongue-tied use of US/American English may contribute to a further shift in the language. Bush-speak could have the world talking about "globic issues," the "East Timorians," and how to make the "highways of the Internet more few" (Franklin 2000).

Globalisation from Above and Below: The Restructuring of the Nation by the State

The public debates and protests over globalisation have highlighted its economic dimensions, foregrounding the pursuit of neo-liberal politics across the globe. The emerging global economy is characterised by market forces enacted by fast capitalism's new online commerce where it is often claimed that this global economy operates beyond the control of nation-states (Axford 1995). Too often the state's role in subsidising, nurturing and facilitating the development of global capitalism is much too understated.

The state is an important mechanism for steering the newly corporatised public sector and the private sector in directions that increase their integration into the regulatory discipline of the global economy. In some countries the nation-building focus seems to be becoming less important. The public service framework of the nation-state is being transformed by the state through the processes of corporatisation and privatisation using mechanisms to ensure compliance with an enterprise culture. The state is responsible for the development of these compliance regimes, the allocation of state funds to subsidise capital, and its legislative decisions to privatise and corporatise public assets. These government interventions on behalf of global capital have radically reshaped English language teaching. For example ELT has been transformed from its civic role of integrating migrants into the nation-state to its commodification for a transnational industry.

From the immediate post–World War II period the Teaching of English to Speakers of Othered Languages (TESOL) in Australia was intended to contribute to the public and political life of the nation and state by integrating migrants into a democratic and increasingly multicultural society. The teaching of English to European migrant labor was initiated in 1947 as a mechanism for constructing a collectivised Australian identity as well as serving the nation's political interests of (re)forming the allegiances of its newly recruited citizens. TESOL was a key mechanism through which European immigrants were invited, sometimes even coerced to imagine themselves as being stereotypical Australians and members of the Australian nation-state. Such teaching played its part in helping to forge a sense of national political consciousness that sought to link a disparate immigrant population with the dispersed, ambiguous, and contested iconography of Australianness.

The shift toward user pays, competitive tendering, and delivery by private ELT providers has intensified with the election of radical neo-liberal governments. These market mechanisms have displaced the civic roles of the state and resituated ELT as a commodity within an internationally oriented business framework. The nation-building agenda has been replaced by market-based regulation and the collective common wealth has been lost through the processes of state, sponsored privatisation. At the macro level this has involved leveraging financial controls on exchange rates and interest rates from the nation-state to concentrate profits in transnational markets. It has also led to the imposition of a narrowly conceived business culture on English language teaching which was once seen as a non-commercial vocation. The public's social and economic security has been downsized to subsidise the participation of business and commerce in the global economy.

In Anglophone countries across the world the costs of these initiatives are paid for by the impoverishment of people at both an individual and a social level. The costs associated with this radical neo-liberal concern to maximise profit above all else have been displaced onto marginalised constituencies, including unskilled migrant workers, the rural and urban poor, and the aged. The alienation and disaffection generated by "globalisation from above" which have led to the erosion of people's security have prompted and extended "globalisation from below" (Falk 1999). The possibilities for global civil society are well illustrated through the alliances and collaborations that characterise the environmental and language rights movements. As the ability of nation-states to influence political and economic affairs has diminished, the emerging organisations of global civil society have been able to utilise the new communications media to mount new forms of intervention around issues of inter-generational language rights.

Ironically the end of the Cold War and the promise of greater individual liberty and prosperity shifted much of the political discourse to considerations of international human rights, broadening the issues away from simply civil and political rights to also include economic, social, and language rights. These shifts have witnessed the emergence of issues and representations by groups suppressed under the confines of nation-state politics. National unity based on coercive mono-cultural and mono-linguistic boundaries is showing signs of dissolving under the weight of transnational processes. This has seen Indigenous rights and the legacy of social injustices meted out to these people under colon-ialism move onto the global stage at a time when the power of nation-states has been reconfigured to serve transnational economic interests. This reorientation of the state strengthened the global consciousness of Indigenous communities whose lives, lands, and languages have been stolen or otherwise destroyed during the years of building nation-states. The new technologies of human interaction, reflection, and knowledge production, combined with the resources of global English, have created new possibilities to take issues of Indigenous human rights beyond the boundaries of nation-states. Paradoxically, the nation-state's dispossession and impoverishment of Indigenous and ethnic minority groups confronts processes of globalisation from above. These nation-communities organise transnational alliances beyond the nation-state to fight the state for human and linguistic rights: "The right to have and use languages located in a subaltern position by the discourse of the civilising mission and the public policy of the state is one of the restitutions claimed under language and human rights" (Mignalo 1998, 44).

Shifting the Costs of Globalisation: Destructuring the Nation-state

One view of globalisation emphasises the emergence of transnational spaces and processes as a replacement for the nation-state as the major framework for social life and security. Another view holds that the nation-state is serving as an important means for the creation of these systemic transnational properties, and thereby sustaining its own legitimacy, globally if not locally. The intensification of "globalisation from above" (Falk 1999) has given the nation-state a new geo-political role in negotiating tariff reductions, redistributing the burden of taxation to consumers, subjecting labor to the forces of the global market, and effecting the de-regulation of the state's environmental controls.

For much of the twentieth century Anglophone governments had a preference for an organised corporate state which sought to intervene in social, cultural, and economic issues. It acted as an intermediary between social interest groups, especially the peak organisational representatives of employers and employees, to strategically support investment, industrial development, and the expansion of domestic economic activities. A key feature of the Cold War corporate state was the continued cultivation of mass support through policies providing for social and economic security enabled some of the material benefits of economic expansion and international stability to be distributed beyond the wealthy to the rest of the population. This was done through progressive taxation, a "safety net" for the financially distressed, general health provisions, public education, pension schemes and public indust-ries, banks, communications, power, water, and transport.

In response to the radical neo-liberal project of "globalisation from above" these policy settings have been challenged and reinterpreted as uncompetitive. The role of the state has been reconstituted (Lo Bianco 1996, 5–14). It has now taken on the task of reducing the public sector to a residue of its former self and corporatising the public sector through the imposition of auditing regimes that enforce the elaboration and legitimation of an enterprise culture. The costs of administering the state's compliance regime have come to consume much more of ELT providers' budgets. The state now intervenes in social, cultural, and econ-omic issues within the nation on behalf of the global market, typically acting in concert with unrepresentative world economic interests that determine global economic policies to redistribute wealth upwards. The state now intervenes to implement increasing levels of compliance-driven enterprise culture that favours global market regulation; the privatisation of public assets and affirmative action for business while arguing for reduced levels of state investment in security for its citizens.

Neo-liberal opponents of the welfare state that characterised Anglophone countries claimed that it was facing a crisis. The increasing demands for security made upon the state had allegedly escalated beyond its capacity to meet more than the interests of the working class. Other marginalised groups were now making demands on the state, including women, the aged, ethnic minorities, rural and regional communities, Indigenous peoples, and those with disabilities. For a moment the location of state power seemed to evaporate. As interventions by the state tended to destabilise society, it became less able to offer security in terms of trade, jobs, drug control, health services, or ecological concerns. In Australia's case the response to this crisis has been a substantial weakening of the nation-state's commitment to its founding social contract; the project of creating a common wealth has been abandoned, because so much of the national estate has been privatised. This destructuring of the nation-state and structuring of the state-global capital nexus has been explained in the following terms:

> State intervention by command was reduced but at the same time states sought to increase the scope and scale of the market. Many government services were open to competition. Competitive tendering between the public and private sectors and then ...many state owned industries were [privatised]. ...They also partially surrendered their sovereignty by participating in global and regional organisations. (Waters 1995, 100)

Politicians now justify the destructuring of the public sector and the failure of their policies in terms of the effects of economic activity elsewhere in the world—typically the strong US/American or Japanese currency or stagflation in either country. Just as global environmental issues have highlighted the need for democratising international governance to secure a sustainable future for all, the same argument applies to the sustainability of the world's linguistic diversity (Nettle and Romaine

2000). Insofar as politicians blame global industrialisation for the problems of the environment and see the solutions in global terms, then the informed and active citizens involved in the language rights movement are shifting the focus of their civic efforts to the transnational political arena. In turn the nation-state seems to be becoming less relevant.

Certainly there is some criticism of "globalisation from above" concerning the diminishing sovereignty and independence of the nation-state in the face of fast capitalism. There is also mounting concern that some countries are increasingly less able to devise and implement policies that are contrary to or mitigate the interests of the international markets and global corporations:

> The capacity of political democracy to discipline capital—to restrict capital flight, for example—to levy effective taxes on capital, or to enact environmental or social legislation perceived by capital as disadvantageous has declined dramatically. (Winant 1994, 276)

Sociologist and advisor to the Blair Labor Government Anthony Giddens (1994) does not see an absolute loss of sovereignty for the nation-state due to globalisation, certainly not in England's case at least. Instead he anticipates an increased sense of security in the institutionalisation of that sovereignty by these forces of globalisation. International relations continue to affirm the integrity of individual nation-states, providing a secure framework in which they (or parts of them) can prosper. Nevertheless, in the wake of the restructuring of the world economic system, there is the possibility of the disintegration of the nation-building projects of some states. Certainly, the globalisation of England's vernacular is threatening the use other states make of their own vernacular in creating a nation.

Transnational corporations are now often larger and more powerful than many of the nation-states in which they operate, so much so that they undermine the legitimate and democratically established authority of the nation-state to make independent decisions. Further, nation-states are now surrendering some of their sovereignty to control economic matters—currency regulation, financial transactions, terms of trade—to the global market or supranational organisations. At the same time they are protecting political controls on the movement of people—especially asylum seekers.

The redefinition of national socio-economic problems as global problems serves to undermine the sovereignty of nation-states in three ways (Axford 1995; Waters 1995). First, it redirects the political preferences and actions of citizens to global civil society; second, it delegitimises the nation-state as a problem-solver; and third, it sets up new international organisations to which some elements of the states' sovereignty are gradually surrendered. These structural changes are generating new conditions and promoting changed conceptions of the national interest and people's identities. At the beginning of the twenty-first century the world order is still based on its division into sovereign nation-states, although many are being reconstituted. Nation-states continue to be restructured and destructured in response to and as active agents of globalisation (Beck 1999).

The reworking of nation-states is an important contribution to globalisation and the development of supranational groupings such as the European Union (EU), the African Union, the Asia Pacific Economic Council (APEC), and the costly North American Free Trade Agreement (NAFTA). These supranational identities have been formed to create economic efficiencies promoting boundary-less but not so free "free trade" arrangements that suit the interests of transnational corporations. The larger nation-states and these supranational regional economic blocs have more power relative to countries

> in the emerging world order ....The sovereignty issue involves not only juridical rights and the question of citizenship and accountability, but also the allocation of resources and life chances, insofar as these are associated with the capacity for human autonomy and social choice ..."core", "semi-periphery" and "periphery" ...reflect the hierarchy of states and stages of socio-economic development (and the constraints and possibilities this entails) ...such concepts might apply within, as well as across, states. ...There is not just uneven socio-economic development across different regions, but also within regions, and even within certain cities. (Gill 1993, 11–13)

The political economy of the Cold War era of superpower global relations proved to be particularly beneficial to countries such as Malaysia. The European imperial powers were forced to relinquish their colonial territories out of a fear that anti-colonial resistance and insurrection would see them defect to communism. Having gained independence, these postcolonial nations learned that their survival depended on the ability of the Third World alliance to play the superpowers off against each other in order to secure regional economic development. With the victory of capitalism over communism in the late 1980s Euro-American support for the prevailing political economy collapsed as it set about destroying all remnants of Russia's economy and opened the world to the regulatory force of globalising markets. Speaking at the 54th session of the United Nations General Assembly in New York Prime Minister Datuk Seri Dr Mahathir Mohamad said that "free market" global

> capitalism [sees] no more need to be gentle in spreading their systems or in profiting from them. No one would be allowed any other political economic system by the sole dominant bloc. The true ugliness of Western capitalism revealed itself, backed by the military might of capitalism's greatest proponent. For the small countries the demise of the Eastern bloc is a major disaster. Now they are exposed to pressures which they cannot resist. And very quickly they learnt that the free marketeers intended to milk them dry. ...The currency manipulation and short-term investors of the rich soon impoverished these countries through devaluing their currencies and share prices. Impoverished and politically unstable they were forced to borrow from the IMF (International Monetary Fund). Whether by design or through sheer lack of understanding the economic regime imposed by the IMF destroyed their economies further. ...And so for the small, independent countries of the world the future looks bleak. (Mahathir 1999, 19)

Globalisation impacts differently on each country given the inequities of the global economy:

> market forces now take on the role of rating the performance of governments, accusing governments of poor governance, of lack of transparency, of corruption, etc. Declaring that they need to discipline governments and change ways of doing business, they pulled out the capital they had invested and began to sell the currencies of these countries to devalue them. The result of massive outflow of capital and devaluation is to impoverish these once-prosperous countries. Millions have been thrown out of jobs, bringing about social and political unrest. (Ismail 2000, 5–6)

Many nations have been subjected to processes of recomposition: Australia did it to itself, the World Bank did it to Indonesia. Typically, this has involved the restructuring of public education along crude business lines. The internationalisation of ELT provision is indicative of the wide range of radical, economically driven changes that have been initiated since the 1980s (Singh 1998b). In 2001 this scenario has led to suggestions that Australia forgo its sovereignty by joining NAFTA or establish a free trade agreement with the US. None of this means that Australia is going to disappear as a nation; but it does give legitimacy to a trend toward "national" interventions by its governments, which favour the integration of Australia into the global economic and military interests of the US. These interventions have included radical reforms to the training and education systems, including ELT providers in order to develop an internationally competitive enterprise culture in this sector (Kell 1998). Claims that suggest there is a decline of the nation-state need to be treated cautiously.

The notion of "economic crisis" should also be used conditionally since the dramatic growth of Asian economies like Malaysia coincided with the decline of the economies of the United States and the European Union. The economic growth that fuelled the expansion of the "Asian tigers" was in part a transfer of investment to the Asian region from the European and North American markets. In this region economic conditions for growth were enhanced by development-oriented nation-building governments. Malaysia, Thailand, Korea, Singapore, Taiwan and Japan achieved high levels of sustained growth through substantial government intervention (Daly and Logan 1999). The role of government was not in the command mode but a policy mix directed to export development. This involved the provision of significant levels of tax subsidisation, generous credit arrangements for large corporations from state banks, high tariffs, protected internal markets as well as minimal labor and environmental regulations.

The active support of the state in providing the investment and business environment conducive to production and export was a key foundation for Asian economic development. Unfortunately, this form of state intervention was mythologised as a "miracle" in Anglophone countries as neo-liberals refused to acknowledge the direct role of the state in shaping these achievements. The social and environmental costs of the "not-so-free trade" regimes of the United States ensured that these emergent economies experienced dramatic growth. Anglophone countries experienced the deflationary and contracting effects of monetary policies that assigned a residual role for the state in economic matters. In contrast, the interventionist policies that characterised the administration of Prime Minister Dr Mahathir ensured that Malaysia became a significant trading nation with a growth rate hovering at 7 percent throughout much of the 1990s.

Expanding the Knowledge Economy, Shrinking Cultural Lifeworlds

"Globalisation from above" is a neo-liberal political project that is accelerating the process of change across three interconnected arenas. It is leading to the integration of the work of English language teachers into a worldwide economic system; to the subjugation of national ELT businesses to the regulatory force of transnational markets, and spurring on the project of globalising English through popular consumer culture. The global transformation of production, finance, and exchange challenges the ELT industry's political relationships and its economic organisation. Economic globalisation is characterised by the integration of the ELT industry into a world market that makes an exclusively nationally bounded ELT business meaningless. The ELT industry is now asked to imagine itself operating in a "borderless" world economy. ELT products and services are developed, distributed, and delivered within a worldwide market operating against competing national interests and within new compliance regimes that enforce competition.

Accompanying these economic notions, political globalisation can be seen as the reorganisation of authority, surveillance, power, authority, and diplomacy to control the movement of peoples and to support the development of a borderless economy. These political changes include major restructurings of the nation as the state realigns its interests to more closely serve the economic imperatives of globalised markets. As English is now the language of the global economy there is relentless pressure on nations speaking other languages to learn English. To become linked to the global knowledge economy they also have to replicate the structures, cultural norms, and economic relations of the English-speaking world. Postcolonial projects of nation building in countries such as Malaysia, Vietnam, and Cambodia once centred on local "national" languages. Now these countries are under increasing pressure to accept English as the language for participating in the global knowledge economy. Despite a willingness to accept English as the language of international commerce and communications, conflicts often arise regarding the status, survival, and symbolism of national languages in postcolonial nations.

Cultural globalisation is finding expression in English language communications, publications, performances, teaching, entertainment, displays, public demonstrations, data accumulation and transfer, exhibitions, advertisements, and spectacles (Waters 1995, 8). There are key questions about the threat that globalising English has in creating a homogenised world culture and subordinating, or even extinguishing, localised cultures and languages. The socio-political and economic processes of global restructuring entail challenges to the locally established structures, ideas, and practices of language education. The contradictory pressures and interactions between these domains serve to promote, as well as constrain, innovation in ELT.

The emphasis on the economic importance of education for increasing the competencies of human resources has given English language teachers a significant role within the transnational labor market. The high value of English as intellectual capital is linked to the production of knowledge and its dissemination through English-only teaching and learning. English is a complex multicultural language, only some versions of which are internationally recognised. English is also a global commodity that is traded worldwide. As a commodified product English is an accessory for entry into highly sought after lifestyle opportunities and transnational mobility. This status as a globalised product is reshaping the products and services in the ELT industry and the teaching of English. What makes the study of "English" attractive in some countries is its use as a marker of personal status and signification of cosmopolitan ambience as well as its value as a symbol of the nation-state's desire to modernise and internationalise (McArthur 1998, 16). English is seen by both individuals and nations as a passport to wider opportunities, and so its acquisition is seen as a valuable investment with the potential to return high dividends in education, jobs, travel, and migration—all of which have increased in speed.

New Technologies of Human Interaction, Reflection, and Knowledge Production

Perhaps the most distinctive features of the current era of globalisation are speed and the compression of time. Contemporary globalisation involves the phenomenological shrinking of the planet, such that increasing numbers of people have a changed sense of the world in terms of time and space relationships. As the time to travel between physically distant places shortens then space itself seems to shrink so much so that the new technologies of human interaction, reflection, and knowledge production have made the connection between geographically distant places almost instantaneous (Singh 2001). For the transnationally mobile and cyber travellers space itself virtually disappears.

Likewise, time can be synchronised around the world so that there is the virtual elimination of space. Time/space compression is a process in which time is organised so as to minimise the tyranny of distance and vice versa. Increasingly, the time taken to travel or communicate is being reduced and in turn this is reducing the apparent distance between those places integrated into the global communications network. The process of time/space compression has been occurring in punctuated, incremental bursts in response to changes in technological, economic, and political conditions. The compression of time has almost wiped out space such that new satellite technologies have made the time to communicate between various distant places virtually instantaneous. The demands on time and space create advantages for a language like English that can easily be compressed in truncated and abbreviated forms without losing its meaning. Being the dominating language of computerised technologies the English language is claimed to be the foundation of these new global digital relationships. The English language occupies a dual role being useful for both the communicative purposes of effecting human cooperation and for making production and exchange possible (Thiong'o 1994, 440). Capitalising on its origins as the language of imperial interconnectivity, English is in daily use throughout the world in music, television, movies, road signs, business names and products, advertisements, hotels, civil aviation, shipping lanes, professional publications and computers.

At the beginning of the twenty-first century, a new millennium according to Christian reckoning, English has taken over as the official language of transnational political relations (e.g., UN, ASEAN, NATO, OPEC) along with most transnational scientific and sporting organisations (e.g., UNESCO, IOC). Many of the world's periodicals, magazines, and academic journals are produced in English, including those newspapers published for a transnational readership such as the *International Herald-Tribune*. Media developments in advertising, satellite television, block-buster motion pictures, and popular music give expression to and contribute to the global spread of English. Transnational travel, trans-portation, accommodation, and hospitality, for business, holidays, pilgrimages, conferences, political rallies, sporting competitions, and military service, are increasingly mediated by the use of English (Crystal 1997, 95–97). The language most often used for air and water safety in the transnational transport industry is restricted, specialised versions of English. Likewise English is the major language of electronically trans-mitted information used in electronic mail (and accompanying viruses) and the not always accessible World Wide Web. But even in the world of virtual reality global English can take on a quite restricted form:

> the transnational language, the one designed to end all barriers between speakers, the speech that everyone can pronounce and that cannot be translated or incorporated into another tongue, turns out not to be Esperanto but rather IBM-speak, the language of [US]American corporate technology. (Nakamura 2000, 22)

There were several reasons as to why English dominates the Internet and seems to threaten the ultimate in colonisation of virtual reality. First, most of its pioneering users were North Americans because that is where the technology was developed by the military. Second, those who design-ed the Internet used the American Standard Code for Information Exchange (ASCII), which made computing in non-Roman alphabets or characters difficult if not impossible. Third, the Internet also increased the need for people to communicate in an international lingua mundi. Together these factors strengthened the position of English along the frontiers of new technology (Warschauer 2000, 156–157). However, despite the originating ASCII code for the Internet being in English, this is a centrifugal technology spinning off a diversity of languages (Singh 2001b). Web browsers are being developed in an increasing range of languages and character sets. While global communications using the Internet are still conducted in English, there are increasing opportunities for the use of other languages to access Web sites or online discussion groups. Despite imaginings to the contrary the prospects for an English-only Internet are diminishing; as the Internet is globalised it is becoming more localised by way of content, culture, geography, and languages (Taylor 2000). The multi-channel capacity of the Internet means that the production of a Web site in more than one language is relatively easy and inexpensive. The Web is now being used to support communications in English and other languages, including Indigenous languages spoken by limited numbers of people.

The growth of electronic commerce has not expanded at the huge rate techno-evangelists had promised resulting in online companies experiencing difficulties in establishing themselves as viable businesses. Few if any e-commerce ventures made a profit in 2000, while computer makers and microchip manufacturers experienced a slowing in computer sales and a resulting fall in their share price. Even Stephen King's online novel, *The Plant,* has yet to deliver on the promises of this new cargo cult.

Businesses and consumers alike are experiencing fatigue from the pace of technological change. The novelty of the Internet is wearing thin as users become frustrated with its fragility and slowness; the speed of information transmission has not been able to keep pace with the volume of information (text, visuals, sound, graphics) now available on the Internet. Some users have even found that the real world has more to offer their lives than the virtual. They are questioning the costs of this technology, especially the frequency with which computer hardware and software has to be upgraded. The expense of upgrading computing systems, Internet service provision, and telephone bills compound the reasons for people logging off. A technology that was supposed to make life easier has overwhelmed people by the excess information created via electronic mail; the intensification of pressure for an immediate response to each and every electronic communication; and the imposition of unrelenting compliance demands, new productivity regimes and surveillance mechanisms in the workplace. There has also been an increase in the number of face-to-face meetings now needed to resolve the flame wars which erupt via electronic communications. While people wanted access to the Internet, they now find its presence inescapable. Whether we use it directly or only indirectly the never-never-net has deeply permeated the lives of many people and we are never-never going to escape the virtual age.

The World Wide Web is directly challenging institutionalised education through students' sale of their assignments, lecture notes, book summaries, and answers to examination questions for online provision. Web sites such as whereitsat.com.au have forced universities to employ new computer software to spot cheating, to use only examinations for assessment purposes, and to pursue Web site designers and producers for copyright infringements. More creative teachers are using the resources of the Web, including those providing online "study aids," for the purposes of reflection and knowledge production rather than just reproduction.

Global Consciousness: Reflexivity, Critical Reflection, and Action

Globalising English involves a range of risks. For instance, many of the risks the world's languages face today are the product of linguistic imperialism of the superpower languages such as English and Mandarin Chinese. For some languages the effects of colonising English are irreversible, causing irreparable damage to linguistic diversity (Nettle and Romaine 2000). The newly industrialising countries (NICs) are buying their economic prosperity by accepting these linguistic risks and even ignoring their consequences. This "language death" policy is slowly making humanity's linguistic diversity an unthinkable cause of political and economic inefficiencies. However, it is also destroying the knowledge, identity, and history of humanity, and as such the legitimacy of those ELT providers that contribute to the extinction of other languages and the governments that allow this "knowledge destruction" to occur.

Increasing consciousness of the risks of language death is encouraging global governance because one possible solution to these risks requires supranational action and transnational cooperation (Crystal 2000). The multiplication of risks to linguistic diversity on a global scale is producing a worldwide language rights movement aware of and actively engaged in combating their dangers. These risks are, in part, directly attributable to globalising English and are multiplied by the impact of the globalisation, commodification, and technologisation of ELT. In turn these risks have prompted the development of innovations in ELT in order to make ethical and educationally sound responses to these challenges.

Terralingua, for example, is an international, nonprofit organisation concerned about threats to the world's biological, cultural and linguistic diversity (http://www.terralingua.org). To support the perpetuation and development of the world's biolinguistic diversity, Terralingua explores the connections between linguistic, cultural, and biological diversity through research, information, applied work, and advocacy. The basic ideas that led to the creation of Terralingua in 1996 and which have guided its work since are that:

- the diversity of languages and their variant forms is a vital part of the world's cultural diversity;
- cultural diversity and biological diversity are related, and often inseparable, perhaps even causally connected through coevolution;
- like biological diversity, linguistic diversity is facing rapidly increasing threats that are causing a drastic loss of both languages and the knowledge of which they are carriers, including knowledge about the environment and sustainable resource use; and
- the continued loss of linguistic, cultural, and biological diversity will have dangerous consequences for humans and the earth.

Globalisation is a reflexive process such that as people become self-conscious about the risks facing the planet they reorient themselves to the world on a global scale. The reflexive aspects of globalisation is evident in the language that teachers use to talk about the world: "transnational education," "online distributed learning," "global alliance," "Internet literacy," "language rights," and "cyber English." This reflexivity is captured in the ELT industry's new vision: "Act and think globally to ensure local viability." This growth in global consciousness means that there are increasing numbers of English language teachers who now address themselves to the entire world rather than to their provincial nation-state loyalties. More teachers are now giving greater consideration to global markets, while others, through their participation in organisations of global civil society, are expressing their concerns about the abuse of language rights, including threats to the world's knowledge economy through language extinction. As members of many different global villages, teachers everywhere are becoming conscious of humanity and the environment in its entirety. As English language teachers teach about the world as a whole, so they help to produce it as a single unit in their students' consciousness thereby increasing the probability that this is the way in which their students may conceptualise it (Waters 1995, 45).

While globalisation can provide English language teachers opportunities to amplify localised issues in wider transnational forums, the driving force of "globalisation from above" has created uncertainties and tensions between the neo-liberal doctrine of globalism and neo-conservative appeals to regressive localism. The responses of regressive localism and neo-liberal globalism differ between time and place, being contingent on many strategic and political factors. Together they present several potentially dangerous reactions that are emerging as local responses to globalisation.

Inglstan Rules Forever? Postmodernist Anglocentrism

One response English language teachers can have to the uncertainties of globalisation is to view the changes in English from an exclusively Anglophone perspective. This creates and perpetuates a "postmodernist Anglocentrism" (Morley and Robins 1995, 206–208) that sees the English spoken by Others as "backward," "less advanced," "deficient," or "improper". This form of Anglocentrism sees people from other social and cultural backgrounds, with differential access to different forms and quantities of the cultural capital provided by the English language, as fragmented identities. This deep and powerfully Anglophone perception of the changes occurring to English is particularly evident in the demand that the "benefits" of English imperialism should be accounted for in any critique of colonialist and colonising English. However, Anglocentric constructions of nostalgic images of past glories are

> problematic because of the view of colonialism that it puts into play through a liberal apoliticism that seeks to see "both sides" of things. ...[when] there is still a pressing need to write against the massive history that has extolled the benefits of [English] colonialism for so long, and, second, this history cannot be reduced to some even-handed balance sheet in which some things were lost and others gained. ...Having myself watched—and in some sense participated in—the micro-politics of colonialism, the constant dismissals, inequalities, putdowns, racisms of everyday life in Hong Kong, I see no good reason to go looking for the "good" [in English] colonialism. (Pennycook 1998, 25)

But for Alistair Pennycook (1998, 25) the real point is that the most dramatic impact of English colonialism was the destructuring of African, Asian and Australian societies, their languages, and knowledges. The globalisation of the English empire and its language halted their development by excluding Indigenous peoples from participation in making decisions that controlled their lands, family ties, languages, knowledges, identities, and histories.

Postmodernist Anglocentrism assumes that the dislocation, hybridisation, and displacement of English, the creation of postcolonial Englishes, are remarkably unique. For the peoples of Malaysia and the Indigenous inhabitants of Australia, and many other countries colonised by English—these experiences have a long historical resonance that this perspective fails to take into account. This postmodernist Anglocentrism decontextualises the teaching of English, flattens the significant differences in English languages, and ignores the multilingual needs of people in different situations. It assumes that everyone has access to English as a key tool of global interconnectedness, and that they are well served by the opportunities it claims to provide to enhance their life chances. Not surprisingly it is for this reason that postmodernist Anglocentrism has been characterised as "intellectual escapism and therapy ...fitting snugly and smugly within the mould of increasingly neo-liberal and consumerist times" (Phillipson and Skutnabb-Kangas 1999, 20).

US/American Cultural Imperialism

In the last fifty years there has been a changing of the guard. The networked villages of the globe are now subject to symbolic and linguistic domination by US/American English that competes with and generally overpowers all other Englishes and challenges other languages. The superhighway that tracks through these global villages is signposted in US/American English. Because these Internet-linked villages are, for the moment, still largely controlled by US/Americans, the conversations engendered there are typically occurring in US/American English. Furthering the cultural, linguistic of the United States and economic imperialism, has been a deliberate and explicit strategy of US foreign policy (Morley and Robins 1995). Its influence has been launched through a heavily state-subsidised motion-picture industry, which has become a form of export-led advertising for US/American Englishes, US/American consumer products, and media imaginings of the US/American way of life.

US/American English has always been part of the entertainment and media exports used to promote the political and cultural interests of the United States at home and abroad. The joining of its economic strength with the control of the new technologies to shape the public opinions of the world continues to be essential to maintaining the international power of the US. The linkages are firmly established between this medium of communications and the organisation of the global political economy. The defence of the freedom to speak, in US/American English, enhances

> the opportunity of the US/American mass media to disseminate their message throughout the world arena [in US/American English]. ...Free trade [costs as it] is the mechanism by which a powerful economy penetrates and dominates a weaker one, then the free flow of information [in US/American English] is the channel through which the life-styles, [language] and the values of [the USA] have been imposed on poor and vulnerable societies. (Morley and Robins 1995, 221)

The seductive technologies of the media industry were unavailable to English imperial expansionism during that era of globalisation. The new technologies of human interaction, knowledge production, and reflection offer a revolutionary form of linguistic imperialism which sees such things as popular music becoming a vector for learning US/American English, consuming US/American products, and reinforcing political messages about competitive individualism and credit-driven consumption. It is little wonder that US/American cultural products in the form of music, film, and dance are resisted in localities seeking to sustain linguistic diversity.

Regressive Parochialism

For some the politics of resentment have provided a false sanctuary against the uncertainties of globalising English and the globalisation of ELT. In the face of the project of globalising English there have been calls for a return to the mythic project of linguistic purification and regressive linguistic fundamentalism. The emergence of racist, anti-immigration groups in Australia and Europe have their parallels in the emergence of radical manifestations of Islamic fundamentalism in Malaysia as elsewhere. These manifestations of regressive parochialism seek to insulate their particular nations from the regulatory forces and destructuring of lives created by "globalisation from above." In part regressive parochialism can be attributed to the erosion of the protectionist umbrella of the nation-state, the Cold War superpower alignments and the western European imperial infrastructure—legacies of previous eras of globalisation. As the state relinquishes its regulatory and institutional capacities for protecting its citizens' economic and social security to global market forces, there are heightened levels of desire to reproduce the attitudes, behaviours, and practices which were once associated with the protectionist nation-state. While many of these have long ceased to have symbolic relevance and meaning, they are revived in a wave of nostalgic resentment politics.

In Australia the emergence of the One Nation/White Nation/English-only movement in 1996 was an effort to revivify images of a tarnished White Australia politics. Although necessarily responsive to the electoral pull of this regressive parochialism, Australian governments have used this movement to mask the socio-cultural consequences of their radical commitment to neo-liberal globalism. The emergence of Islamic opposition parties in Malaysia has been portrayed, mostly by the ruling elite, as an attempt to retreat toward a more secure and morally pure nation-building project based on religious principles. Advocacy of mono-religious politics is an attempt to insulate the nation-state from global influences that seem to undermine its moral economy.

This resentment politics is stimulated by the global restructuring of the world economy and its failure to address the miseries of the poor and marginalised. However, it strikes out against racialised others rather than those imposing "globalisation from above." Regressive parochialism redefines the legitimacy and authenticity of the nation-state around exclusionary criteria: racism, fundamentalism, chauvinism, and xenophobia. This backlash politics is a response to and expression of globalisation from above, and has moved from the margins to structure "meanstream" politics:

> opportunistic politicians have tended to build on grass-roots discontent by contending that jobs were being lost to overseas markets where labor conditions were horrible and that immigrants were driving down domestic wages and exerting pressures on public services. ....Such backlash politics have become a structural feature of this period, present in virtually every advanced industrial society. It fosters chauvinistic and xenophobic types of nationalism that are essentially intolerant of differences, and hence radically inconsistent with the sort of juridical nationalism that is the ideological taproot of the modern secular state, including its stress on the citizen as an individual member, purged for political purposes of secondary identities and pledged to reconcile private concerns with the promotion of the public good for the whole of society. (Falk 1999, 161–162)

The project of globalising English is not without tensions or problems. Globalising English is a challenge to local languages, identities, knowledges, and histories, and is seen as a revival or extension of Anglo-American colonialist domination. There are also anxieties created over claims about the ownership of English that trigger the political backlash nurtured by regressive parochialism. Globalisation has provoked fear and resentment often within nations such as England, the US, Australia, and Canada (which see themselves as native speakers) at the very idea that others—Singaporeans, Filipinos, Malaysians, or Indians—might have increased control of English and enter the transnational ELT business (Graddol 1999). While the English and US/Americans do actively assert control over the English language, David Crystal (2000, 117) observes that the global spread of English is such that "no one can be said to own it—in the sense of having a recognised right to direct its development. English is now used in so many places by so many people that it no longer has a single centre of influence."

The reaction of Anglophone nations has been to secure the legitimacy of claims to the English language by resorting to nostalgic and outdated views about standardised Englishes and promoting the sale and distribution of ELT products, services, and methods that reinforce these views. Such attempts to revive this Anglophone agenda is a regressive reaction to what are perceived as threatening forms of English language hybridity and competition by othered languages. While Anglophone colonialist desires have not disappeared, there are alternative perspectives on the global/local nexus that accept the displacement of English-speaking natives. The idea of appropriating English offers a certain amount of optimism given that it promotes a critical orientation to the globalisation and localisation of multivocal Englishes.

Developing Global Optimism Locally

Much of the radical, corporate-friendly restructuring of education in Anglophone nations is continuing from the end of last century. Increasingly, countries like Australia and Malaysia are engaged by worldwide socio-political, cultural, and economic forces, most of which are beyond the control of established state institutions. The continuation of an English language curriculum centred on the nation-state, such that it excludes the global connectedness of Malaysia or Australia or ignores new forms of multivocal Englishes, is now seriously out of tune with current trends and thereby fails to meet students' changing needs. In responding to these changes students of the English language and those learning how it is taught will not benefit from ELT policies or practices framed in terms of postmodernist Anglocentricism, US/American cultural imperialism, or regressive parochialism. Nostalgia for the past of the English empire or the fundamentalist pursuit of White Australia politics will not help either.

On the contrary, English language teachers who examine the possibilities presented by globalisation from above and below will be able to make an advantage of the opportunities flowing from the risks of globalising English. This orientation is needed in order to make "global optimism" a reality of ELT students rather than confirming hopelessness that leads to either passivity or the resentment politics that exploits racist and religious fundamentalism. It could prove valuable for ELT businesses to make links with democratically inspired organisations of global civil society oriented to language rights, moving beyond regressive parochialism, cultural imperialism, and postmodern Anglo-centrism so as to make "hope practical, rather than despair convincing" (Williams 1983, 240).

In order to make global optimism a reality, English language teachers can work with their students to examine the possibilities presented by global restructuring and look for the opportunities in the global difficulties we face. An approach to ELT that is informed by a perspective of global optimism may help in thinking beyond economic reductionism and parochial, Anglo centric interests.

The opportunities and challenges posed by the sustainability of language diversity globally can be explored in ELT classrooms. This is necessary not in the least because an image of a future filled with hope is needed to enable students to make meaning out of, and to give fullness to, their lives (Turner 1994, 147). The confusion and bewilderment that make risks to other languages borne of globalising English now seem an inevitable part of the world's future, of our students' futures, is being challenged in small but nonetheless significant ways by initiatives that emphasise bilingual education and the sustainability of global multilingualism. Such educational initiatives are among the resources that English language teachers can gather for "a journey of hope. If there are no easy answers, there are still available and discoverable hard answers, and it is these that we can now learn to make and share" (Williams 1983,

268–269).

While there are certain risks associated with the current processes of global restructuring and the compression of time/space relations, it is also necessary to explore the opportunities that these create for innovation. For instance, global forces, including those based both on governments and on citizen groups, have served to constrain the actions that undermine people's language rights. Perhaps more importantly, this type of activity may result in a form of global citizenship with the power to press for the enactment and enforcement of language rights legislation regionally or even globally. The development of the transnational ELT industry offers significant educational opportunities for teachers to nurture an optimistic global consciousness. This provides a valuable opportunity to engage with the tensions between the role of education in addressing local concerns and their connections to and embeddedness in global concerns. It would be an educational disappointment if national efforts to build monolingual societies overrode the possibilities for sustaining the world's biolinguistic diversity created by global restructuring. Should ELT be framed solely and exclusively from the perspectives of Anglophone interests or should a more global perspective be developed? Transnational ELT is caught in a tension between a commitment to globalising English in order to serve Anglophone economic interests, and the opportunities English language teaching has for adopting an innovative educational role within global civil society.

CHAPTER 3

Trends in the Business of Teaching English

> A language which has come to be spoken by as many people as English has, has ceased to be the property of any of its constituent communities. Nobody owns English now—not the British, with whom the language began, nor the Americans, who are now its largest mother tongue community. The total number of mother tongue speakers in the world is some 400 million, is actually falling as a proportion of world English users. (Crystal 2000, 52)

A major theme in the conceptualisation of globalisation is its economic dimensions. Globalism is a neo-liberal political project to impose economic reductionism across the globe. Accordingly this neo-liberal ideology is promoting an integrated global economy regulated by market forces, operating through state sponsorship and enacted by new transnational institutions such as the global alliances constructed around the producers, distributors, and deliverers of infotainment. While the production and dissemination of the English language (and how to teach it) are still key functions of ELT providers, such knowledge increasingly has value and legitimacy insofar as it attracts global (fee-paying) clients and serves the interests of money-making enterprises (Singh and Singh 1999). This is due to the increasing privatisation of education and training where more and more aspects of teaching and learning are being commodified. English language teaching (ELT) curricula, courses, instructional materials, tests, methods, and theories are being transformed into saleable products and online deliverables. This privatisation, in countries such as Australia and Malaysia, has featured a shift away from situating ELT as a civic good linked to nation building-goals, toward that of an individualised market relationship where English is a way of securing economic advancement, elevated status and prestige, and trans-national mobility.

These changes in rationale have been accompanied by new, complex sets of relationships involving clusters of ELT providers spanning both the private and public sector and operating in a competitive global market. These new educational markets integrate state ELT providers in universities and further education colleges with multinational tele-communications and media organisations, private ELT providers, the cultural agencies of government and businesses producing popular consumer commodities (Kell 1999). The diversity and scope of these ELT providers reflects and gives expression to shifts toward the internationalisation of education markets and the complex shifts in the nature of English. Moving from a parochial provincial language "owned" by a small group of "native" speakers English has become a global language owned by an expanding and diverse range of speakers. This chapter explores the escalation in the importance and competitiveness of the ELT industry and its changing character in the context of the global commodification of English.

The Diversification of ELT Providers

While the great diversity in the global ELT industry can create confusion, there are a series of emerging markets that are serviced by carefully differentiated providers. The global ELT market splits into a variety of providers ranging from national flagships to hybridised enterprises through to shopfront colleges. These groupings are not exclusive because many ELT providers like Australian and English universities relate to, benefit from, and contribute to the operations of the national flagships as well as the emerging hybrid enterprise structures.

The *national flagship* providers operate transnationally and are funded by the governments of countries where English is the primary language to deliver cultural programmes, educational services, and English language teaching. These flagships integrate their cultural, educational, and language activities with their political and economic roles of furthering the national interests of their respective governments in a specific region. One of the longest established flagships is the British Council, which is directly funded by the English government. IDP Australia is funded through Australian universities and is indirectly an agent of the Australian government. Both organisations are charged with promoting their nation's image internationally and selling their nation's education and training products. While there is direct competition between these English and Australian flagships, there are also mutual interests which lead them to collaborate. Most notably the British Council and IDP Australia have a shared interest in preserving the integrity and status of the International English Language Testing System (IELTS) as a measure to standardise language, as a quality assurance instrument, and as a business activity.

The emerging integration of public and private organisations is operationalised via consortia of *hybrid enterprises*. In the global education market ELT providers are becoming increasingly involved with non-education providers such as publishing, multimedia, and Internet firms. These hybrid enterprises now include the private arms of universities as well as international franchised language schools such as those owned by Study Group International. There is a growing range of hybrid enterprises that have resulted from partnerships between publishing, multimedia, and information technology firms and newly corporatised education providers such as universities. Numbered among these hybrid enterprises are such partnerships as the Global University Alliance and Universitas 21. As ELT providers are using new technologies of learning, these partnerships take on a strategic imperative to mobilise resources and expertise to address English language teaching globally.

There are a growing number of small independent *shopfront colleges* with fewer than 10,000 students providing a range of ELT services. Many of these operators are long established organisations that are privately owned and located in inner city locations. Shopfront colleges are varied in sise, ownership, and program delivery but are heavily reliant on securing "native speakers" for their teaching staff to maintain market credibility. They are also dependent on ELT curriculum, methodology, and products developed by national flagships. Their marketing edge often lies in lower pricing, more accessible hours, and established, reputations. In the face of strong competition some of these colleges are subject to significant criticism about quality assurance. As a consequence, long established and reputable college operators are keen to enter into partnerships that typify those of hybrid enterprises.

National Flagship: The British Council

The ELT industry is intensely competitive. However, it is dominated by the flagship of England's national interests, the British Council. The Council offers those working in the globalised ELT industry some useful insights into the cultural dynamics of the emerging transnational education order. While the Council correctly claims to be an independent, non-political organisation, registered in England as a charity, at another level it is also an arm of the English foreign office and as such an instrument of the English government's cultural and economic policies. Through spreading the study and use of English worldwide the Council seeks to further the business and political interests of England throughout the world. It does this by providing access to English ideas and expertise through English language education, testing, books, and information on English arts, science, and technology. In 1995 the Council launched the English 2000 Project as part of its strategic investment and business development program to

> facilitate informed debate about [and to forecast] the future use[s] and learning of the English language worldwide [...] and to help develop new means of teaching and learning English. The project team works to position British English language teaching goods and services to the mutual benefit of Britain and the countries with which it works. (Graddol 1997, i)

The British Council, a long-standing participant in the global ELT industry, has shifted away from merely offering English courses toward a more sophisticated integrated strategy providing a suite of ELT products and services. Originally established in the 1930s as a propaganda arm of the English government, the Council was charged with combating fascism throughout Europe. It has moved from its origins as an organisation featuring the "gentleman diplomat" to representing the global economic interests of England. The British Council has been a vital conduit for retaining contact with former colonies of the English empire through the funding of technical programmes and institutions. Whilst the Council's priorities have moved beyond these large-scale programmes, it still values the relationship between ELT and national development. Evidence of this is to be found on the British Council's Web site, where the dilemmas of development are summarised as follows:

> Language is an essential component in development. Without *the ability to communicate* what their real needs are, people risk having *solutions imposed* on them and being denied *access to information* which will assist them being *empowered* to make their own decisions. (http:www.britishcouncil.org/english/ lang/dev/index/html)

The characterisation of the English language as an imposition by "globalisation from above" is counterposed by claims that assign English a prominent role in people's empowerment:

> What type of communication and in which language will depend on a variety of factors; often the first language will be most appropriate, at other times the regional or national language and at yet others English—as the main language of global communication and business, will be most appropriate. (http:www.britishcouncil.org/english/lang/dev/index/ html)

Here English is strategically linked to the enhancement of national economic development and modernisation. For English to be used as a means of alleviating poverty the proposition is put that there must be a combination of low-cost reading materials and trained teachers capable of using those materials. The Council's approach establishes an integrated market involving ELT materials, teacher education, professional development, and the methodologies needed to support them.

In the context of a transnational market for the Council's ELT services and products, the most recent growth areas are Central and Eastern Europe and other countries that emerged out of the political and economic collapse of the former Union of Soviet Socialist Republics and its satellites. These new markets complement the traditional Asian and African markets which emerged in the decolonisation period of the 1950s as a consequence of the British Council's commitment to development under the "Winds of Change" doctrine of Prime Minister Harold Macmillan. These policies ensured that the Council and its programmes had a significant presence in the former English colonies and this has helped keep the gaze of these former colonies focused on London, even when post-colonial regional interests dominate national policy debates.

National Flagship: IDP Australia

The cultural and educational arms of other governments have replicated these institutional shifts. For instance, the Australian national flagship is the International Development Program (IDP Australia), which is funded and owned by all 36 of that nation's universities. Like the British Council it aggressively markets Australian university education including English language courses; some of these are run by IDP itself such as the Australian Centre for Education (ACE) in Cambodia.

In 1999 IDP assisted some 11,000 students from 29 countries to study at Australian education and training institutions. Although headquartered in Canberra IDP has offices in 31 countries where it represents some 250 Australian educational organisations. IDP recently reorganised its operations to devolve greater responsibility to its localised offices and to develop alliances with other providers including media organisations. Like that of the British Council, IDP's role is threefold: acting as a marketing and recruiting agent for providers, a quality assurance agent for inbound students, and a cultural agent for Australia overseas.

ELT services and products constitute a large and lucrative globalised market that is increasingly characterised by substantial international competition and ambiguity over changing priorities. IDP Australia is experiencing intense competition from media organisations and private providers using new digital technologies (*Campus Review* Vol. 10, No. 20). New overseas competitors such as Belgium, France and Germany, and existing competitors like the British Council, are challenging the interests of Australia's educational business throughout Asia and eroding its market share. In response to this global competition, IDP is seeking venture capital loans and equity shareholding, and developing robust and strategic partnerships to enhance its participation in the global marketplace. Recognising that Australia's share of the ELT market is dependent on IDP's performance it is now working to become more skillful in its use of marketing, promotion, new technologies, and virtual sites.

Increasingly the survival of ELT providers is evaluated by their ability to join in global alliances to share in an expanding market. The development of collaborative partnerships capable of spanning the globe is already evident among Australian universities. Melbourne University has merged with New Zealand's Active English Language Academy to form a private company with branches in Vietnam and Taiwan. In 1988, when the Australian education industry began to enter the international market in earnest, globally the market for ELT products and services generated approximately $US9.5 billion (Pennycook 1994, 155). This market was divided between England (16.4%), North America (32%), and Asia and the Pacific (32%). Since then the dimensions of this market have grown dramatically, fuelling increasing competition to the extent that "by the late 1990s intensive English language courses for overseas students constituted nearly one quarter of Australia's 'export' education industry and generated some $750 million for an industry estimated to be worth $3 billion a year" (Abbott 1997, 12).

By 2000 Australian ELT providers such as IDP were experiencing a boom in traditional markets such as Malaysia and newer ones in Cambodia. In Malaysia applications to study in Australia escalated in the first six months of 2000 by 132%. At the IDP managed Centre for Australian Education in Phnom Penh there were over 2,000 students enrolled in English language programmes including English for Academic Purposes (AEP) as well as vocationally oriented courses. In 2000 Australia's RMIT University and ACE commenced the delivery of award courses in business management with over 100 students in the first intake. This alliance between RMIT University and IDP's Australian Centre for Education is another instance of the new and complex organisational arrangements that now typify the globalised ELT market.

The New Hybrid ELT Enterprises

Many of the organisational shifts that have happened in the education and training sector have been amplified in the ELT industry owing to the heightened competition and the need to operate in more cost-effective configurations than the heavily bureaucratised, corporate universities. The education bureaucracies that characterised the nation-building era of providing for public social and economic security are rapidly being transformed into new hybrid learning enterprises. Even in Asian countries where the state has steered developments in education, increasing numbers of public education institutions, including those involved in the delivery of ELT programmes, are entering into strategic alliances and forming consortia with private providers. For example, in Malaysia these hybrid enterprises include twinning and articulation arrangements between Sunways, a private corporation, and Australia's Monash and Victoria Universities through a joint campus in Kuala Lumpur. In Cambodia, Malaysian universities are also teaming up with local providers to compete against Australian providers. For instance, the Universiti Utara Malaysia conducts business courses in Phnom Penh in collaboration with the Cambodian National Institute of Management.

These "hybrid organisations" blur the boundaries between the private sector and the corporatised public sector. These new hybrid education enterprises of multiple partners are developed as subsidiary companies to increase flexibility and to expedite innovation in their parent organisations. In the ELT industry where there is substantial demand and increasing competition, these joint ventures create the capacity to conduct operations in accordance with government compliance regimes that enforce the relocation of public education within the regulatory force of the global market. This enables the private arms of public universities to set differential employment conditions and student fees, and to pay profits as dividends to partners (Kell, Balatti, and Muspratt 1997). With the globalisation of the production and markets for increasingly corporatised and privatised ELT services has come the need to develop global marketing strategies based on more effective uses of existing assets and the provision of products that satisfy customer needs.

To effect market advantage new arrangements are being made by ELT providers for credit transfer for studies undertaken at "feeder" institutions. They have also developed hybrid courses, such as offering the simultaneous study of both the English language and new technology skills. Joint venture enterprises have negotiated to recruit students from these countries to undertake fully articulated or even jointly badged courses. Typically, these joint ventures offer students the cost-effective opportunity to undertake a greater proportion of their education within their home country. Where visa provisions permit short, intensive courses billed as mini-conferences travel, and accommodation costs for students can be minimised. In Malaysia, for example, these courses are marketed using a 3+l formula to represent a course structure with three years of study in the student's home country linked to one year of overseas study. Such courses are hopeful of assistance from Web-based technologies to deliver ELT materials and to facilitate student interactions in order to provide flexible student-centred learning. English is the dominating language of the hardware, software, authoring languages and the information super-highways that are part of these new domains of flexible learning.

Major challenges arise from the emergence of international partnerships involving multinational corporations, global media, and telecommunications organisations as ELT providers. Mega-corporations are key agents in reshaping the delivery of ELT by their use of sophisticated forms of the new technologies (Lepani 1996; Kenway 1995). New alliances involving consortia of ELT providers and media giants like Foxtel are setting new standards for production, distribution, and delivery. However, much of the money made in electronic commerce through businesses such as Yahoo!, an Internet portal which has experienced financial difficulties, comes from advertising. Most ELT providers are fixated on selling course content.

The Universitas 21 alliance comprises eighteen universities from around the world, and includes Australia's Melbourne University, which has a significant presence in Malaysia. Universitas 21 is a major player in the $US100 billion international education market with a combined total of over 500,000 students and 44,000 staff. This alliance has formed a partnership with News Limited Corporation and plans to establish a delivery network using new technologies by accessing some of the $US40 billion in capital controlled by Rupert Murdoch's communications empire. Similarly new international venture capital is financing *J & R Educational Media*, *Global English*, *Then*, and *Learning Smith*, education businesses that combine learning brokerage, online learning, and adult education.

Questions have been raised about the role of these hybrid business ventures as vehicles for privatising public education services and assets. There are dilemmas concerning the tensions between the differential responses in the commercialised context of private sector competition and its financial bottomline and the requirements of social and cultural responsibilities associated with more traditional public sector roles. The latter was mostly associated with building and nurturing the security of the public. These tensions are now emerging in Malaysia where some 360 private providers were approved in 1999. How these new hybrid organisations will manage the tensions between equitable social outcomes across racial and communal groups, and their own need for profit remains a focus of considerable debate. This drive for profitability and the incremental privatisation of the ELT industry has considerable implications for the social injustices that threaten the global sustainability of biolinguistic diversity and issues associated with the widening digital divide.

Radically new forms of inequality are emerging in the global knowledge economy based on the new digital technologies (Beck 1999, 117). In

Australia only 20 percent of low-income families are likely to have access to the Internet, while over 50 percent of higher income earners have such access. This division is worse for those living in regional areas remote from densely wired metropolises where the possibilities for the formation of community are being fragmented across an indeterminant range of cable and satellite communications networks (Singh, Harreveld, and Hunt 1997). Globally 20 percent of the world's population constitutes over 90 percent of the world's Internet users; in other words 80 percent of the world's population is presently excluded from this new knowledge economy (Conhaim 2000). While one-third of the Australian population is likely to be marginalised from the world's virtual communities, the situation in countries throughout South East Asia and beyond is far worse. Technically, it is possible for

> people in the remotest locations will have the potential capacity to be educated through the Internet at a fraction of the cost of traditional methods, having access to the best minds in the world ...while sitting in Nong Khai in Thailand, Kuala Nerang in Malaysia or Phuntsoling in Bhutan. But sadly, many marginalised people will be further marginalised. (Ismail 2000, 7)

It is not only a matter of accessing the net culture where global poverty is encountered but also in the information and speed hierarchies structured into its usability. The cost of using personal computers, the language used on the Internet, and other exclusionary factors mean that this medium is thus far dominated by a relatively wealthy elite, with most of the world's people shut out from using it. Internationally, the Internet remains dominated by users in the United States and other industrialised countries. Access in developing countries remains rare: "The poor in developing countries are not likely to go online soon, as 80% of the world's population lacks basic telecommunications facilities, let alone computers" (Warschauer 1999, 17).

The propensity for the exclusion and marginalisation of many people has much to do with the differentiated marketing of English to promote access for mobility in the transnational labor market. The educational use of digital technologies is being developed on the promise that they will actually address inequalities in provision by enhancing access and reducing the tyranny of distance. In particular, work-integrated action learning projects are being developed for the delivery of flexible learning experiences to the desktops of workers. The staff and management of large transnational companies are being recruited on the promise that flexible learning can provide for retraining and up-skilling without the associated costs of travel and subsistence or the loss of productive time. Strategies such as these have become all the more important as the competition in the international marketplace for ELT grows and have made continuous innovation in ELT products and services a driving force. These developments are changing the culture of teachers' work. Not surprisingly, there is a sense of uncertainty and confusion about teaching, knowledge, and the institutions in which English is taught and learned.

The New Forms of Selling English

The products and services of the new transnational education order are increasingly being commodified: that is, designed, packaged, advertised, and marketed in ways similar to that of manufactured goods. The view that English and English language teaching are commodities is not new. However, that they are now so widely and deliberately marketed as such is something that has only occurred since the late 1980s following the collapse of the Soviet Union and its communist allies. ELT providers are seeking to expand the global markets for their products, the learning of the English language, and new methods of teaching it, using the digital technologies of human interaction, knowledge production, and reflection to pioneer educational innovations.

Diversifying ELT Products and Services

The knowledge-intensive industries associated with the new transnational education order are increasing the global market for ELT products and services. In the weightless or immaterial knowledge economy of digital capitalism, ELT businesses revolve around and are integral to "word processing, email communication, database queries and information retrieval" (Graddol 1997, 35). The focus is on teaching students the new technologies and the ability to frame questions to search electronic data banks and to know which services to secure. The screen-based ELT industry now sees knowledge workers dispersed at great distances around the globe, albeit with telecommunications connections stretching from Melbourne to Penang, from Ho Chi Minh City to Johannesburg. This has increased the pressure for cheaper, non-regulated but skilled labor to work in the knowledge-intensive, ELT industry.

The transnational ELT business is a massive industry that supplies a diverse range of products and services to speakers of other languages, prime amongst these being varieties of "standardised English." Knowledge of English is now a product to be sold to consumers worldwide. Here it is worth noting that the process of standardising or rationalising spoken, and then written English, in order to achieve "linguistic correctness" began in England several centuries ago and continues to be a matter of considerable dispute even there (Williams 1965, 237–253). This process of fabricating standardised Englishes was initiated by the rising middle class of England who were involved in developing a "model" (rather than common) English language for both functional convenience and to assert class distinctions. These social divisions have since been misinterpreted and mispresented as distinctions between the educated and the uneducated—an issue confronted by many bilingual students, including those studying abroad.

Raymond Williams (1965, 247) defined standardised British English as a tool that made some English people "capable of the vulgar insolence of telling other Englishmen [sic] that they do not know how to speak their own language." This quest for standardised or "proper" English confronts emergent local varieties of English, an issue highlighted in former Anglophone colonies such as Australia, Canada, New Zealand, and the United States, which are considered to be "native" speakers of English. Speaking of these changes John Mulhall, the Chair of the Australian Broadcasting Standing Committee on Spoken English, explains how this diversification of English informed that public television corporation's policy making:

> Australian English has moved on, it's diverged from British English, we've made a deliberate decision, as long ago as the 60s, I think not to preserve some kind of Oxbridge accent on air, because we need to sound Australian. We need to sound relevant to our audience, which is extremely important so part of it is using Australian pronunciation for English words. (Sheil 2000, 8)

The *Macquarie Australian English Dictionary* has reinforced development of standardised Australian English having catalogued distinctively Australian idioms, phraseology, and grammar. Not surprisingly the development of a standardised Australian English draws on a diverse linguistic heritage that merges elements of Afghani, Cornish, Gaelic, Hindi, Welsh, Polynesian, and Indigenous languages, including the languages of the Torres Strait, to name but a few. The emergence of local Englishes creates challenges for the durability and robustness of ELT products structured around standardised British or US/American Englishes.

In addition to varieties of standardised Englishes, other worldwide exports include English language teachers in search of pleasure and sustenance; theories and methods of ELT, as well as ELT materials, books, and courses. A particularly important product is English for Special Purposes such as business, science and technology, health and medicine. English language examinations and the training of students to sit for these exams are among other highly marketable ELT products and services. Much of the money generated by Australia's ELT businesses comes from overseas clients, particularly students from Asia. They are keen to take English language examinations and to purchase English language instruction as an investment in either a financially rewarding career and/or transnational mobility as skilled migrant labor.

Selling Enterprise and Heritage Englishes

There is increasing pressure on ELT providers to adopt an entrepreneurial orientation in order to attract mobile global consumers and their capital. The marketing of English, and its associated images of English enterprise and cultural heritage, is intensified by competition between global cities. Success can be short-lived due to increased competition or rendered moot by alternative innovations. Thus, when we speak of ELT as a business we are speaking of both the co-joining and disarticulation of enterprise English and cultural heritage English. Most of those involved in the businesses of creating ELT products and services have been drawn into entrepreneurial initiatives and the English of enterprise. Enterprise English is constituted by knowledge of the language relating to global business and the new technologies, and other dimensions of English are abandoned. Cultural heritage English is marketed to those seeking to manufacture differentiated class identities, and is

> centred around the creation of an image, a fabricated and in-authentic identity, a false aura, usually achieved through "the recuperation of history (real, imagined, or simply re-created pastiche) and of community (again, real, imagined, or simply packaged for sale by producers.)" (Morley and Robins 1995, 37)

Viable ELT providers and their products are increasingly embedded within a relatively integrated global economic system. This new era of global restructuring requires that the linguistic particularities of localities, say standardised Australian English, are constructed in relation to the market needs of consumers worldwide. The meaning of "local" ELT activities is being recast in terms of global markets rather than merely the nation-building task of educating migrant labor. The local ELT product is being reconstituted in and through global marketing. In the case of the Australian and New Zealand ELT products, these compete on unequal terms in the global marketplace against British English (particularly in the former colonies of the English empire) and US/American English (in a range of Asian countries including Taiwan, Japan, and the Philippines). Australian and New Zealand ELT providers not only compete as supplicants in this context but are also in competition with other local ELT providers such as Malaysian marketers of English. Capturing investors (e.g., joint venture partners) and clients in these circumstances is especially difficult. ELT products from any given locality are vulnerable to abrupt changes in the movement of people and investment, and the increasing production of a global consumer culture mediated by US/American English. Thus, while some local ELT providers respond to these challenges with introverted, parochial nostalgia, most have worked to embed their ELT operations in a transnational enterprise culture.

It is no longer viable to make ELT products for a national market alone. The privatisation of public services and their increasing regulation by the global market is displacing nationally centred services by a new generation of ELT producers operating in the emerging transnational education order. The teaching of English globally involves international trade in cultural experiences leading to the enhancement of the profile and refurbishment of the image of distinctively local ELT products so that they are strategically oriented to globally dispersed contexts. Australian ELT providers are working to differentiate their cultural assets from British and US/American Englishes. They are exploiting the entrepreneurial capacities of their English language resources especially as these relate to the new technologies and bilingual capacities for the translation of cultural differences and the interpretation of the processes of cultural hybridisation. In a world where US/American globalisation seems to be erasing differences, the commodification of local cultural heritage (e.g.,

British English) is about creating distinctive products and services in the eyes of global consumers (Morley and Robins 1995, 119–120). In order to position themselves in this new global context, Australian ELT businesses are working to "re-image" and progressively "re-imagine" themselves as innovative purveyors of enterprise English.

Reimaging Consumption: Reimagining Approaches to Selling English

The selling of ELT products and services has been under way for many decades. As early as 1968 the British Council stated that there "is a hidden sales element in every English teacher, book, magazine, film-strip and television programme sent overseas" (The Council cited in Pennycook 1994, 145). In helping to sell British English worldwide through spreading its study and use, the Council simultaneously tries to develop students' cultural understanding of English literature, arts, and politics, and to further the interests of England as its influence in many regions changed after granting independence to countries like Malaysia. Pennycook (1994, 147–148) explains that the spending of public money on this cultural heritage English, or "cultural propaganda," has been justified by its political and economic significance to England. Other cultural arms of the English government, including the British Broadcasting Corporation (BBC), have harnessed it in developing products that have appeal in enhancing the global status of British English. The popularity of British English is evident in the large numbers of videos, tapes, and compact discs available in Malaysian retail outlets that are produced and marketed by the English. These range in style and substance from videos such as *The History of the English-speaking Peoples* by Winston Churchill, through the classist *Thomas the Tank Engine* for children, to audio-cassettes to help parents teach English to their children.

Politically, English cultural agencies sought to use ELT commodities to influence the views of elites in the former colonies of the English empire as part of the Cold War struggle against both communism and the global flows of "Third World" peoples to "First World" nations. Economically, the British Council sought to further the use of British English as "the language of transnational commercial promotion, opening the world more readily to [England's] salesmen [sic]" (The Council cited in Pennycook 1994, 149). Attention has now shifted away from the preoccupation of the global conflict between capitalism and communism toward a range of other struggles including that between the project of globalising English and the language rights movement's efforts to sustain biolinguistic diversity globally.

In this context it is, therefore, not surprising to learn that the Australian government has in recent decades been promoting the sale of ELT commodities. While less attention has been given to the problems arising from efforts to resurrect White Australia politics, the government expects Australia's ELT businesses to promote this country's preferred cultural imaginings and to secure trade and investment for it. In 1999 the Minister for Foreign Affairs, Alexander Downer (Junior), raised the idea of establishing an Australian equivalent to the British Council:

> We have to understand in this country that promoting our culture is promoting an image of Australia; it's about promoting our diversity of society, the creativity of our society, and when it comes to the national interest, yes, it can help with trade, it can help with investment, it can help make Australian cities more attractive to multinational companies setting up regional headquarters. (Downer cited in Osmond 1999, 3)

In seeking to compete with England and the United States, Australian and New Zealand ELT providers have tended to replicate the structures, attitudes, behaviour, and products of their competitors. Australia has developed agencies such as IDP to sell ELT services and also uses such agencies as the Australian Broadcasting Corporation (ABC) as its cultural ambassadors. This is likely to accelerate as the ABC pursues a new role in the delivery of educational products, building on the success of Open Learning Australia's use of radio and television. ABC management envisions a role for itself in the Web-based delivery of an identifiably Australian form of education provision throughout Asia.

Because the English language speaking diaspora of the United States, Canada, South Africa, Australia and New Zealand have developed their own national varieties of English, the international market for England's ELT business would seem to be shrinking. Graddol (1997) argued for a re-examination of the work of English providers of ELT goods and services in terms of the competitive advantage they might secure through promoting a global brand image for a specifically "British English." Creating such a brand image through selective associations with English cultural heritage and a client-centred corporate image is one way of adding the value needed to make it possible to extract additional market share and increased revenue. Establishing a brand image for "British English" and "Education UK" more generally integrates enterprise English and cultural heritage English thereby creating the possibility of enhancing its market leverage. "British English" is a commodity marketed internationally to provide England a commercial advantage in the global knowledge economy. The vision for "British English" is to enhance its position as a resource that will produce even greater economic benefits for England by giving it a linguistic advantage in the international marketplace over its competitors offering other brands of English and other languages.

What is involved in creating a corporate brand image for cultural heritage English? The Foreword to the English 2000 report gives us an idea: "The British Council's task is to promote Britain and the English language throughout the world...I commend this work to all who are concerned to see a strong and vigorous future for our language" [i.e., British English] (Graddol 1997, i). The Foreword, authored and signed by His Royal Highness the Prince of Wales, draws on England's regal cultural heritage as a way of adding value to British English. The English monarchy is now being put to work in the international market for ELT products and services. Cultural heritage assets—including remnants of empire and royalty as much as nature, photographic works, video products, writers, and sporting legends—are exploited to create a positive sense of product(ive) difference in order to attract students to England's ELT products and services.

For many bilingual students the learning of English may be matter of advancing their material well-being, or of enhancing their possibilities for transnational mobility. However, the prospect of learning "British English" is being sold as having the additional benefit of acquiring even greater symbolic value, that is, the ability to give linguistic expression to a chosen source of aristocratic identity and social class differentiation. That "British English" is a differentiated, marketable commodity is related to the development of a global consumer culture (in which the teacher is the "supplier" and the student is the "customer") as much as the historical legacy of the English empire (Waters 1995, 139–145). The consumption of elite cultural goods bearing English brand names is being used to nurture consumers eager to play with the images, symbols, and meanings of England's regal heritage. The creation of this consumer culture by entrepreneurial brokers of ELT products and services also involves the development of social technologies (Featherstone 1995, 75–78). In particular this involves the rationalisation and re-ordering of the previous work practices of both ELT workers and their students around the new technologies and the new pedagogies that create or enable this to happen.

That transnational ELT providers transmit knowledge that has value and legitimacy is a matter of contestation. The British Council acknowledges that its current market advantage owes much to a colonial heritage whereby the global dimensions of the English empire established English as a compound of language varieties on which the sun has not yet set. However, the situation continues to change. After the Second World War British English found itself in increasing competition with US/American English which emerged to take significant global influence, largely because of the seductions of its popular, consumer culture. Organisations such as the IMF and the World Bank, and US/American colonisation of the Philippines, its occupation of Japan, and its military actions in Korea and Vietnam, contributed to this shift in the control of English. In the heat of the post–Cold War years regional trading blocs and multilateral political affiliations have emerged to upset the global structuring of the two worlds sustained by opposing super-powers, and those who met in Bandung in 1955 in search of a third way, a third world. The emergence of English as the language of Europe may mean that the European Union rather than the United States, provides the main economic and linguistic force shaping the future development of English globally. However, the history of England being the central authority for the English language is not a market advantage that it will easily relinquish.

Students from South East Asia pay a fee of (Aus) $14,000 to Australian universities for one year to study good, practical courses in new technologies and English. Other supplementary benefits to making an investment in Australian education attractive to these students and their parents include the promise of safety, good lecturers, and the opportunity for work experience. Moreover, it is cheaper than the more costly UK and US alternatives and also closer to students' homelands. Those returning home have the benefit of an internationally recognised degree and improved English to compete in the labor market against students with local university degrees. For those under 30 years of age, postgraduate study in Australia is sold as a pathway to permanent residence in Australia and its high standard of living, significant employment opportunities, and its reputation for fairness and equality.

Despite this Australia is losing 20,000 technology graduates each year, particularly to the United States in the global competition for new technology workers. To help Australia's new technology companies recruit some 35,000 staff a year for the next few years, the Australian government is looking at deficiencies in its immigration policies and procedures. Because many countries in Asia are gazetted as "high risk" technology graduates from there, even those who have studied in Australia experience excessive delays in obtaining work visas (Cope and Kalantzis 2000, 259–272).

Increasing Competition for ELT Products and Services

So how do we explain these trends in the ELT business toward international marketing, the selling of new products, and new tactics for securing sales? ELT providers from the Anglophone diaspora are more than a little anxious about those countries in which English is a second language but which have now made English their language. Indeed this anxiety is heightened by the recognition that there are fewer first language speakers of English than there are multilingual speakers of English. This has increased the competition in the international ELT market (Graddol 1999). Countries such as India, Malaysia, Singapore, and the Philippines are emerging as major competitors in providing education courses in English for students from Asia, Europe, Africa, and Latin America. These countries have generated a quite different expression of values and identities from those of Anglophone cultures and have further extended their English use to create intellectual properties and exports in English language goods and services. In India this is now evident in the new ELT products that are emerging from the exploding information technology industry centred in Bangalore and Hydrabad. This represents a challenge to ELT business prospects in Anglophone cultures, albeit a challenge that is somewhat mitigated by the asymmetrical power relations which privileges "First World/Northern" over "Third World/Southern" nation-states.

Postcolonial Alliances and Dangerous Competition

ELT providers in Australia are troubled by the increasing competitiveness of Asian and Latin American economies relative to those in the OECD, particularly in those products which typify the new technologies and practices of the ELT market. To date English has been dominated by the interests of its monolingual native speakers. This is expected to change when the majority of users of the English language throughout the world increase their sense of authority in its use as a second language (Graddol 1997). As already noted the English are losing control of the English language as the majority of its speakers in the world today are at least bilingual. These bilingual peoples who speak English as a second language are already teaching the language, in some cases they have developed models of correctness for local Englishes and a few are already emerging as centres of authority for the speaking and writing of English (Canagarajah 1999). Clearly this gives Anglophone entrepreneurs cause for worry: who, if not the English and their Anglo-ethnic disapora, will decide the future of English globally?

Countries where English is spoken as a second language are emerging as competitors with Anglophone nations in the ELT business and in the global market for the cultural resources and intellectual property available in English. As high technology and datacast media industries are developed in countries such as China, India, and Malaysia, the situation for monolingual "native" speaking ELT providers is coming under increased competition. The possible success of the struggles by Spanish speakers in the United States is likely to affect its future and that of English as a major world language. This is so despite the English-only movement's political and legislative tongue-tying of speakers of other languages, especially Spanish (Macedo 2000). The English language is taking on new forms as a result of both contact with other languages and changing communication needs and possibilities (McArthur 1998; Pennycook 1994). It is worth reiterating the point that the number of people speaking English as a second language already outnumbers those for whom it is a first language. Those who speak "English as a first language" are becoming minority stakeholders as English expands to become a global resource. As a consequence, Anglophone cultural resources might no longer provide the focus for the project of globalising English.

India and the Philippines are using new technology and English-speaking staff to create thousands of jobs and develop a range of global service industries including those in customer relationship management, answering customer e-mails, account payments, payroll management, the review of insurance claims, processing mortgages, and call centre services. Customer service management is especially important given that so many Internet transactions are abandoned before completion due to the lack of customer support. US/American businesses are outsourcing their customer support services to companies such as 24/7 Customer.com in Bangalore and New Delhi. India has an abundance of English-speaking graduates whose labor can be bought at comparatively lower cost to that paid in the United States. Indian customer service workers are specifically trained to speak in selected US/American English dialects and learn how to match the needs of US/American customers and their shopping habits.

The English-speaking diaspora is becoming increasingly aware that the franchise on the future of English as a global language seems to be passing into the hands of others; in Asia this means Indians, Sri Lankans, Malaysians, Singaporeans, and Filipinos. There is a growing consciousness that the ownership of English (and therefore ELT products and services) is passing into the control of bilingual speakers for whom English is a second language. The old story took the view that Australia was part of the modernising English-speaking world and that Malaysia was part of an exotic and underdeveloped world. This view has been thrown into crisis by Malaysia's economic successes. The dynamic hub of the world economy is now seen as moving from the Atlantic to the Pacific, from Euro-American countries to Asian-American countries. Here the English-speaking nations of Asia are emerging as a problem for Australia, occupying an ambivalent position of threatening competitors and significant market opportunities. Australian ELT providers now face the difficulties of living with the English-speaking countries of Asia and making a living out of Asians wanting to learn English.

Competition from Othered Languages

Anglophone concerns have also been heightened by the competition arising from the provision of languages othered through English in schools in various Anglophone countries throughout the world. The growth of global cities, such as Shanghai, is increasing the challenges to the project of globalising English as they develop their own powerful economic and cultural base around Mandarin. Anglophone ELT businesses operating in Asia are likely to be challenged by the strengthening role of global Chinese. The growth of intra-regional trade and financial dealings throughout Asia among the Chinese diaspora is already having an impact. Given that the 2008 Olympic Games will be held in Beijing, consider for a moment the implications and opportunities should the following advertising claim by accenture.com come true: "Chinese to become #1 Web language by 2007."

Anglophone businesses face significant competition from other languages. If the OECD countries become proportionally less important in the world economy, this could mean that there might be a comparable reduction in the demand for English. This is because if people's desire to learn a language is related to the wealth of a country, then the languages spoken in rich countries are much more rewarding to learn. However, English-speaking countries such as England and Australia have to date been less than successful in meeting the need they each have to operate in bilingual contexts.

The dominance of English in global telecommunications may soon reach saturation point. The growth of the Internet in terms of English language speakers may have already reached a critical mass. Given that in 1997 Internet usage was highest in the United States, it is not surprising then that English was seen as the dominating language of this new communications technology. However, this is unlikely to continue to be the case. Internet use began later in Europe and elsewhere in the world where it is now experiencing rapid growth. In Europe, for example, Germany is expected to become the largest Internet user. These developments suggest a possible shift in the dominance of English as *the* language of the Internet. The growth of Web sites and Internet news-groups making extensive use of languages othered through globalising English is expected to reduce the proportion of computer-based communications in English to less than 40 percent within the next decade (Warschauer 2000, 156). ELT businesses are acutely aware that as "communication infrastructure improves and relative costs fall more telephone conversations around the world will be held in languages other than English" (Graddol

1997, 37). Communication technologies such as the Internet will be encouraging new forms of transnational affiliation around globally dispersed communities speaking an increasing range of languages. In the new global economy integrated media corporations

> seek to maximise their market share by shaping their products to local conditions. Thus, while CNN and MTV originally broadcast around the world in English they are now producing editions in Hindi, Spanish, and other languages in order to compete with other international and regional media outlets. (Warschauer 2000, 157)

The new technologies of human interaction, reflection, and knowledge production are becoming increasingly customised, with marked improvements in the possibilities for them being used in languages othered by English (Singh 2001a). Whereas once Latin writing systems were the dominating forms for computer programming and use, the development of new technical vocabulary has provided increased potential for communication within and across countries in many different languages. Of course, Asian languages such as Bahasa Malaysia, Vietnamese, and Bahasa Indonesian, which use Roman script, have not found this to be a problem. Not only can documents be generated in different scripts it may soon be possible for rudimentary machine translation to be made of some of those in English into other languages and vice versa. With the possibility of controlled, restricted language texts being translated using new technology, the need for learning English as a second language may take a different path. The close link between computers and English has already been broken:

> Internet anglocentricity continues to provide the originating language principle, but fractures are spreading and creating marginal non-anglophone spaces on the Internet. The Internet, born and nurtured in cyber-English, is in the process of market segmentation and gradual maturation ...reconceptualizing the nets as a set of linked human languages that actualise heteroglossic norms, not simply as a domain of market segementation and software localisation from an English norm, will aid in propelling minoritarianism from out of the electronic shadows. (Lockard 2000, 176, 177)

It is no longer possible to think of ELT provision in terms that assume the continuing dominance of English-speaking countries over others. Despite the 1997 financial crisis which gave renewed impetus to Euro-American colonialism by interrupting growth in East Asia, Asian economic development continues to bring about a shift in global power relations (Daly and Logan 1999). As newly authorised participants in world trade, China and the Chinese diaspora throughout Asia are seen as major challenges. The concern here is for the intensification of competition from new ELT intermediaries. This competition will test the ability of Anglophone ELT providers to maintain the stability of the symbolic hierarchies that have given British English and US/American English positional advantage. Their vision of a global order in which their Englishes and their knowledge economy have prevailed for so long may recede or the risks of global English may continue unchecked.

CHAPTER 4

The Risks of Globalising English

> "Global" is a trendy word nowadays. But without cynicism, what I mean is that we can teach English, through the environment, without teaching. "Englishness" or "Americanness" or whatever cultural values we might accidentally or deliberately put across to our students. We do not have to provide an un-questioning diet of fast food, pop and fashion to interest teenagers; nor do we have to impose our view of the role of women in society upon those who happen to think differently. (Etchells 1995, 1)

Many of the risks affecting and caused by the project of globalising English have a paradoxical quality. The risks to ELT providers are accelerating as the global spread of English loses its monopoly on the world's technologies of human interaction, reflection, and knowledge production. The danger for ELT providers from countries where English is the "primary" language grows dramatically as the currency of English consumes global communications and its popularity furthers the colonisation of virtual reality. The native's loss of ownership of the language has accompanied the globalisation of English (Graddol 1999). Increasingly Anglophone providers of ELT products and services find themselves facing a more complex and risky agenda involving public interests across a number of countries.

"Primary" language providers of ELT products and services which assume that English is "their property" are now worried about how to reorganise their businesses as other users of English change its nature and character. Risks are now multiplying as second language learners become ELT providers and enter the transnational market as competitors (Singh 2000). These risks arise not because of any shortages, but rather from an overabundance of the demand for English and the technologically mediated ability of ELT providers to transgress the boundaries of space (rendering national borders negotiable) and transgressing the boundaries of time (effecting the intergenerational transmission of languages). These risks are integral to and an unavoidable consequence of the expanding transnational ELT industry itself, even though their effects or the opportunities for innovation they create may not be immediately obvious in the short term.

The risks identified and discussed in this chapter are stimulating new levels of critical reflection, interrogation, and monitoring as both ELT producers and consumers attempt to balance the need to reduce their consequences and to further the appropriation of English. During an earlier era of globalisation the rich and militarily powerful English empire could insulate itself from these risks by the force of arms but now these risks haunt those who produce them. In promoting English as the global language ELT business finds themselves "burdened with ethical responsibilities concerning linguistic rights and the management of associated contingencies" (Graddol 1997, 3). Recognition of these risks is now stimulating questions about the role of the ELT industry in sustaining biolinguistic diversity and in preventing language death. The risks described in this chapter refer to the pedagogical and instructional inadequacies that emerge from a dependence on an outdated and rigid English-only paradigm.

Endangering the Peoples and Languages Othered by English

There is a danger that globalisation involves the creation of a homogeneous world system in and across every locality. In Chapter 2 we discussed the prospects for a single, unified global language—English. This view suggests that the new transnational education order is oriented to the production of graduates who speak a single global language (English), who hold to a unified Anglo-American worldview, and who have all experienced online distributed learning. In this way the globalisation of ELT can be regarded as a new colonial project where the cultural capital and social values of rich Anglophone countries are imposed on poorer multilingual ones. By taking over the cognitive domains of education, information, and entertainment the project of globalising

English colonises the space of the languages it others. In occupying an important evangelical and marketing role for English, ELT businesses could also hasten the disappearance of other languages and the people who speak them. The project of globalising English could make some languages and their endangered speakers seem unnecessary and peripheral to the economic and political purposes of globalisation. Historically, the loss of these other languages has usually been accompanied by considerable depopulation and an irreversible loss of knowledge, history, and identity (Crystal 2000; Nettle and Romaine 2000).

A serious limitation on the exportability of ELT products arises from the well-founded fears people have of being swamped by Anglophone culture (Morley and Robins 1995, 44). By the end of the twenty-first century we can expect the extinction of a large proportion of the world's estimated 6,000 languages. David Crystal (1997, 17–20; 2000, 1–26) anticipates that 60–90% of these languages could disappear, leaving humanity with as a few as 600 languages. This reduction in linguistic diversity will, if current trends continue, greatly effect those people who are relatively powerless such as Indigenous and dispossessed nomadic communities (Nettle and Romaine 2000). Not surprisingly speakers of other languages are increasingly concerned. Referring to Bahasa Malaysia, Tagalog and Bahasa Indonesia, Razail Ismail (2000, 4–5) warns that

> the imperatives and compulsions of an economic driven world will try to sideline and marginalise the varied strands of cultural and linguistic diversities. ...[Much has already] been lost in terms of linguistic and cultural richness through modernisation that has disenfranchised the Indigenous, forest dwellers and the *orang asli* ....The challenge is placed squarely on those who must continue to fight [for] and promote our cultural and linguistics affiliations.

Will the ELT industry contribute to marginalisation linguistic diversity and disenfranchisement of speakers of other languages? How might the ELT industry contribute to efforts to sustain humanity's linguistic diversity? The prospect of a single world language in the form of English provokes considerable resistance (Phillipson and Skutnabb-Kangas 1999). The capacity of globalising English to swamp other languages, knowledge, cultures, identities, and educational opportunities is a source of fear among some of those who do not speak this language. It has also caused organisations such as the British Council to anticipate the rise of vigorous language rights movements campaigning against the role of

English in the destruction of the world's biolinguistic diversity (Graddol 1997, 39). These movements associate the death of their language with the project of globalising English. This worldwide movement advocates views that oppose the global dominance of English. While it is possible to explore productive opportunities in the risks created by the globalisation of English, Zawiah Yahya (2000, 28) argues that Malaysians

> have every right to fear globalisation as a direct consequence of the expansion of Western culture across the planet via colonisation and cultural mimesis. In a globalised world where electronic communication is fast putting an end to geography, we have every right to fear for our national sovereignty. In a world in which the minds of individuals are focused on mass-mediated Western images and models, we have every right to fear that our values and identities may in the end be under siege. In a world in which English has become the common public language of the globalised communications system, we have every right to fear that the role of national language as a tool of nation-building will be undermined.

Throughout the world, from Asia to Europe, from the Americas to Africa movements have arisen to defend local languages against the encroachment of globalising English (Warschauer 2000, 155). For instance, in Italy campaigns of active resistance have been initiated against the infiltration of English into the Italian language where it is seen to be causing a decline in knowledge of Italian vocabulary and affecting that language's grammatical functions and structures. English language grammatical constructions are being imposed on the Italian language rendering the words nonsensical (Crystal 2000, 22–23). The concern here is that the globalisation of English is undermining the Italian language/s, people's knowledge, and community identities. Many of the English words that are being directly incorporated into Italian come attached to the new technologies (e.g., Internet, netiquette, chat-line, e-commerce) and through US/American popular culture (e.g., blockbuster, pet therapy, new age, fusion, infotainment). While there are appropriate Italian words for hobby, gloves, and hairdresser, and the language has the capacity to generate new words for changing realities, the social status of English makes its infiltration into Italian very seductive. Of course, the process is neither straightforward nor one-way; for Italians "thriller" becomes "thrilling" and "non-stop" becomes "no-stop"; and where would the peoples of global, cosmopolitan cities be without their "caffe latte" and "mozzarella"?

Not only has globalising English led to the loss of a range of languages the notion of standardised English has been used, unsuccessfully, as a tool to eradicate non-metropolitan dialects, accents and vocabulary. In the United States special speech clinics have been established to eradicate what is seen as the unfashionable drawl of those people who live south of the Mason Dixon line. The use of standardised Englishes in mastering the narration of people's lives began in England. The movie version of Bernard Shaw's play *Pygmalion*, *My Fair Lady* (1964), offers an interesting account of the (unsuccessful) efforts made to socially engineer the "disappearance" of local dialects from England; this theme is repeated in the US/American film *Miss Congeniality* (2001). This attack on linguistic diversity has been integrally associated with the growth of global cities such as London; increases in English language teaching; the widespread dissemination of English language media of all kinds; increases in travel; and the press for (transnational) social mobility (Williams 1965, 248–249). In *My Fair Lady* Eliza Doolittle (Audrey Hepburn) is a lower, working-class flowergirl who speaks cockney English. Higgins (Rex Harrison), a professor of phonetics, sets out to turn Eliza into a gentrified, aristocratic lady by teaching her "correct diction." Despite a resistant student the professor eventually realises his material, sexual, and political desires. Professor Higgins wins his bet, gains Eliza's affections, and reasserts the aristocracy's power to exercise control in standardising its model of English.

This marginalising process can easily be seen in Australia where the use of languages othered through English has been used to incite suspicion among Anglophones about the intent and motivations of speakers of these languages. In an incident indicative of this widespread linguistic politics a talk back radio host "described it as 'ignorant and arrogant' that Chinese-[Australian] people would speak Chinese at a party in Australia. [The radio shock jock suggested that] these people are ignorant if they sit there and they talk in another language, in Australia we have English" (Wilmoth 1999, 15). This situation highlights some of the dilemmas for English speakers who triumphantly cite the linkages that English-speaking culture has with a long history of democracy. This tradition is contradicted by the propensity for English to censor and overwhelm other languages including Indigenous languages. This situation helps sustain reluctance by Anglophones to engage with and learn other languages. Insofar as English language teachers are not required to learn other language/s, this epitomises

> ethnocentricity and anglocentricity, the belief that our culture and language is universally relevant. ...How can anyone be an expert on the language learning needs, steps and strategies of a set of learners without in-depth knowledge of the culture and languages that the learners bring with them to the classroom and the learning operation? This sort of professional competence goes without saying in foreign language education throughout the "Western" world but is regarded as superfluous in dominant [English] language learning paradigms both in the home market in the "North" and in its export variant. (Phillipson 1997, 245)

All too often speakers of other languages who are learning English are constructed as "passive, rote-learners, whose logic follows a strange [non-linear] pattern," a construction that is deeply rooted in colonialist English (Pennycook 1998, 161). Such English language teaching, testing, and policies are located within the legacy of colonialist English present in films, books, and day-to-day conversations as much as they are in the workings of ELT. Colonialist English has produced representations of the speakers of other languages which have gained fixity over time, such that selected, negative constructions of the Orang Asli, the *bumiputra,* Tamil, and Chinese Malaysians are replayed and recirculated in a range of English cultural products. The dominating English images of the speakers of other languages, images handed down from the days of the English empire to today, tend to articulate with the broader colonising interests of Anglophone powers to intervene in and change their lives (Said 1978). Colonialist English promulgated images of the speakers of other languages as passive, complacent, unchanging, and inferior. The continuing use of this derogatory negative English is as much an expression of cultural arrogance as it is a legacy of colonialism.

Using English as a Tool for Disempowerment

In today's world access to English language and literacy skills are key criteria for participation in the global economy. To share in the new wealth of globalisation then the lack of English is a disadvantage in the transnational labor market. The stratified class-based nature of former colonial societies is becoming more exaggerated in this era where English is a tool of the new economies of globalisation. Indeed the dispersal of economic opportunity is closely related to the type and way in which English is spoken. Those who do not speak the model, class-based standardised dialects of English are in a position of relative powerlessness and economic disadvantage.

This is perhaps most noticeable in the rise of global English-speaking cities, such as Penang and Melbourne, and the decline in many non-metropolitan, rural areas in Malaysia and Australia, as elsewhere. The global movements of students in search of English language education, the creation of marketable electronic ELT commodities for their consumption (such as *Planet English*), and instant Internet-based communication across the globe are leading to challenging new opportunities. However, these developments are also aggravating existing inequalities and creating a new polarisation of economic opportunities and disadvantages. There is good reason to raise concerns about this connection between power and ELT commodities, because the project of globalising English:

> suggests one is worthy of being heard only if one speaks in [standardised] English. ...[This] disempowers those of us who are just learning to speak, who are just learning to claim [the English] language as a place where we make ourselves subjects. (hooks 1994, 174: 168)

English is not only the language of the "new" knowledge economy, it is also the language of the new technologies of human interaction, reflection, and knowledge production. However, the price of entry to the superhighway is very expensive and often the exclusive property of the rich and influential Anglophone nations. The costs for accessing Internet services and maintaining the infrastructure to support them greatly undermines the promise that the new technologies could be a global resource capable of producing new riches for all and a new era of global democracy. Those in poorer, over-exploited developed countries experience considerable difficulty in gaining access to the knowledges available through these new technologies. These inequalities in access relate, in part, to an earlier era of globalisation:

> The pattern of unequal access is partly a colonial legacy: information is piped around the globe by fibre-optic and coaxial cables along the same routes as taken by the Victorian telegraph which linked the [English] empire ...the areas of the world closest to the information superhighway are those which the telegraph first reached. (Graddol 1997, 39)

A cumulative disempowerment is occurring through a combination of historic disadvantage in terms of technology, its dispersal, and the capital needed to acquire and maintain it. These developments tend to "wall off" many of the fruits of prosperity to a privileged minority who might speak and are comfortable with standardised Englishes. Given that over 30 percent of the sources of the Internet are primarily and predominantly from the United States, Japan, and Western Europe (94.3%), Razali Ismail (2000, 3) raises the question of

> whether an Internet-worked world will encourage global cultural diversity...[especially] given the highly politicised nature of the international community. ...There is the danger that an Internet-worked world would also make it easier for a few multinational companies to own and operate global media, thereby introducing and enforcing cultural homogenisation.

The historic legacies of conflict and contestation which typified much of the expansion and defeat of the English empire has left a residual bitterness in countries like Cyprus, Eire (Irish Republic), Kenya, and Burma (Myanmar) to their former colonial masters and the English language. While there are some in these countries who have fond memories and deep associations with English colonialism, others share a deep resentment and hostility to the colonial era and interpret the project of globalising English as a new colonialism. To participate in the new global economy these nations now need the tools of the new technologies that are owned by their former colonisers. Moreover, they also find themselves dependent on the English language.

Those engaged in transnational ELT business are becoming increasingly aware of the disempowerment that people in different countries' experience through or because of English. ELT products and services are not value free and benign but in some instances are hostile manifestations of (neo)colonisation. This is particularly so when ELT is linked to the fundamentalist missionary efforts to secure converts. An example of this sense of disempowerment is found in Burma (Myanmar) where English is known as the "killer language" (Phillipson 1997, 243). Likewise in Turkey some linguists, religious groups, and nationalists worry about "the unstoppable influx of English" being alarmed by its dominance of Turkish culture and its tendency to erode cultural and linguistic diversity (Dogancay-Aktuna 1998, 35).

The products and accessories of popular English language culture can create tensions with local cultures that are challenged by the seductive and materialistic US/American values embedded in them. Many English language products are viewed as a threat to other cultures and languages.

This view of English does not necessarily mean outright antipathy to globalisation but can involve a different orientation to and focus on global values and norms. These developments create a sense of danger associated with globalisation that threatens cultural values and in some cases the very existence of some languages and their speakers. In the case of Malaysia its association with Anglophone nations stands in tension with its worldwide connections to Third World nations.

Languages are the archives of human knowledge giving expression to events that formed people's past, and the resources for making judgments about present actions and future developments. The loss of one's language means the loss of that knowledge and the exclusion of that record from considerations about the present and the future (Crystal 2000, 40–43). Consider for a moment two reasons for the inattention to Australia's Indigenous histories. This forgetfulness is, in part, incited by Anglo-fundamentalist politicians and scholars. They dismiss as inconsequential the negative facts of the twentieth-century social experiment of creating a Whites-only, English-only Australia. Just as importantly the inattention to the histories of the crimes committed against Indigenous Australians (the stealing of their lands and the destruction of their families) is associated with efforts to remove their repositories of living memory—Indigenous languages.

English is a "cultural nerve gas" (Crystal 2000, 78) which is infiltrating everywhere with the ample reinforcement from the mass media, especially television, music, and the Internet. A sociopolitical context which is antagonistic to Indigenous peoples, their knowledges, histories, and languages incites policy decisions which minimise resources for vernacular language education (Lo Bianco 1999, 40–51). There are those working in TESOL who have mounted counter-arguments against the myths promulgated by the sociopolitical project of the English-only movement, highlighting its divisiveness and alienating effects on linguistic minorities (Dicker 1996). The importance of this point necessitates quoting David Crystal (2000, 87, 102, 136) at length:

> In Australia, the presence of English has, directly or indirectly, caused great linguistic devastation, with 90% of [Indigenous] languages moribund. ...Throughout the 1990s, there were several reports of language support programmes becoming endangered through budgetary cuts. ...In Australia, at the end of 1998, when the Northern Territory Government announced plans to phase out bilingual education for its

> Aboriginal communities, replacing this by English-teaching programmes. ...If their only experience of speech and writing in school is through the medium of the dominant language, it will not be surprising to find that the Indigenous language fails to thrive.

Not only are languages important for encapsulating human identities and providing historical interpretations of human existence, but they also provide a wealth of human knowledge. This knowledge is so important to the "new" global economy. What precious knowledge of holistic environmental sustainability has Anglophone Australia lost through its suppression of Indigenous Australians and their languages? Those few Indigenous languages which have survived English invasion and colonisation have taught Anglo-ethnic zoologists, botanists, and military personnel to distinguish between species of pythons, kangaroos, wallabies, insect larvae, and plants they otherwise thought were the same by using different taxonomies, for instance, based on movement rather than static appearance (Crystal 2000, 44–54). The teaching and learning of Indigenous languages would increase the human resources available for the globally important knowledge economy.

What valuable knowledge of environmental sustainability could Anglophone Australia gain through the struggle for Indigenous rights and the carrying forward of their languages? Countries like Australia could promote the revitalisation of endangered languages by following Colombia's lead. This would see the provision of public socio-economic benefits being thought of as a reward for speaking, writing, and teaching Indigenous languages and extending Indigenous knowledges (Crystal 2000, 125, 134). As in the United States, Australian Indigenous languages should be given official status as a national asset with the legal protection of the state.

Ignoring Anglocentrism and US/American Cultural Imperialism

The conceptual and practical inadequacies of ELT are most starkly manifested by its continued tendency toward Anglocentrism. Alistair Pennycook (1994, 158–159) argues that too often ELT instructional materials, teaching methods and theories have been weighed down by Anglocentrism, rendering many of these services inappropriate for culturally different clients. The danger of these products is that they present a distorted and nostalgic view of the world organised around redundant views of the English empire and US/American neocolonialism, perpetuating a global, racialised hierarchy radiating from Anglo-American interests. In this context Anglo-American things are seen as culturally superior, characterised as being of great social worth, held to be an indicator of significant economic advancement, and celebrated as the product of superior evolution. There are profound social, cultural, and political risks that accompany the continuing durability of such Anglocentrism. These manifest themselves in the arrogance that repeats images of the Other as "backward races" and restate Kipling's "white man's burden." The imagery, practices, behaviours, and attitudes of colonialist English are transported, imparted and absorbed by the commodities produced using the new technologies, marketed using controversy-driven publicity (Ow 2000). The inculcation and acceptance of Anglo-American ideas is perhaps one of the greatest "successes" of colonialist English.

Anglocentric attempts to capitalise on the nostalgic imagery of Englishness is a key part of the ELT industry and is evident in the selection of various business logos and livery. Some companies have appropriated the cultural capital associated with the "branding" of English universities and the global images of these prestigious learning institutions. One company operating in Taiwan, Australia, and Canada trades under the name of the "Cambridge" Language School, a name that evokes an association with one of England's elite universities. The logo of this organisation uses traditional heraldic livery of open books, rampant lions, and shields to represent and market English as a vehicle for accessing a business or communications education. Other providers use brand names such as "Thames" and "St Marks" as part of their marketing strategy to capture students or parents keen to invest in nostalgic Anglocentrism.

These images look harmless and even quaint. However, they neglect some of the negative historic legacies of the colonial policies of the English that were based on a strategy of divide and rule. Racial groups in various colonies were subject to differential treatment. Some groups were seen as vital to the strategic and economic interests of the English colonisers and were accorded privileges that were not afforded to others. They were cultivated as allies and enlisted to actively assist with the mechanics of colonisation and rewarded for their loyalty. Those who were seen to have the capacities and resources to aid the economic administration of colonies and maintain the hegemonic domination of the English were rewarded with rights, wealth, and power in colonial society.

English colonies were characterised by highly stratified class and racial systems that clustered around those who were indispensable to the economic and political interests of the colonisers. A key feature of these colonial hierarchies was the use of English as the language of social and economic intercourse. The possession of standardised English was required for entry into the elite economic cockpit of colonial society. In some situations labor from English-speaking countries was imported in preference to using Indigenous labor because the latter's refusal to learn English made their control more difficult. This meant that both contact with the English and the acquisition of English language skills were minimal requirements for the acceptance of some ethnic and racial groups; otherwise they were seen as peripheral to the needs of the colonisers. This is a point made by the current Prime Minister of Malaysia, Dr. Mahathir, in his 1970 book, *The Malay Dilemma*. Recalling the colonial era in Malaya, Mahathir argued that the English regime:

> did not merely divide the Malays from the Chinese, but went on to divide the rural Malays from the town Malays. It is true that the division was already there, but it was the [English] who severed the tenuous links that town Malays had with the rural Malays. ...Taking advantage of the lack of cohesion between town and country Malays, the [English] created further conditions to keep them apart. Having encouraged white-collar jobs among town Malays, they made these people feel that their status was above that of manual workers and peasants. The few Malays who remained in the towns were then provided with an elementary English education which was at the same time denied the rural Malay. (Mahathir 1970, 26–27)

The point here is that nostalgic views of colonisation not only ignore the dispossession and oppression that were strategies of control in English colonies but they also ignore the creation of stratified social structures which have endured past colonial times. These structures provided access to and enhanced the possession of English language skills. In some places this has since inspired a backlash against English and those who speak it. The tendency to enlist "English as a weapon to silence and censor" (hooks 1994, 172) provides a rudimentary explanation for the emergence of the worldwide language rights movement.

The retreat to a nostalgic Anglocentric past and an accompanying unwillingness to engage with a more contemporary understanding of global shifts presents epistemological and practical risks for ELT providers. What is at stake here for Anglophone ELT businesses is a challenge to a very powerful but dated England-centred view of the world. The world no longer rests on outright dominance by England. However, global relations are now more influenced by US/American hegemony which, in turn, is contesting the emergence of influential countries such as China. Following its "success" in facilitating the collapse of the USSR, the United States now seems to be applying the same technique to China; it is caught in a tension between inciting China to spend on military defence rather than to continue to invest in social and economic reforms. The shift in the focus of economic and political events away from Anglocentric perceptions presents a postmodern narrative crisis.

The grandiose sense of crisis captured in the idea of postmodernism offers a peculiarly Anglocentric view of globalisation. When speaking of the "end of history" postmodernism is a signifier for the challenges to Western Europe's dominance of the world. Postmodernism is limited where human history is seen largely in terms of the ascendancy and dominance of Western Europe. The claims for the validity and rationality of Western European culture have been shown to be a mirage to legitimise and protect its economic domination and political hegemony. Anglocentric postmodernism is symptomatic of

> the crisis of the downwardly mobile white intellectuals of Western Europe, working in the decaying public sector of those economies, during the period of the long slump that began with the oil crisis of 1973 ...a crisis specifically of the authority vested in Western European culture and its institutions. (Morley and Robins 1995, 206)

These comments highlight the risk for ELT providers of retreating to literacy practices and epistemological orientations that privilege an exclusionary monolingual environment. To do so means neglecting the shifts in the world's political, economic, and cultural balance as well as the continuing changes in the English language itself (Colebrook 1996). Anglophone ELT providers are likely to benefit from the recognition of and engagement with other Englishes, and an acknowledgment of other cultures, other languages, other knowledges, and other identities. The work of interpreting and translating hybridised languages and cultures is now integral to the delivery of ELT products and services. If space for the appropriation of English is to be found, then what is required is an enhanced ability to engage in deconstructing the concept, authority, and sense of primacy associated with the project of globalising English. Conversely rigidly locating ELT practices in the nostalgia of Anglo-centrism creates risks of relevance and engagement for clients that will rebound on the providers themselves.

Failing to Engage the Specifics of Local Contexts

There is a need for less Anglocentric English language teaching and more need for locally engaged teaching that explains and contrasts differentiated Englishes, local languages, and regional cultures, especially in relation to technology, business, diplomacy, and the professions. The relationship between the local and the global is open to differing and contrasting interpretations. One view holds that globalisation involves the creation of a single, unified, homo-geneous world system. At one level this means the spread of fast food chains throughout the world, while at deeper level it involves the spread of consumer credit culture and the MacDonaldisation of work practices throughout the world (Ritzer 1996). Another view of the local/global nexus focuses on the specific and disjointed ways in which global flows of ideas, media, finance, technologies, people, and risks affect and are affected by particular and diverse localities (Appadurai 1996). According to this view, the interdependent processes of globalisation and localisation create hybrid forms of English and ELT as global influences meet up with local languages, educational traditions, and working conditions. For instance local languages such as Bahasa Malaysia influence English, giving rise to a new hybrid language variety called Malaysian English (Nair-Venugopal 2000, 45–72). Malaysians who speak English as their second language are changing the English language itself in terms of rhythm, pronunciation, vocabulary, and grammar as a result of the influence of their first language and culture.

The view that the "local" is "here" and the "global" is "out there" now seems all too simplistic. A richer and more complex view sees the local as inescapably embedded in the global, and increasingly we see situations where the local is disembedded and redistributed globally. There are dangerous contradictions in celebrating the global and local as inherently separable and one or the other as either inherently good or bad. First, it is necessary to recognise that certain global conditions, such as UNESCO's Endangered Language Project, are necessary to enable people, their languages, their knowledges, and their cultural heritages to survive locally. Second, there is a need for global bodies to prevent the might of the powerful transnational corporations from usurping the rule of democratic power. Some global forums and international networks, such as the International Clearing House for Endangered Languages at the University of Tokyo, are necessary for advancing the struggles for inter-generational language rights (http://www.tooyoo.l.u-tokyo.ac.jp/ichel.html). Therefore we have to address the question of what kind of (ethical) globalisation/localisation is desired? We have seen in Seattle, Melbourne, Genoa, and elsewhere increasing opposition to the over-whelming dominance of the politics of globalisation by neo-liberal econ-omic reductionism, as people begin to explore other forms of global/local interconnectedness and alternative imaginings of globalisation/localisation (Beck 1999).

A third view, the one which is explored in *Appropriating English,* not only sees the presence of English in local languages as evidence of globalisation, but also sees globalisation as a particular construction of locality (Morley and Robins 1995). In this view processes of localisation are positioned as responses to, and expressions of, the processes of globalisation. This broader definition of globalisation focuses on linguistic shifts and the manner in which multilingual landscapes are transformed in a variety of uneven and chaotic ways, perhaps most noticeably in the project of globalising English and the extinction of non-metropolitan languages and death of their knowledges (Nettle and Romaine 2000).

There are globalised ELT providers who fail to engage with local socio-political and cultural contexts preferring to remain anchored in and dependent on ELT services that feature nostalgic Anglocentric legacies. Sometimes these products tend to be vacuous and trivial, being meaning-less and irrelevant to the contemporary experience of their students. There is a "blindness" to the loaded and biased nature of many ELT materials that perpetuate the myth that these commodities and products are value-free. In many instances this leads to their inappropriate deployment in a range of culturally diverse contexts. A historically pertinent example reported by Alistair Pennycook (1994, 151–152) concerned the unfor-tunately named "Madras Snowball" project of the 1960s that was "a colossal and...disturbing failure" because of its irrelevance to the Indian context. Since then many ELT providers have repeated this project's failure to recognise and engage the specific uses of English in India that includes the multilingual context of English language use and the socio-linguistics of Indian society where multilingualism is a national resource.

Even today ELT providers use materials that depict English social settings of the 1950s, being totally irrelevant to the experiences of contemporary, vocationally oriented students. This creates a situation where the global export of English, English language teaching, and English textbooks leads to cultural conflict because the norms presented in the texts are in direct competition with local social and cultural values (Pennycook 1994, 176). This situation is not aided by the use of teaching methodologies that both demean the experience of learners and, in some instances are confronting for students (Canagarajah 2000).

While globalisation creates patterns of inter-dependence and inter-connection, it does not necessarily do so in any uniform or homogeneous way. Consider for a moment popular cultural representations of Anglophone ELT. Adrian Cronauer (Robin Williams) in *Good Morning Vietnam* (1987) gives over-the-top English language lessons, teaching "New York Street English" to Vietnamese adults during the US/American war in Indochina. No consideration is given to the uses to which his students want to put English or the knowledge they want to access, let alone the street language of Vietnamese peoples themselves. Bilingualism and transcultural understanding are not part of the repertoire of this radio announcer impersonating an English language teacher; exotic sexual conquest is his objective. ELT will benefit from being attentive to the dangers caricatured by such Anglocentrism and decontextualisation.

Promoting Inappropriate Teaching Strategies

There is the risk of using English language teaching methodologies, theories and practices that fail in culturally and linguistically diverse settings. This is partly attributable to the continued export of inappropriate ELT strategies that are dependent on assumptions of cultural superiority, albeit couched in the language of neutrality. Many of these approaches are reliant on programmes and methodologies that have a generic quality, asserting that there is "one best practice" that fits all student needs and cultural contexts. TESOL language acquisition models are based on second rather than foreign language environments, grammar instruction is emphasised despite the needs of non-native speakers to develop communicative skills, and too often socio-cultural factors are ignored. Given the range and breadth of the ELT industry, both geographically and culturally, not all types and varieties of ELT products are exportable to different people to the same degree. ELT products rooted in one socio-cultural environment and attractive to that locale may have diminished appeal to people in other locations. Some find it difficult to identify with the styles, values, beliefs, and behavioural patterns represented in this generic material.

There is a tension between generic ELT products and methodologies with an assumed universal application and customised approaches designed to meet the specific needs of particular groups. The high cost of investment required for developing customised packages for specialist niche markets leads to the generation of ELT products with little linguistic content, such as multimedia products. These are easier to export than those having a heavy dependence on written words as do cultural heritage products based on English literature. This process of "cultural discounting" (Morley and Robins 1995, 62–63) applies in different ways to different types of ELT products. While these more seductive multimedia products tend to reduce language barriers with their attractive visual and graphic appearance, there remain risks of offending cultural norms and values: when selling English in China should a world map show China and Taiwan in the same or different colours?

In some countries and for some students there are pedagogical problems with ELT strategies such as informal interaction, conversation, and games. For some students who consider they already have reasonable English language skills these strategies are as paternalistic (Canagarajah 1999). These problems stem from the mistaken assumptions that national development occurs along a uni-dimensional line, and that all the ELT products and services that are exported from Anglophone countries are culturally superior. They are assumed to be more "advanced" relative to ELT products emerging from multilingual settings in Asia or elsewhere. The tendency to develop generic ELT materials and methodologies is based on a business preference to use a "unitary, prescriptivist model of standardised English" (McArthur 1998, 79). However, some of their clients find that this approach is an impediment to language learning rather than an aid to improving their knowledge of English or how to teach it. English-only education may create learning problems for students and negatively affect their scholastic achievements. For instance, for

> large numbers of students in Hong Kong schools, an education through the medium of English is detrimental to their overall education: they learn little English (which is generally irrelevant to their daily lives) and inadequate subject matter. Furthermore, with English filling such an inordinate amount of the school curriculum, students are often left with inadequate skills in Chinese. (Pennycook 1998, 196)

Some ELT methods are excessively reliant on explicit grammar translation techniques, texts representative of monolingual Anglophone communities, rote learning, and limited oral activities. Typically ELT materials and methodologies are designed by native speaking monolinguals for native speaking monolingual teachers, and in doing so fail to draw on local cultural and linguistic knowledge. Their use throughout Asia displays the frustrating shortcomings of "the rigid and often restrictive ways in which Latin was conventionally taught during most of the last two centuries in English-speaking countries" (McArthur 1998, 184). The communicative teaching methods celebrated in ELT unreflectively induct students into foreign Anglophone culture in a manner that is often insensitive to the ideological implications of doing so. Not surprisingly these limited and restrictive techniques do not meet with the approval of all clients and in some cases provoke hostile resistance. The adaptation of ELT materials by means of teacher research for use by bilingual teachers or for use in multilingual contexts is an important innovation in internationalising the ELT curriculum (Colebrook 1996). The inappropriateness of ELT strategies has been explained in the following terms:

> A debilitating monolingual/monocultural bias has revealed itself in the insistence on [standardised] English as the norm, the refusal to grant an active role to the students' first language in the learning and acquisition of English, the marginalisation of "non-native" English teachers, and the insensitive negativity shown by the pedagogies and discourses toward the indigenous cultural traditions. (Canagarajah 1999, 3)

With the US/American overthrow of local authority and its colonisation of Hawaii in 1893 came laws banning the use of Ka 'olelo Hawai'i. Those who spoke this language were punished. These repressive measures, along with the reduction of the Hawaiian population by nearly 90 percent through introduced diseases, would have contributed to this language's virtual extinction had it not been for the language rights movement and language revitalisation projects (Warschauer 1999, 84). Despite opposition to English-only politics, support for vernacular language education, and advocacy for biolinguistic sustainability, many in the ELT industry have come to see English-only classes as "natural" and even as "commonsensical" (Auerbach 1993). While these might be seen as benign lapses by poorly theorised teaching, Ngugi wa Thiong'o (1994, 438) reminds us of the ideological imperatives driving the history of English-only pedagogy and the inequities in power relations and the violence associated with what is now regarded as inappropriate ELT strategies:

> In Kenya, English became more than a language: it was the language, and all the others had to bow before it in deference. Thus, one of the most humiliating experiences was to be caught speaking Gikuyu in the vicinity of the school. The culprit was given corporal punishment...or was made to carry a metal plate around the neck with inscriptions such as "I AM STUPID" or" I AM A DONKEY". Sometimes the culprits were fined money they could hardly afford. ...The attitude to English was the exact opposite: any achievement in spoken or written English as highly rewarded. ...English became the measure of intelligence and ability. ...English became the main determinant of a child's progress up the ladder of formal education.

Rather than create synergies that meet students' needs, the move toward generic ELT practices heightens the risk of alienating them. It also tends to reduce the potential for ELT businesses to engage with local contexts. New difficulties are being experienced by the trend toward the development of and reliance on generic ELT packages. The increased commodification of ELT is related to the entry of large multimedia development, delivery, and distribution corporations into the industry. Many transnational corporations such as the *Daily Mail*, News Corporation, and the BBC have significant interests in the ELT industry. These corporate players have created standardised ELT products to be used in varying locations and culturally different contexts. This move toward generic ELT programmes is known as "harmonisation," which is a strategy for economising on delivery costs across a global organisation as well as a way of effectively monitoring distribution.

The corporate quest for "global harmonisation" has produced prepackaged responses to ELT challenges; in particular, teaching is simplified into an instrumental activity. This technical deskilling of teachers, which is discussed further in Chapter 8, is contradicted by an emerging trend to develop discrete ELT markets. These "niche markets" require responses capable of meeting the local needs of students and clients:

> Global corporations do, indeed, acknowledge differentiated markets and customise for specific market segments...this is combined with the search for opportunities to sell to similar segments throughout the globe. ...[It is increasingly important to target] consumers on the basis of demography and habits rather than on the basis of geographical proximity; marketing strategies are "consumer driven" instead of "geography-driven." (Morley and Robins 1995, 110)

Global ELT providers treat all their strategic markets with similar attention, positioning themselves at an equal distance from all their customers. In order to boost its market share in Taiwan's highly competitive cable television networks the Hong Kong–based Star TV, owned by the Murdoch News Corporation, has had the Canadian young adult television program *South Park* translated into Mandarin (Chu 2001). Kenny is still killed as the show's signature lamentation says: "Tian-ah! Kenny bei guagiao!" The English script for *South Park* has been markedly changed as the voices have been dubbed into Mandarin. This is part of Star TV's strategy to use the show's popularity to build a following for its other North American popular televisual commodities broadcast in English throughout Asia. While under contract to retain the spirit of the original, the process of localisation, of taking a North American commodity and remaking it into something the Taiwanese can recognise, means that more than half of the dialogue, including the lyrics, have to be rewritten. North American jokes and slang are replaced by allusions to Taiwanese popular culture, current events, and politics. This localisation strategy is enhanced by the program's (re)writers meet-ing regularly with groups of Taiwanese youth to discuss issues they face and to pick up on their use of language. Having developed a winning formula for (re) producing a successful animated program, the Taiwanese television producers and writers are in a position to capitalise on this expertise with their own local production.

Sanctioning Linguistic Complacency among Anglophones

In Anglophone countries the project of globalising English has engendered linguistic complacency by undermining the motivation, opportunities and funding needed to learn other languages. Anglophone antagonism to the languages othered by English is often coded as humour:

"You know you're in Sydney when...you take a bus and are shocked because two people are carrying on a conversation in English." Because of efforts to spread ELT products and services worldwide Anglophones are less inclined to put an end to their monolingualism, and instead have used it to mobilise an English-only politics (Macedo 2000). As already noted Australia's Northern Territory Government is, despite resistance, pursuing English-only politics through the closure of bilingual and vernacular language education programmes in regional Aboriginal communities. The language of English colonialism deemed many Indigenous languages as foreign or even alien in their own countries and then made outlaws of them (hooks 1994, 169). However, in economically hard-pressed times, success in boosting exports and attracting transnational investment can depend on subtle factors. The diverse languages spoken throughout multilingual nations are now particularly important in the quest for worldwide trading opportunities. Statements and funding from "influential politicians and administrators" are necessary for creating both the resources and a "climate of opinion about the importance of [second] language learning" (Crystal 1997, 16).

In the early 1970s Australia officially recognised the government of the Peoples' Republic of China, then known by the ice hot Cold War label of "Red China." However, this new relationship was not supported with the resources needed for teaching Mandarin or Chinese social and cultural studies. The same monolingual complacency is still evident even thirty years later:

> there has never been a permanent head of the Australian foreign service fluent in an Asian language, or, for that matter, of any other Australian government department. The same goes for the vice-chancellors of all the Australian universities, the general editors of our major newspapers and magazines and heads of television stations, the general staff of the defence forces, and the heads of our major and most of our minor corporations. (Fitzgerald 1997, 12)

David Crystal (1997, 12–20) observes that English-only politics tends to "cultivate an elite monolingual linguistic class...dismissive in their attitudes toward other languages." The lack of knowledge of Asian languages among monolingual, English-only Australians is because, Fitzgerald (1997, 12) argues, "the acquisition of Asian languages is too much trouble, because we're doing all right in Asia anyway, or so it's believed." He characterises monolingual, Anglo-ethnic Australians as self-indulgent and complacent in their orientation to second language education. Complaining that Anglo-ethnic Australians "have been lazy about Asia to the point of irresponsibility," Stephen Fitzgerald (1997, 10–11) asserts that this "lazy country" has been encouraged by indulgent policies and legislation governing welfare, working hours, and wages. Most citizens have seen these as a matter of ensuring the public's social and economic security, and are experiencing and giving political expression to their alienation and disaffection with governments that have now robbed them of these. There is, however, another more significant reason for this disinclination among Anglo-ethnic Australians to learn an Asian language, namely that White Australia politics has made it difficult for them

> to have an easy relationship with Asian countries and peoples. ...fear, aggression, condescension, insecurity, over-friendliness in its patronising and servile forms, possessive paternalism, and the possessive arm of "mateship" around an unreciprocating Asian shoulder. [These symptoms of regressive parochialism underlie] reservations about Asia, and even about race, in the ranks and in the heart of the [Howard] Coalition Government, and a nostalgia for an international order long gone. (Fitzgerald 1997, 29, 60)

Stephen Fitzgerald (1997, 137) asks, "Could we bring ourselves to look at Asia first, on fundamental issues? Or do we still hanker after a white man's answers and a white man's world?" However, in raising legitimate concerns about the continuing cultural power of White Australia politics on relations with Asia, Fitzgerald constructs an exclusionary notion of "we," reproducing that which he claims to be questioning. He too fails to recognise that not all Anglo-ethnic Australians hanker for a Whites-only Federation, and that not all Australians are Anglo-ethnics. Nevertheless, his argument for second language education has merit. Throughout much of the world bi-lingualism is assumed to be the norm. Even if English is a major global language, bilingualism is a valuable skill, as globally oriented employers become more inclined toward qualified bilingual job applicants.

Baron de Coubertin of France founded the modern Olympic Games. In memory of his contribution all Olympic functions, such as the opening of the Games, use French and English as their official languages. However, Australian dignitaries hosting the Sydney 2000 Olympics Games disappointed many when they refused to follow Olympic protocol. Instead they insisted on the use of English because, they claimed, it is the "native" tongue of Australians. That the Australian representative of the Head of State is a monolingual Anglophone who is not prepared to honour the Game's founder is perhaps an indicator of political antagonism toward languages othered through English, more than complacency.

Ironically, during the Sydney Olympics Games liquor, photographic film, and cosmetics products from China were widely promoted to the world's Chinese diaspora on the global television networks without having to pay any advertising or sponsorship fees. Chinese businesses deployed "cheer squads" at key events, such as badminton and volley-ball, to sing the praises of their companies' products. While the Games' organisers had rules prohibiting just such non-funded advertising, this "ambush marketing" involved slogans and chants in Mandarin. It was made possible in Australia where the cultural press is directed toward speaking English-only. Monolingualism is a disadvantage for business and regulators and a deprivation in the multilingual global marketplace.

Resistant Consumers and the Appropriation of English

ELT products do not have any simple or straightforward colonising effects on students that can be easily anticipated from an analysis of their content or production history. We cannot assume that there will be a "hypodermic" impact through the consumption of Anglophone cultural products by culturally different audiences (Morley and Robins 1995, 126–127). It cannot be predicted that students of English will be passive recipients of ELT products or that they will automatically comply with the norms, rules, and linguistic practices associated with standardised Englishes.

Local social and cultural differences influence the take-up of ELT products and services. This leads to a situation where students in diverse settings reinterpret or otherwise appropriate the ELT materials they encounter. The agency of second and foreign language learners in reshaping English may partially mitigate the risks associated with the homogenising influence of the project to globalise English. This makes "one sise fits all" ELT products problematic. To be widely exportable generic ELT products operate at a high level of abstraction and the price of this abstraction is that students have the space and capacity to make new and alternative expressions of English. The greater the level of abstraction, the greater the chance that ELT products are open to appropriation by linguistically different students and teachers.

Let us now turn our attention briefly to the complex ways in which some of those colonised by English have viewed and have been affected by being taught English to assess the level of contestation, hybridisation, and appropriation of English that now confronts Anglophone ELT providers. The voices of students from Nigeria, Kenya, India, and the United States of America alert us to the uses they have made of their English language during different eras of English global dominance. Chinua Achebe, Ngugi wa Thiong'o, Gauri Viswanathan, Salman Rushdie, and bell hooks (aka Gloria Watkins) are all cosmopolitan commentators on the teaching of English language, literacy, and literature. They provide valuable reflections on the risks associated with ELT products and services; their critiques provide platforms for the appropriation of English that recognise the emergence of local hybrid-ised Englishes.

Ngugi wa Thiong'o (1994) used the English he learnt to create new meanings and understandings by refusing to accept the categories, norms and standards that his colonialist education provided. For Thiong'o English became a site of struggle, contestation and appropriation rather than compliance and passivity. His use of English involved its replacement with local Kenyan cultural specifics as he sought new ways of saying things and new things to say in a way that powerfully critiqued colonialist and colonising English (Thiong'o 1994, 441). By rupturing standardised American English Black Americans made English into more than the language of those who had enslaved them by creating a language of their own (Ebonics). Not only did this enable Black Americans to resist racist White supremacy, but through their trans-formative work they

> created an intimate speech that could say far more than was permissible within the boundaries of [standardised US/American] English. The power of this speech is...that it also forges a space for alternative cultural production and alternative epistemologies—different ways of thinking and knowing that were crucial to creating a counter-hegemonic worldview. (hooks 1994, 171)

Ngugi wa Thiong'o (1994) and bell hooks (1994) offer those working in the transnational ELT business a conceptualisation of languages as mutually constituted and informed, moving beyond an understanding of

English as being a static, reified, and essentialist entity. Their accounts add weight to the argument that primary, secondary, and foreign language speakers are not really neat separate entities. The elimination of polarised attitudes to linguistic diversity and cultural differences can help reshape ELT. For example, thinking of Chinese-Malaysian students in Australia as belonging to absolutely different cultural entities from their Anglo-Australian peers can lead to a view of transnational ELT that addresses language and cultures as if they are forever fixed in time and space, and separated by an incommensurable and insurmountable barrier. It now seems unhelpful to think that these students can simply be stacked up alongside each other and treated in ways that see them as belonging to absolutely different linguistic and cultural groups (McCarthy 1998, 155). Transnational ELT involves an engagement with inter-penetrating hybrid Englishes and the seeking out of commonalities. While successful strategies for internationalising ELT typically seek to ensure a reflection of multiple voices and diverse perspectives, there may also be a need to challenge any assumptions students have about their cultural separateness.

Innovative Opportunities Created by Risks

The dilemmas created for ELT providers by the risks canvassed in this chapter can be understood as threats representing dangerous socially explosive hazards. Nevertheless, out of this analysis of the socio-cultural impact of the project of globalising English, and the despair this engenders, we must mine the resources of hope (Beck 1999, 65–69, 151–152). An optimistic understanding of these risks recognises in them opportunities for innovation. The opening up of the ELT industry and its products and services to scrutiny by those concerned about the risks wrought by the project of globalising English makes this realm available for innovative decisions. Here it is also important to recognise and investigate the ways in which innovation in the ELT industry is constrained by the dominating epistemology and regulatory regime within which it operates. However, global restructuring does create possibilities for reconstructing the definition of English as a global risk and thereby opens up possibilities for innovative ways of framing the management of the risks it creates for other languages. This is made possible through the work of organisations of global civil society raising people's consciousness of this endangered and dangerous world, and in particular the civic courage and vigilance of the transnational language rights movement.

In responding to and in giving effect to globalisation ELT providers are addressing unprecedented transnational legal, ethical, and epistemological risks, and in doing so reshaping their businesses in profound and irreversible ways. The problems they confront include furthering inequalities in people's access to power, unquestioningly legitimising linguistic hierarchies, stigmatising and downgrading the languages "othered" by English as well as sanctioning the mistaken belief that English is better suited to global economic, intellectual, and human development (Phillipson 1997, 239–240). A new generation of ELT providers is emerging in response to and as an expression of the challenges of globalisation involving partnerships between primary, second and foreign English language teaching businesses (see Table 1).

Such responses to these risks are not an optional extension to their current work, but necessary innovations created by the ethical dilemmas and investment risks ELT providers now face.

That ELT providers transmit knowledge that has value and legitimacy is a matter of contestation. The market for ELT products and services thrives on contradiction. On the one hand, humanity is confronted with the dangerous possibility that the globalisation of this market is contributing to the homogenisation of the world's cultures and the death of a huge number of its languages, and the extinction of knowledges at a time when knowledge is essential for the new economy. On the other hand, ELT providers are becoming more heterogeneous—multicultural, Asia literate, and multivocal—in order to capture "local" markets and to expand existing ones. In these circumstances ELT may be used to embrace the knowledge produced by others, to strive to transcend the partiality of local particularities, and to join the intellectual strivings of culturally diverse peoples. The challenge of the new transnational education order is a test of the capacity of ELT providers to embody applications of local cosmopolitanism wherever they seek their markets.

The experiences of Chinua Achebe, Ngugi wa Thiong'o, Gauri Viswanathan, and Salman Rushdie suggest that before the era of cost-conscious, full-fee paying students, ELT was also used by the colon-

Table 1: From English-only Pedagogy to Sustaining Linguistic Diversity

English-only	Driving force for innovation	Sustaining linguistic diversity
Second language acquisition • English language skills for teachers • oral and written discourses • second language learning	Technology • hypertextual reading and writing • teacher/learner aide	Language acquisition in multilingual contexts • bilingual or immersion education • vernacular language education • multiliteracies • new technologies of interaction, knowledge production, and reflection
Teaching methodology • theory and practice of English language teaching • second language pedagogy • classroom management principles	Commodification • heritage and enterprise Englishes • English teaching business	New pedagogies • Real world action learning • relational pedagogies • 3D teaching
Curriculum materials • evaluating teaching resources • practical use of technology	Globalisation • global/local Englishes	• multi-vocal English dictionaries • popular cultural studies
Language planning and policy • curriculum principles and program design • project implementation and formative evaluation • international language communication and reflective practice	Risky opportunities • containing language death • redressing knowledge extinction	Sustaining biolinguistic diversity • ethics of teaching English • negotiating cultural affinities and hybridities • language extinction and knowledge death

ised to acquire new skills. They learned the skills needed for transnational entreprenuership to facilitate on-going transnational mobility and to establish useful global networks. Their experiences suggest that it will become increasingly difficult to continue to divide students into administrative categories of "them" and "us," into "local" and "international." The notion that there are certain students who can be classed as "primary" while the rest are "second" or "foreign" speakers of English distorts our understandings of students' cosmopolitan experiences. What it means to be an ELT student now seems to be about becoming worldly, transnational, or even cosmopolitan, and bilingual.

CHAPTER 5

Converging Responses to and Diverging Expressions of Globalisation

> Not, then without their reward have been the services of Great Britain to the Malay Peninsula. The time may come, as it has elsewhere, when, filled with a new sense of their own value, the native races may spurn the ladder by which, if at all, they have reached the height to which they have attained; but in Malaya, so far as one can see, generations will pass before such a state of mind comes about. (Eggerton 1921, 239)

The refractions and reflections of contemporary globalisation can benefit from an examination of sites where English is dominant and where it is emerging. Many parts of the old English empire can give Anglophone nations an insight into their own multilingual future. Australia's relationship with Malaysia, and vice versa, has a number of historical and contemporary links around family and kin, and shared regional strategic interests. These friendships and associations have been shaped in such disparate fields as education, regional diplomacy, and military engagements. Malaysia and Australia's relationships have been melded by enduring links that have seen them working together as regional partners in global capitalism and allies in war. There have also been salient points of tension and conflict that represent the differing aspirations of each nation in the period since the decolonisation of South East Asia.

These points of conflict represent sites of divergence in a history typified by convergence. These tensions reflect changing interpretations about the positioning of each nation in the growing economies of the Asia Pacific region. Politicians in both countries have sought to position their respective nations as regional leaders, a tendency that has led to occasional outbreaks of competitive tension. These skirmishes have tended to highlight the ambiguous attitudes of each nation's leadership to each other and to their relative status in the region. As each nation has sought to occupy a position of economic and moral leadership, small incidents have escalated to foreground and accentuate imagined differences.

Most of the sources of tension circulate around the conflicting interpretations over whether Australia is part of South East Asia. The resolution of these continuing tensions is not assisted by the ambivalence of Australian governments toward Asia in recent years. Since the recognition of the People's Republic of China, Australia's withdrawal from the US/American war in Indochina, and the growth in Asian immigration to Australia, these developments have seen a change in its relationships with South East Asian nations. After the English decision to join the European Common Market in the 1960s and its subsequent withdrawal of troops garrisoned east of the Suez Canal, Australia has been forced to take a different role in securing regional partnerships.

Locked out of the European Union and without the defence infrastructure of the English navy Australia has had to seek new policy settings to replace its reliance on English markets to sustain its economy and the "forward defence" view of its engagement with Asia. Up to the early 1970s, Australia's relations with Asia emphasised its distance from the region, albeit forever tyrannised by its proximity. This policy had its origin in the founding vision of the Federation in 1901, which was grounded in White Australia politics.

By the late 1980s a new engagement with Asia shifted the orientation from a colonialist paradigm in support of English imperial interests to an economic, political, and military framework shaped by an aspiration for regional cooperation. The long-standing interactions with Malaysia, the most sustained and direct in the Asia Pacific region with the exception of Papua New Guinea, has created a special relationship between Malaysia and Australia. Unfortunately, each nation has tended to undervalue or even ignore this relationship at times. Both are former English colonies, federated states headed by constitutional monarchs, and have legal systems based on English courts. Both countries are currently members of the Commonwealth, each having hosted the Commonwealth Games. In Malaysia's case Kuala Lumpur hosted the 1998 Games, handing the legacy of the games to Melbourne to host the 2006 event.

Regional Rivals and Allies

Regional rivalries have mostly centred on the key question of whether Australia is an "Asian nation."Malaysia under the leadership of Dr Mahathir has used the recurring outbreaks of advocacy of White Australia politics to question Australia's credentials as an "Asian nation" and its membership in regional forums. With respect to membership of ASEM, the Asia-Europe forum, Australia is excluded on the basis that it does not constitute either an Asian or a European nation. Australia's attempts to join this body were vetoed by Malaysia. Other members of ASEAN not willing to fracture a consensus about what constitutes "Asia" supported Malaysia's stance. Similar exclusions have been applied to Australia in relation to its claim for membership of the East Asian Economic Caucus. This exclusion has forced Australia to seek a more active role in the Pacific Economic Cooperation forum (APEC) which Mahathir has called a "white man's club" and what Fitzgerald (1997) has referred to as the "Clayton's Asia" due to the membership of Canada, New Zealand, and the United States. Indeed contemporary Australian government notions of "Asia" have been framed around orientalist definitions of "east" and "west" at a time when global restructuring is making such a division even less plausible. The tensions over what is and what is not "Asia" and "Asian" have engendered testy relationships between Australia and Malaysia.

This exclusionary stance led by Malaysia parallels what Stephen Fitzgerald (1997) has identified as an uncertainty about Australia's engagement with Asia. The inappropriateness of Australia's membership has been confirmed in the eyes of the country's Asian critics by the claims of White Australia politicians. Since 1996 Australia has been swamped by "One Nation/White Nation/English-only" policies aimed at reducing Asian immigration and disengagement with Asian trade and investment. The anti-Aboriginal, anti-Asian advocacy of this movement is an instance of regressive parochialism which is itself a response to and an expression of contemporary globalisation. The comments by Prime Minister John Howard that Australia is not an Asian nation and that engagement with Asia should be pragmatically based on economic and strategic priorities alone has confirmed Australia's preference for isolation from its immediate regional neighbours. Howard's statement that Australia should play a "deputy sheriff" role to solve the region's problems through the use of its military forces drew significant criticism from the deputy prime minister of Malaysia in 1999. This doctrine governing current Australian engagement with the region positions it in a superior, overseer relationship and weds it to a dated colonialist policy of "forward defence" as conceived during the Cold War era. The Bush-Powell administration has sanctioned this view of Australia's role of a "stalking horse" for the United States in South East Asia. The continuing struggles over regional leadership in South East Asia have not been assisted by such political support, which has merely heightened tensions between both nations.

Australia and Malaysia's macro-political concerns have been played out through political crises generated around micro issues. An illustration of this was the television series produced and screened by the Australian Broadcasting Commission (ABC) called *Embassy*. This drama program depicted fictional events in an Australian embassy in an unidentified, imaginary "Asian" country. The program tended to portray the fictional nation as subject to endemic corruption and instability, while characterising its inhabitants as untrustworthy, conspiratorial, and backward. The program drew significant protests from Malaysia including calls for its withdrawal from broadcasting and sanctions against the ABC. The furore caused a diplomatic crisis with the Malaysian government calling for action from the Hawke Labor Government and one of the ABC producers of the drama being banned from Malaysia.

The tone of these diplomatic exchanges was not helped by the execution of two Australians in the early 1980s for the importation into Malaysia of illegal drugs. After a lengthy trial and appeal process Malaysian authorities executed prisoners Barlow and Chambers. In response to the executions an emotional Australian Prime Minister Bob Hawke referred to it as a "barbaric act," drawing a caustic response from Malaysia.

Another major crisis in 1992 has been variously referred to as the "Gillespie Affair" in Australia and conversely as the "Raja Bahrin Story" in Malaysia (Bahhrin and Wickham 1997). Raja Bahrin had studied at Geelong Grammar before undertaking a degree in architecture from

Melbourne University and marrying an Anglo-Australian woman. The affair in the Australian press was referred to as a "kidnapping" of two young children by their Malaysian father, after his failure to gain satisfactory judgments in the Family Law Court of Australia. The Australian media concentrated on the dramatic and illegal escape of the father and demands for the return of the children to Australia. The complexities associated with Islamic marriage customs and conventions, which added to the already tense and irreconcilable issue of marriage breakdown, were forgotten in a media feeding frenzy. Indeed the claim by Raja Bahrin, a member of the royal family of Terengannu, that the children had been kidnapped by their mother from Malaysia were ignored in the Australian media. The affair escalated to the extent that it became the subject of talks between the prime ministers of Australia and Malaysia; however, the issues involved remain unresolved to the present day (Kitley and Mules 2000; Schofield 2000).

Perhaps the most memorable dispute between Australia and Malaysia concerned former Prime Minister Paul Keating's remarks made prior to the 1993 Seattle APEC meeting when he criticised the absence of Malaysia's prime minister. In a hurried press conference at the Boeing works Keating, in his colourful invective, said APEC was bigger than any one country whether that be Australia, the United States, or Malaysia, Dr Mahathir or any other recalcitrants. This remark about "recalcitrants" unnecessarily inflamed the already hot issue of Australia's role in peak Asian bodies. It provoked the banning of the ABC from Malaysia in response to these comments about Malaysians. This diplomatic incident led Malaysian authorities to review links with Australia and to place the long-standing defence alliance between the two countries in jeopardy for some time. The Mahathir Government adopted a disinterested stance for the duration of the Keating Government until its defeat by the Liberals and the election of John Howard.

Anxious to maintain an ongoing dialogue with Australia the Malaysian government ensured that a state visit by newly elected Prime Minister Howard was conducted early in the government's term. The generally placid relationship since 1996 has been interrupted briefly by criticism over the handling of the arrest, imprisonment, and trial of former Deputy Prime Minister Anwar Ibrahim by human rights organisations in

Australia. Relations were further soured as a result of Australia's participation in the UN's peacekeeping forces in East Timor. The subsequent claims by John Howard that Australia had a "deputy sheriff" role in preserving law and order on behalf of the United States in South East Asia did not help. Howard was caricatured in the local press as a reincarnation of Inspector Gadget (*The Star* (Penang) 30th September 1999, A, 17). Mahathir responded by saying Howard was not welcome in Malaysia, arguing that Australia should "sort out its treatment of Aborigines before it lectures nations in the region" (Mahithir 2000, 1). Mahathir commented that if Australia wants to be a friend of Asia, it should stop behaving as if it is there to teach Asians how to run their countries, reconfirming well-established criticisms of Australia's paternalism toward the region.

These incidents have highlighted the competitive relationship be-tween Australia and Malaysia as ambitious administrations in each country strive to position their respective country as a regional leader. In a climate of competition small controversies have had a tendency to escalate into major diplomatic incidents. The history of goodwill between these countries has been negated by their rivalry in regional forums, competition for recognition as regional leaders, and the tendency by each nation to view the other suspiciously.

While there are enduring associations across a range of activities, two fields have dominated the relationship between Australia and Malaysia. This partnership emerged out of a key military alliance that assisted in the creation of an independent Malaysian state and more recently through significant educational collaborations. This military alliance is explored briefly as part of the discussion on the character of the Malaysian state setting the scene for consideration of the role of English and ELT in independent Malaysia.

Australia's Part in Malaysia's Struggle for Merdeka

The emergence of the Malaysian nation-state was not a trouble-free road. In a sense Australia's changing policy settings in South East Asia have mirrored Malaysia's journey to nationhood. Malaysia's early years featured significant regional conflict with the communist insurgency of the "Malayan Emergency" closely followed by "confrontasi" with

Indonesia. More recently there was also the suppression of sucessionist movements in the northern border states of Kedah and Perak.

As part of the Commonwealth defence alliance of Australia, New Zealand, and the United Kingdom (ANZUK), Australian troops participated in these campaigns with varying intensity. The "Malayan Emergency" (1948–55) involved a significant deployment against communist guerillas in the jungles of West Malaysia. Australian forces were engaged in action on the ground, air, and sea. The anti-colonialist "Malayan Emergency" erupted after World War II as part of the numerous global struggles between the communist and capitalist superpowers played out in Third World nations. The communist insurgents tied down significant Commonwealth and Malayan forces including English paratroops and Gurkhas. The large garrison of Commonwealth forces was not able to prevent spectacular military actions such as the assassination of the governor general of Malaya, Sir George Gurney. However, without the support of rural Malays, the communist movement, which largely grew out of the Chinese-Malay wartime resistance movement, eventually collapsed. Confined by the tactics and techniques of agrarian revolutionaries the communists required the support of a rural constituency: this was not forthcoming from rural Malaysians or the Orang Asli, many of whom were forcibly separated from the guerilles in concentration camps. The struggle and pressure to decolonise Malaya through the United Nations enabled the eventual declaration of the Federation of Malaya in 1957.

The federal state of Malaysia was declared in 1962. This involved the incorporation of the former English colonies of Singapore and North Borneo, the latter now being the East Malaysia States of Sabah and Sarawak. The neigbouring countries of Indonesia and Philippines opposed the integration of North Borneo into Malaysia, citing a lack of consultation and supervision by the United Nations. Although the Philippines was eventually satisfied with UN involvement, the Indonesian leader President Sukarno declared "Confrontasi" or a defacto state of military confrontation. Sukarno argued that the formation of Malaysia, then containing Singapore, Sabah, Sarawak, and the Peninsular states of the Federation of Malaya, was a political move by England to preserve its imperialist and colonial influence in the region. In the era of the fading English empire and the superpowers' global Cold War the ANZUK alliance deployed troops to protect the emerging state of Malaysia. Citing concerns about Sukarno's pro-communist leanings, Australian military forces were involved in operations in Sarawak, Sabah, and surrounding waters—a deployment that lasted from 1963–65.

Throughout these campaigns Australian forces were based at Singapore, Tenendek in Melaka, and Butterworth in Penang State. For over 30 years the Royal Australian Air Force (RAAF) operated a base at Butterworth in mainland Penang. This enabled strong connections to develop between Malaysian and Australian defence personnel. Such was the presence of Australian military personnel in Malaysia that the area close to Tanjong Bungar on the eastern side of the island of Penang is called "Australian Heights." The friendships at individual and national levels established during the military deployment of Australian forces in the period from 1945 to 1973 operated in parallel to a growing educational relationship.

Malaysia since Merdeka: The Syncretic State and Language Policy

Concern about the ability of the newly emergent and independent nation of Malaysia to preserve its unity as a multi-ethnic country in the context of internal and external conflicts prompted the English colonial authorities in the Foreign Office to place conditions on Malaysia's political structures. The conservative Macmillan administration institutionalised the requirement that Malaysia's political structures and parties had to be multi-ethnic in composition. To qualify for independence the dominant Malay party, the United Malay National Organisation (UMNO) formed the Barisan alliance with Malaysia's Chinese and Indian political parties as partners. This alliance has held office for the entire 43 years since Merdeka, constructing a political environment which Case (2000) describes as a "semi-democracy."

Malaysia is a "syncretic state" insofar as it merges ideological orientations and political practices in managing a society typified by diversity and complexity (Jesudasoon 1996). The syncretic state merges coercion with democratic procedures; propogates religion as it pursues secular goals; engages ethnic mobilisation while inculcating nationalism; and utilises a range of economic strategies spanning liberalism, state interventionism, and rentier arrangements. One of the noteworthy achievements of the Malaysian ruling elite has been to manage the mix of ideological orientations to secure a relatively stable and prosperous state. In a short period their nation-building efforts have produced substantial improvements throughout the country. The post-independence Malaysian journey has been characterised by skilful management of apparently contradictory policy settings. The country's leadership has successfully promoted conservative national symbols and communal virtues grounded in the Islamic faith while institutionalising secularism and a pro-active, sometimes skeptical engagement with globalisation. The leadership has also been successful in mediating anxieties between ethnic and racial communities in Malaysia through utilising the state as a mechanism to steer economic opportunities for the *Bumiputra,* but less so for the Orang Asli, the Indigenous Malay peoples.

Anxieties about economic inequalities between the *Bumiputra* and the Chinese-Malaysians have, particularly since riots in 1969, been recognised by what Prime Minister Mahathir (1970) termed the "Malay dilemma." This dilemma identified a historic lack of economic influence, employment, educational opportunities, and confidence among the *Bumiputra*. Since 1970 Malaysia's umbrella New Economic Policy has been typified by interventionist strategies to create a renewal of the *Bumiputra* identity and to redress historic inequalities of opportunity which grew from English colonialism. The latest manifestation of this policy has been captured in the concept of the "new Malay" (Melayu Baru), a rejuvenated ethnic identity that responds to the contemporary neo-liberal ideology of globalism. These state policies are intended to ensure access by *Bumiputra*, on the basis of population sise, to finance, education, and job opportunites. In material terms there has been a vigorous effort to sponsor the mobility of *Bumiputra* into the capitalist classes; this has resulted in an expansion of the middle class from 20 percent in 1970 to 33.5 percent in 1993 (Jesudasoon 1996).

The imposition of quotas based on ethnicity to redress inequities in many aspects of economic and social life has been achieved with stunning rapidity but not without criticism. Quotas are used to limit the number of qualified Chinese-Malaysian applicants who gain university entry so as to make provision for *Bumiputra* applicants. This system continues to be criticised for limiting development opportunities for Malaysia. In particular there are concerns that this quota system has benefited only a select few among the *Bumiputra*. Related criticisms of this policy have been that it accelerated the development of private education providers and the popularity of overseas studies among Chinese-Malaysians and Indian-Malaysians.

The *Bumiputra*-dominated Barisan national alliance has successfully managed the politics of Malaysia by mobilising a triangular relationship around ethnicity, democracy, and development (Loh 2000). This political management strategy operated largely unchallenged until the economic crash of 1997. Then a combination of factors such as concerns about the administration of justice sparked by the conviction of Anwar Ibrahim and the economic inequalities between rural and urban communities in Malaysia produced significant fractures. In the 1999 elections the Mahathir Government withstood a significant challenge from opposition parties and retained power in spite of losses to the Islamic party (PAS) in the northern and rural regions.

Language policy and the relative status of Bahasa Malaysia and Bahasa Inggeris (the English language) in Malaysia have also been influenced by the orientation of the syncretic state. These policy settings have been used to rejuvenate the status of the *Bumiputra* and their culture and to respond to and give expression to globalisation. This prompts a question that is the focus of recurring debates throughout Malaysia. How is it possible that the struggle for national liberation is being undercut by the language of the coloniser so many had fought to vanquish? Dr Mahathir writes of the link between the English language and English colonialism in the following terms:

> In colonial days the use of English in all government documents was taken for granted. Those who could not understand English were expected to find their own interpreters. Signs, notices with few exceptions, were in English, and if at times these signs were only useful to a handful of people this was expected and tolerated. Malay even in the colonial days was used more frequently and better understood than English. It is even more so now. (Mahathir 1970, 138)

Mahathir was writing shortly after the 13th May 1969 riots in Kuala Lumpur. This was a period when Malaysia was lurching toward civil violence mobilised around economic inequalities and which found expression in racism. However, the quest for national unity was secured through the government's active reaffirmation of the language of the *Bumiputra* as the national language:

> In a multi-racial nation like Malaysia, unity, can therefore be achieved provided agreement can be reached as to the choice of language and the related culture. Provided the language is accepted, a multi-racial nation can mould national unity by employing accessory methods such as the projection of a focus on loyalty to king, the teaching of national history, the veneration of national symbols in the form of the flag, the anthem, the colours etc and last but not least the law and the constitution. (Mahathir 1970, 102)

Mahathir (1970) referred to English as an "immigrant" language in his book *The Malay Dilemma*. It was not regarded as the most appropriate language to provide a unifying force in Malaysia since its use and teaching was generally restricted to those urbanised communities with close contact to the commercial and political networks associated with the English colonial administration. These colonial practices ensured that other languages such as Chinese and Tamil were the responsibility of the communities who spoke them and not the colonial administration. The status of Malay and English was firmly established by the 1951 Barnes Review of Education in the colony of Malaya which recommended that instruction in schools be restricted to Malay and English. While these recommendations were later modified by the Fenn-Wu Commission (Malay (Federation) 1951), English became the language of instruction from the sixth year of school in Chinese schools and the fourth year in Tamil schools. After independence free primary schooling was mandated for six years using each of the nation's four main languages of Malay, English, Chinese, and Tamil (Pandian 1999). This trend has been preserved since independence albeit with increasing emphasis being on enhancing the status of Bahasa Malaysia as the nation-forming language. This nation-building mission is clearly present in Malaysia's philosophy of education, which states that:

> Education in Malaysia is an on-going effort toward further developing the potential of individuals in a holistic and integrated manner, so as to produce individuals who are intellectually, spiritually, emotionally and physically balanced and harmonious, based on a firm belief in and devotion to God. Such an effort is designed to produce Malaysian citizens who are knowledgeable and competent, who possess high moral standards, and who are responsible and capable of achieving high level of personal well-being as well as being able to contribute to the harmony and betterment of the

> family, the society and the nation at large. (Kementerian Pendidikan Malaysia 1998, vi)

Aspects of this nation-building orientation are evident in Malaysia's recognition of the relationship between moral values and literature in providing a framework that enables teachers to infuse these as integrated elements into the materials and activities of their English language lessons (Kementerian Pendidikan Malaysia 1991, 3). As well teachers are expected to "use materials that emphasise the principles of good citizenship, moral values, and the Malaysian way of life" (Kementerian Pendidikan Malaysia 1994, 3). Moral values are stipulated for each year level:

> The moral values selected for the upper secondary school level are self-reliance, moderation, justice, diligence, public-spiritedness and rationality. At the lower secondary school level, the moral values selected are courage, honesty, charity and unity for Form 1; kindness, cooperation, friendship and selflessness for Form 11; and patriotism, neighbourliness and gratitude for Form 111. (Kementerian Pendidikan Malaysia 1991, 2)

In Malaysia English is a second language taught in government and non-government primary and secondary schools. It is taught for communicative purposes relevant to certain job situations; the meaningful engagement of Malaysia in local and international trade and commerce; and as a means of accessing academic, professional, and recreational materials (Kementerian Pendidikan Malaysia 1990, vii). Students' skills in Bahasa Inggeris are developing through learning about the nature of the language using certain content and text types. The expectation is that all such language learning experiences will be framed within a new technology orientation with links to contemporary globalisation (Kementerian Pendidikan Malaysia 1998, 68). The aim of the Bahasa Inggeris Kurrikulum is to enable students to acquire

> proficiency in the [English] language so as to equip them with positive communication skills and knowledge of English that will enable them to widen their networks of interpersonal relations and have direct access to information for general knowledge and leisure-based purposes (Kementerian Pendidikan Malaysia 1998, viii).

In terms of learning to speak English "the aim is for international intelligibility" (Kementerian Pendidikan Malaysia 1994, 2), while taking "into consideration the roles and needs of English" of Malaysia (Curriculum Development Centre, 1997, 1). Teachers are expected to "use the Malaysian setting as the base to teach the [English] language skills and [English] language contents" (Kementerian Pendidikan Malaysia 1994, 3).

Beginning with the immediate learning environment of students, the learning content or topics "gradually expands in widening circles to include the home, village, town, state, country and the world," including the ASEAN region (Kementerian Pendidikan Malaysia 1994, 2).

The perspective of the Malaysian language curriculum concerning English highlighted in these education policies conforms to the ideological orientation of the syncretic state where the needs for an internally coherent response to the contradictory pressures of nation-building and globalisation are simultaneously incorporated. Key issues have arisen in Malaysia recently that create significant challenges for its language education policies. There is continuing concern and anxiety about the English language proficiency of students throughout the nation and more particularly the competence of teachers. The push to globalisation associated with the knowledge or "K" economy has raised concerns about the role of English, particularly in exacerbating inequalities in Malaysian society. These issues are discussed further in Chapter Six, which specifically addresses ELT provision in Malaysia.

School principal Wong How Chan said that Sekolah Menegah Union recorded a 5.3 percent improvement in the pass rate in the Sijil Pelaqjaran Malaysia (SPM) English examination paper as a result of *The Star* Newspaper in Education (NIE) programme (*The Star (Penang)* Thursday, April 6, 2000, p. 18). The NIE programme reportedly provided useful strategies for students to learn English in an enjoyable way. It uses interesting games and language activities to motivate both students and teachers. NIE was used to improve students, English as well as their general knowledge and awareness of current affairs. Moreover the Great Eastern Life Assurance (M) Berhad pledged to provide the school NIE classes with 100 copies of *The Star* one day a week for 20 weeks. Great Eastern is providing 10,000 copies of *The Star* to one selected school in each state of Malaysia as part of its community service marketing strategy. Prior to receiving this sponsorship the school had to encourage students to buy *The Star* and share it in class.

Tunku Ismail Jewa (Penang) wrote to the editor of the *New Strait Times* (Tuesday, April 11, 2000, 13) urging the Ministry of Education to "take immediate remedial action as English is a complusory second language in the school curriculum," because of the "drop in the percentage of passes in the 1999 Sijil Pelajaran Malaysia examination."

On the same day C. K. J. wrote to the editor (Tuesday, April 11, 2000, 13) raising the following issues. First, that when English was the medium of instruction, lower secondary students had to read abridged versions Robert Louis Stevenson's *Treasure Island*, Jules Verne's *Around the World in Eighty Days,* and Daniel Defoe's *Robinson Crusoe*, noting that there were no examinations on these books. Second, that senior secondary school students did Shakespeare, Hardy, Wells, and the like, but these were never part of the English language test. Third, few students now take literature, as most study the sciences; those who do are stigmatised as "dummies." Fourth, literature has been recently revived as part (20%) of the English language examination and "is now being forced down students' throats" (Sijil Pelarajran Malaysia). Fifth, "the alarmingly low standard in the [English] language is a more pressing matter that needs to be addressed" than is having Form One students "see the light of Shakespeare's Life's Brief Candle." Sixth, C. K. J. asked "whether we [Malaysia] have the teachers to teach literature. I suspect many of them may not even have a good command of the language themselves. ...No doubt the Ministry of Education has been running courses for them but with inservice training lasting a day or two, they could hardly be expected to do a decent job, much less a good one." Finally C.K.J. urged the authorities to review the curriculum materials, poems and short stories, selected for use in schools because of their "unnerving obsession with death and violence," a controversy within the Indian community over K. S. Maniam's *The Return*, and the racialism of Keris Emas' *Jungle of Hope*. While issues of proficiency emerge, there is also uncertainty about what constitutes the English that is taught.

Nasi, baju, hantu, ladang, makan, and kalan? Which of these is not an English word? The answer, of course, is that all of these words are part of the English language. While your computer spell-checker might not recognise them, the *Oxford English Dictionary* (*OED*) does. The *OED* defines nasi as "cooked rice"; baju as "a short loose jacket"; hantu as "an evil spirit or ghost"; ladang as "a piece of land under dry cultivation, often a jungle clearing"; makan as "to eat"; and kajan as "matting made from palm or pandanus leaves." Other (Malaysian) English words include "amok" (engaging furiously in battle, attacking with desparate resolution, rushing in a state of frenzy to the commission of an indiscriminate murder); "sambal" (a highly seasoned condiment); "sarong" (a wrap-around skirt); "gecko" (housed lizard); and "dugong" (a large aquatic herbivorous mammal) are also (Malaysian) English words.

The *OED* has recently incorporated a number of Malay words into the English language. *Bumiputra* (sons of the soil, Malaysian citizens of ethnic Malay origins) and "tun" (hereditary title) are among the 10,000 new or revised words appearing on the *OED* online (www.oed.com) launched in February 2000. The *OED* sourced the origins of "lah" to Singaporean English, much to the disbelief of Malaysians. Nevertheless, where there is good evidence that a word borrowed from another language is in widespread use in English anywhere in the world, it is included in the *OED* as an English word, irrespective of whether it is Malaysian or Singaporean English. "Lah" became part of Malaysian English soon after the English colonisation of Malaysia, a process of linguistic hybridisation which typically occurs when two languages meet. "Lah" acts as a (emotional) modifier to reduce the apparent harshness of a statement, request, or order, or to reinforce a sense of intimacy, friendliness, or amicability. "Lah" is used in informal interactions for comfort and to reduce the social and psychological gap between speakers (Golingai 2000, 3–4).

Learning from Each Other: Educational Alliances between Unequal Partners

In May 2000 Dr Mahathir criticised, the Australian federal government's bullying of neighbouring Indonesia. The Australian Government responded with the claim that while inter-governmental relations may be subject to tension, the relationship between the peoples of both countries was healthy. Side-stepping the inter-governmental tensions, the Australian government claimed this to be so because some 130,000 Malaysian students had graduated from Australian educational institutions since the initiation of the Colombo Plan in the 1950s. Even so the educational contact between the people of the two nations has undergone several stages since the earliest programmes after the Second World War.

In the immediate postwar years the Australian government developed its foreign policy as a support for White Australia politics and its strategies for expanding a Whites-only Anglo-ethnic population. The Colombo Plan, which provided education for students from the "old Commonwealth" countries such as Malaysia, was seen, as have all of Australia's international aid programmes since, as a mechanism for enhancing national security and economic interests. In the summer of 1946 Professor A. H. MacDonald (reported in Borrie 1947, 36) expressed the motivating desire informing White Australia's contributions to the Colombo Plan thus: "We are bound, for our own security and prosperity, to support international schemes for the development of the East in the fullest sense." More than this, the government relied on the Colombo Plan to befriend an Asia it feared: these Asian students were seen as its best ambassadors for promoting "peaceful co-existence" (Palfreeman 1967, 129, 130–131). When confronted with internal and external critiques of White Australia politics, the government pointed to the Colombo Plan and Australia's education of thousands of students from Asia in its defence. The recurrence of this rhetorical ploy indicates the failure of Australian governments to decolonise the legacy of White Australia politics that continues to cloud their thinking.

Between 1950 and 1965 the number of students from Asia studying in Australian universities grew from 1,000 to 5,000 but was limited to the extent that it served the ideological interests of White Australia politics. Until 1966 temporary entry as a student was judged on the technical benefit their course would bring to their homeland and their ability to contribute to its economic growth. In 1973 Australia's anti-Asian "populate or perish" immigration program was replaced by the introduction of a "controlled, multiracial" immigration program which made it possible to lift the limit on the number of Asian students studying in Australia to 10,000 per year. The chief criterion for rejection then became the availability of comparable courses in the students' home country. In the period when domestic student fees were abolished, the number of overseas student positions rose under the sponsorship of Australian Development International Board. Investment in this strategy of security, through students, varied but was estimated to be $Aus70m at its peak. This sum attracted scrutiny from the Hawke Labor Government in the 1980s and resulted in the introduction of a new category of full-fee paying overseas students (Williams 1989). With the end of the Cold War and the struggles between communism and global capitalism, the time when Australia had to buy its political and security interests in Asia seemed to have past, now it could sell education to Asia.

By 1995 the full-fee paying category of overseas students had reached 81,000 (Baker, Creedy, and Johnson 1995). A significant part of this expansion in fee-paying students was the growing market for ELT programmes which in 1995 attracted some 7,398 students from Asian countries. This growth in ELT provision resulted in this sector's enrolments making up 20 percent of all full-fee paying overseas students which had reached 84,600 by 1999 (DETYA 2000). As a result of the increasing reliance on full-fee paying students to bolster Australian higher education and the corresponding increase in the internationalisation of Australian education, the annual contribution to export earnings reached $A3.08 billion by the turn of the century. This growth can be partly attributed to IDP Australia and the establishment of Australian International Education Foundation (AIEF) in 1994 to facilitate the promotion and management of education as a growing export business.

By 1999, 73,000 students from Asia made up the 84,300 international student enrolments, or 85 percent of all the international students in higher education throughout Australia (DETYA 2000). Throughout these changes Malaysian students have been one of the largest national groups, now making up 18 percent of the total. Malaysian students have tended to display a preference for business and commerce courses. A large number of Chinese-Malaysian students from merchant families study in Australia. The quota system for entry into Malaysian universities provides a majority of places for *Bumiputra* places. This ensures that the majority of Malaysia's 60,000 overseas students are of Chinese background (Harris and Jarrett 1990). The strong demand from Malaysian citizens for overseas education has resulted in Australian ELT providers developing twinning agreements with local partners in Malaysia. In 1999 this mode had attracted some 4,800 Malaysian enrolments, a trend which represents a substantial shift in the provision by Australian ELT providers to offshore delivery (DETYA 2000).

The competition for Malaysian students was heightened throughout the 1990s with their relatively high levels of English proficiency and ability to pay fees. Nevertheless, ELT providers in the United States, UK, Canada, and New Zealand proved to be especially competitive against Australian providers. The dimensions of the market are evident from the 75,000 Malaysian students who compete for the 2,500 scholarship places allocated by England each year. Even though Australia is recording steady growth, aggressive transnational competition creates various dilemmas for increasing numbers of ELT providers.

Competitive Disadvantage: White Australia Politics and Selling ELT

The quest for students in some key markets in Asia is intensifying and moving in directions where Australian ELT providers experience recurring vulnerability. These vulnerabilities result from frequent efforts to resuscitate key planks of White Australia politics, at least since the mid-1980s. Despite widespread criticisms from within Australia and from throughout Asia the situation is aggravated by regressive Australian government policies on Asia and Asian student recruitment.

The images of Australia as a reformed multicultural country and that it has shaken off the legacies of White racism toward non-Europeans are regularly tested. There is recurring evidence of a lingering White Australia politics such as the 1984 "All for Australia" campaign and the emergence in 1996 of the racist "One Nation/White Nation/English-only" movement. This movement led campaigns against productive Australian engagement with Asia and against Asian immigration. While the courts declared One Nation a fraudulent political party its influence in reshaping the policies of the major political parties has not diminished. The appeal of regressive parochialism has ignited efforts to refurbish White Australia politics. The One Nation/White Nation/English-only agenda is influencing the policies of parties, both Government and Opposition, toward labor migration, international students, family reunion, Australia-Asia relations, and Australian regional politics. The assessment of Australia in South East Asian countries is that there is now a license to indulge in racist vilification, something former Australian political leaders Malcolm Fraser and Paul Keating tried to oppose.

The success of selling a student experience in Australia to prospective Asian and, more particularly, Malaysian students has been based on the belief that Australia is a safe, multi-racial country with an absence of groups promoting racism. The presence of Asian-Australian commun-ities in major educational centres has created an impression that students could live in Australia free from vilification from groups like the National Front in the UK or the Ku Klux Klan in the United States.

The impression that the One Nation/White Nation/English-only movement has peaked and that Australia's racist culture is benign are disrupted by recurring reports in the Malyasian press of outbreaks of White supremacist politics in Australia. The establishment of a chapter of the infamous Ku Klux Klan in Australia received wide radio and press coverage in Malaysia. Moreover, the manner in which the reports were positioned in newspapers raised concerns among Australian ELT providers.

Malaysian readers of *The Star* on 3rd June 1999 were greeted with the headline "Klan takes hold in Australia." This article was accompanied by a large colour photograph of hooded members of the Australian arm of the Klan. The lead paragraph from *The Star*'s report stated: "The white supremacist Ku Klux Klan, spearheaded by a member of the One Nation Party, has established branches in Australia, sparking a storm of protest." The report said the Klan's aim was for "a white Australia, a fair Australia." *The Star* concluded with the observation that the One Nation/White Nation/English-only movement is "anti-Asian."

While the content of *The Star's* report was alarming enough, its juxtaposition on the same page with other world news situated Australia in a most unfavourable position in the international ELT marketplace. Accompanying the feature on the Klan was a report on the killing of three people during South Africa's second democratic elections. Another story from New York (USA) reported on a janitor who worked by night to help police bust prostitution rings. The clustering of these articles created an impression of racial tension, corruption, and violence in the United States, South Africa, and Australia. A cause for concern among Australian ELT providers was the positioning on the same page of a prominent advertisement for scholarships to study in the (not always) United Kingdom at a university ranked highly by the Financial Times University Index.

For Malaysians considering the possibilities of overseas study for themselves or their children the choices were quite stark. Faced with the prospect of anti-Asian racism, murder, and prostitution in three countries, these newspaper reports offer an additional marketing advantage to English universities. Not surprisingly, Australian diplomatic and education representatives contend that the juxtaposition of such stories help competitors to undermine Australia's advantages of proximity, price, climate, and civility. Commenting on the impact of the efforts by the One Nation/White Nation/English-only movement to resurrect White Australia politics, Australia's former deputy prime minister, minister for trade, and National Party leader, Tim Fischer, a Catholic of German and Dutch background, said:

> we got hell. In the diplomatic circuit we had a lot of our competitors set up straw men. They went out of their way to see that the worst aspects of Pauline Hansonism were on the fax machines to some of the key people making purchasing decisions. ...in the areas of individual decision, in education, in inbound tourism, absolutely there was an effect. Absolutely. (Cope and Kalantzis 2000, 57)

The choice for prospective students from Asia when selecting an Australian ELT provider is, however, made more complex by recent policies of Australia's Howard Government. Restrictive and expensive visa requirements are eroding Australia's competitive edge in a market that is still growing. Delays in processing applications which are almost three times more expensive than those in the United States and the UK, and restrictions on working part-time make Australia a less attractive study destination. Statements by the Australian government that such measures are designed to protect the integrity of its immigration system do not set a positive tone for Asian applicants interested in accessing the country's ELT providers. Pressure from ELT providers, and the education and training sector more generally, is expected to bring changes in these areas if the One Nation/White Nation/English-only movement fails to gain further electoral support.

While Australian policymakers claimed that efforts to resuscitate White Australia politics and its embodiment in the one million One Nation/White Nation/English-only voters had subsided in 1999, their complacency was seriously misplaced. In its section on World News, *The Star* (5th April 2000, 27) reported on the increasing pressure on the Australian government to apologise for its past treatment of Indigenous Australians. It was also reported that the Australian government had denied taking Indigenous children from their families between 1920s and the 1960s despite all the evidence of the government's genocidal policy of race purification through "biological assimilation." The policy was to eradicate Australia's Indigenous population through inter-racial breeding across several generations. The Australian Government ruled out the issuing of a formal apology and paying compensation, despite the long-term social and economic benefits this policy promises to deliver. The Government of the Commonwealth of Australia claimed it was not responsible for this policy and refused to be held publicly accountable.

The Australian Catholic Social Welfare Commission said the forcible removal of even one child under this policy was one too many. Sir Ronald Wilson, Australia's former Human Rights Commission president and co-author of the landmark 1997 report into the Stolen Generation, *Bringing Them Home*, condemned the Australian government's stance. Indigenous leaders, such as Evelyn Scott, the former chair of the Council for Aboriginal Reconciliation, were reported as saying that the government's downplaying of the Commonwealth's biological assimilation policy had caused irreparable damage to attempts by government and Indigenous communities to promote reconciliation and inter-racial harmony.

Jeffery Francis, an editorial consultant for Australasia-Pacific Media, wrote a feature article for the *Sunday Star* (Francis 2000, 34) in which he argued "a simple sorry may end big row down under." The failure of the Howard Government to face up to this aspect of Australian history had, he said, damaged "Australia's reputation as a peaceful, multicultural society" in the lead-up to the Sydney Olympic Games in September 2000. The government responded to criticism neither from home nor from abroad. The Australian government's steadfast belief is "that the present generations of [Anglo-ethnic] Australians should not take responsibility for the mistakes of the past generations on how Aborigines had been treated. No one is really surprised by his stubbornness and uncom-promising attitude. He is the same old Howard who took eight years to apologise for his remarks on Asian immigration during the 1988 election campaign." Aboriginal actor Justine Saunders, who featured in *The Chant of Jimmy Blacksmith,* handed back her Order of Australia to signify her critique of the outrageousness of the federal government's views and inactions.

A few days later the *New Straits Times* (11th April 2000, 18) led its World News section with the headline "Howard moves to change racist laws." National and international criticism of the Howard Government, including a blast from a UN Committee on the Elimination of Racist Discrimination, was reported regarding the handling of Indigenous issues, particularly the mandatory sentencing of Aborigines and the Stolen Generation. The tensions around these issues created by the Howard administration hurt Australia's reputation abroad just prior to the Sydney Olympic Games. Despite pressure for the Howard Government to use its constitutional powers to override the mandatory sentencing laws of the Northern Territory, these laws have not been altered. While RM11.21 million (A$5 million) was promised for a rehabilitation and training program for juvenile offenders, Aborigines, the nation's most disadvantaged group, have not relented in their critiques of the government.

We should fully expect that Australia's second generation of transnational ELT will be subjected to the critical gaze of ELT students who are likely to make problematic Australian notions of "international," "education," and "English." At the very least their critiques of ELT might be expected to disclose the remnants of the English empire and orientalist traditions elaborated in the encounters between countries like Australia and Malaysia and the ever-present but ruinous legacy of White Australia politics. The enriching global movements of ELT students and the flows of information packaged in the new educational media provided by transnational ELT businesses confront the comfortable assumptions of White Australia as a bounded Anglo-fundamentalist community with solid racist borders. The gaze of White Australia politics and its powerful motivating desires remain to be fully deconstructed by students of enterprise English. The One Nation/White Nation/English-only movement reminds us of the need for developing a basic understanding of the ways in which White Australia politics continues to be mobilised as a foil against non-Europeans and the ways it imbues the English language we teach/sell them.

Getting the Edge in the Global Market: Competition between Australia and Malaysia

In this context orientations to ELT that draw on and reproduce the legacy of nineteenth-century colonialist English are now a liability (Pennycook 1998). Efforts to construct a globally oriented enterprise English require the eradication of the cultural power of White Australia politics, and the refurbishment of its ELT products and services. In the face of the continuing power of White Australia politics there has been a trend toward the development of 3+0 courses by Australian ELT providers. The 3+0 formula refers to a program structure of three years study in Malaysia with no attendance requirement by the provider for in-country study abroad. ELT providers offer these 3+0 courses on location in Asia. An example of this is Sunway, a multinational corporation which has twinning agreements with eight universities in the United States, UK, New Zealand, and Australia. Other Australian universities have developed a partnership with the HELP Institute. This is part of their bid to seize on the attraction of the 3+0 formula, with the addition of such marketing techniques as two-week study tours at "no extra cost."

In a way these program innovations seek to avoid the consequences of Australia's tarnished image in Asia. However, it is important not to fail to account for the growing ambition of ELT providers throughout Asia. Some Australian ELT providers have complacently assumed that the prestige of their qualifications will be an enduring market advantage. The Malaysian approach to "badging" in the automobile market provides one possible scenario for future developments in ELT provision throughout the region. The development of the Malaysian manufactured Proton car provides some insights as to how Malaysian ELT providers are acquiring the know-how and image of prestige in the context of an increasing internationalised ELT market.

Malaysia's Perusahaan Otomobil National Bhd (Proton) company began operations in September 1985. To get a jump-start in car production it collaborated with Japanese manufacturer Mitsubishi in order to access designs and technological know-how. Gradually, there was a shift from imported parts to the production of local components, all with Malaysian government support and subsidy. By means of technological transfer, Proton gained experience and knowledge from its partner.

A second phase involved Proton buying an 80 percent stake in Lotus in order to enhance the company's image and to gain access to new technical knowledge. Specifically, Proton drew on Lotus's strengths in suspension dynamics and cultural heritage. To leapfrog ahead, Proton designed its cars in a modular way. It uses a single, standard part that may be fitted into several different model cars. This achieves economies of scale and reduces the overall number of parts needed to be designed and produced. In terms of reliability for vehicles produced by car manufacturers throughout Asia, the Perusahaan Otomobil National Bhd (Proton) company has been rated in the "best" category along with Honda, Mazda, and Toyota. Put simply the acquisition as a majority stakeholder in Lotus assured the Proton corporation of not only designs but also the status and prestige associated with this famous marque.

The question for ELT providers is how various elements of this strategy might be applied in the context of their businesses. As argued in Chapter 3, the pattern of competition in transnational ELT provision is already seeing the development of increasingly hybridised structures. These transnational hybrids involve ownership by universities, private developers, and telecommunications corporations. The impact of increasing transnational ownership on these businesses is emerging as a key concern. Australia, in particular, faces problems arising from the continuing effect of White Australia politics and the image problem regressive parochialism creates for transnational ELT businesses.

The relationship between Australia and Malaysia typifies some of the ambiguities and tensions concerning the engagement with Asia that Australian governments have pursued in the last 30 years. The contradictory tendency toward convergence and divergence of interests is an expression of the competition between the two nations. These tendencies provide insights into the differentiating effects of globalisation and localisation in specific national settings.

Relational Affinities

At least since English colonisation Australia and Malaysia have been part of the processes of globalisation and cultural mixing, all of which have accelerated over time. The move toward the socio-economic integration of Australia into South East Asia has revealed the difficulties it has in developing a more outward looking, less parochial sense of place. The ambivalent positioning of this Anglophone nation in South East Asia derives from its distinctive admixture of Indigenous, European, and Asian socio-cultural relations. Efforts to shift its orientation from dependency on England and the United States as a result of increasing contact with South East Asian cultures is complicated by the colonialist legacy of White

Australia politics. Malaysia and Australia exist in a process of continual negotiation in their efforts to blur the lines of demarcation that were once used to construct a Whites-only, English-only Australia. Today neither of these countries can be thought of as a monolingual, ethnically homogeneous entity, but rather each society has risen out of the interplay between English and American colonialism, nation-building forces pressing toward linguistic, racial, and cultural homogeneity, and local resistance which sustains linguistic heterogeneity.

The dangerous stereotype that holds Malaysia and Australia to be neatly divisible, discrete entities has lost some of its ideological certainty that England's naval base in Singapore may have given them in the 1940s. While oppositional notions such as "east" and "west" tend to make the slightest differences between Australia and Malaysia seem absolute, these ignore the affinities between them, and refuse to acknowledge many significant differences among the countries of Asia and within them. Suggestions that differences between these countries are themselves primordial must be rejected. Important elements that constitute their connectedness include both the global operations of transnational capitalism and the regressive modes of parochialism it incites. While these common elements do not operate in the same way in both countries, what they both learn from these experiences can be shared to improve their interrelationships.

Australia can no longer be understood in isolation from its relationship with Malaysia and other South East Asian countries. Australian studies of Bahasa Malaysia, for instance, need to include a consideration of Malaysia's economic activities in Australia and the implications this has for language teaching. The built environment of Australia is a product of a changing global economy. Houses, office blocks, and factories are built on profits and capital accumulated through trade with and investment by Malaysia. Likewise, students can examine the production of Australian leisure resorts by Asian tourists and investors. This will give them insights into the ways in which the well-being and progress of Australia is being built through the work of Asian people, as well as how and to what degree Australia is now a creation of Asian nations. The encounters between Anglophone and Asian nations have been such that each has been mutually created by the other. Contemporary globalisation is also producing increasing cultural and linguistic creolisation.

The idea that Australia is part of South East Asia tends to bemuse Malaysians. However, its engagement with and integration into South East Asia is now constitutive of the economic and socio-political policies of Australia's local, state, and federal governments. The extent to which this varies from the past reflects Australia's changing global relations and is evident in its selective absorption of a variety of Asian phenomena. The racialised boundary line that was constructed to assert absolute differences between the peoples and cultures of Asia and Australia now appears as a porous border rather than a marker of unbridgeable cultural and linguistic differences. These borders were a way of regulating complex global flows of cultural, social, and ideological information, of demographic movement, economic investment, trade, and the dissemination of technology between Australia and Asia (Appadurai 1996). The move by Australia to rework its engagement with Asia requires the creation within Australia of new identities for Asia, Asian peoples, Asian-Australians, and Asian languages. Now Australia must unlearn its historical sense of racist superiority and privilege, listen to those Asians who have been silenced or marginalised, and learn to speak in such a way that they are taken seriously by Asians. The learning of Bahasa Malaysia and other South East Asian languages should be helpful in this regard.

It no longer seems appropriate to speak of either Asian or Anglophone nations as fixed entities with each having its own essence. Nor is it useful to think of Anglophone nations as the ones which produce knowledge about English, with Asia simply being its passive consumer and object of their knowledge claims (Canagarajah 1999). Because of the Asian presence in Anglophone countries, postcolonial studies of Asian cultures and languages, including English, involves more than the crossing of national borders from one country to another; they include the crossing of an indeterminate number of borders within these countries. To cross the borders that have separated Anglo-ethnic Australians from Asian-Australians is to move in, through, and beyond the powerful motivating desires of White Australia politics. Inevitably this means resisting the comfort of Australia claiming to belong to either Europe or the United States or Asia per se. Australia is a distinctively cosmopolitical product, not un/like Hawaii.

CHAPTER 6

Malaysia Acts Globally to Maintain Local Vitality

> The abnormal practice of the British regime must be recognised for what it was.... In the long run a truly Malaysian national education system must be recognised and accepted by all citizens as the only means of moulding a single, unified nation. Once this policy is accepted and set in motion, it will develop its own momentum. No longer will Malaysia have to insist on it, but all who becomes citizens of Malaysia, irrespective of racial origins and culture, will uphold and impose this educational policy. (Mahathir 1970, 146)

Malaysia is a country that exhibits some of the key dilemmas associated with the globalisation and localisation of English. As mentioned in Chapter 5 there is a long and enduring colonial legacy that has led to English emerging and operating as a second language to Bahasa Malaysia. The relative positioning of English with respect to Bahasa Malaysia is an outcome of a historic settlement concerning the nation-building project of the newly independent Malaysia. The dilemmas associated with this issue highlights some of the trends, relationships, and risks that *Appropriating English* seeks to analyse.

The status of English has been influenced by the government's role in planning the nation's response and contribution to globalisation. Malaysia has embraced the new technology revolution enthusiastically and is pressing ahead with investments and strategies to create a knowledge or "K-Society." This represents a transfer from a production or "P-Economy" based on manufacturing to an economy based on innovations in new technologies and the production of new knowledge. The concepts of K-Society and K-Economy have been used in part to reaffirm the role of

English in Malaysia's information technology and globalisation. As part of its move toward the "K-Economy," Malaysia has developed an ambitious plan for a Multimedia Super Corridor (MSC) between the capital Kuala Lumpur and the entreport of Port Klang. A satellite city, called Cyberjaya, is being developed as Malaysia's version of Silicon Valley.

Part of this national planning also rests on a competence in English, the dominating language for the new technologies. To provide the foundation for this "K-Society" the Malaysian government has commenced a process of educational reform that has witnessed significant growth in the diversity of education providers. This has included an expansion of ELT providers beyond the public sector, particularly the new hybrid ELT enterprises.

The nation's confidence in launching into the new era of globalisation is hampered by anxieties about the quality of English language proficiency. These concerns are not a nostalgic longing for the colonial remnants of British English but represent a troubling perplexity about competence at all levels, including that of teachers themselves. While these concerns are continually hyped up by the press, there is anxiety about policy settings seeking nation-building through Bahasa Malaysia having diminished the importance of English in the school curriculum. In particular, current English language teaching methodologies are seen as inferior to those imagined to exist somewhere in the past.

At the same time there is also ambivalence about the role and status of the local variety of English; "Malaysian English" is not seen as having the robustness and transportability required in the context of globalisation. Those policy settings aimed at positioning Malaysia globally are up against a rising tide of resentment against inequalities that typify rural and regional Malaysian communities. This is in an economy that has demonstrated extraordinary growth and resilience since the 1997 economic crises.

These inequalities and anxieties are juxtaposed uncomfortably in a context where language policy and the very identity of the nation-state of Malaysia is torn between Bahasa Malaysia as a national rallying point and the role of English in making necessary global connections. As the initial contact point with the English colonisers, Penang is situated in the centre of all these developments. This historic port city was developed into a centre for educational excellence with strong backing from the state and federal governments. The skyline of the old colonial port city of Penang is now dotted with manufacturing plants on the mainland which produce computer components. The Universiti of Sains Malaysia (USM), one of Malaysia's oldest and most prestigious universities, provides the research and development infrastructure needed by local industries. The local school system is well recognised as one of the best in Malaysia, being active in promoting international partnerships and hosting international education conferences in conjunction with USM. Penang's status as Malaysia's second city after the capital Kuala Lumpur can be traced to its utility in fulfilling the needs of the colonial interests of the English empire. The arrival of the English not only brought the language of this colonising power but also the social relations to service the economic and social priorities of the English. Here it is worth re-counting the history of colonialism in Malaysia prior to commencing an in-depth analysis of the political, social, and economic context of ELT provisions within this country.

Education and Colonialism in Malaysia

The first contact between English and Malaysians was in Penang. Penang Island was the landing place of Captain Francis Light and marked the first territory in South East Asia to be claimed by the English. After the English successfully negotiated for the island of Penang from the Sultan of Kedah in 1786 Captain Francis renamed it Prince of Wales Island. The British East India Company then began its colonial rule of Penang, a situation that lasted for 171 years. Once the island came under the rule of the British East India Company, Christian fundamentalist missionaries began colonising the minds of the locals, providing a key focus and impetus for English language instruction.

English language education was also initiated to meet the administrative and economic needs of the English colonisers. The English missionaries established schools to educate children as a ruse to create opportunities for conversion. Initially the schools served the Indian and Chinese population since the Malay Sultans forbade their Malay subjects from attending due to well-founded fears of this new brand of fundamentalism. The first schools modelled on the English education system were established to meet the huge demand for junior administration clerks.

The administration of the Malay states was transferred to the Colonial Office in London by 1867. The English administration in Malaya began to take more interest in creating a centralised and co-ordinated approach to the education system. To fulfil this unifying role the Isemonger Committee was formed in 1869 to report on a possible budget for education in the Straits Settlements. The report stated that education was failing due to the active or passive resistance among the Malays, as much as the lack of encouragement from the English administration (Straits Settlements Committee 1894).

The British Colonial administration responded with the creation of the office of the Inspector of Schools and A. M. Skinner was subsequently appointed as the first Inspector of Schools, Straits Settlements. Skinner's efforts did not immediately contribute to a more unified system. Indeed Skinner's first actions were to stop financial aid to Indian and Chinese vernacular schools and to be direct aid only to the Malay vernacular and English language schools. These haphazard efforts did little to challenge the problems of colonialist education. As well as exacerbating inequalities across racial groups, they increased the disparities across regions with Perak state being advantaged over all the other Malay states.

In the colonial system English language schools were adequately resourced so that they could be the best organised and most developed in the country (Koh 1967). The English language schools could be divided into missionary and government aided schools. These schools were largely confined to the urban areas because of the restriction on Muslim participation. Indian and Chinese students attended classes in these urban schools. Demographically it was an era when the Chinese and Indians populated the urban areas. These schools created a supply of educated young locals to fill the swelling ranks of clerical positions in the colonial administration and created a racially segregated colonial structure.

The English language schools were also advantaged by the linking of their students into the scholarships awarded for study at Oxford and Cambridge in England. The elites among the colonised were largely the ones who enjoyed these colonial "achievements." This reinforced significant divisions in colonial society:

> The major weakness of the (English) schools was the basic alienness of the cultural values transmitted. While vernacular schools manifestly served to reinforce the group identity of each of the three major groups, the English schools effectively weakened the traditional cultural loyalties of those who became, in varying degrees, westernised. Thus the outstanding result of the quadrilingual educational system was the social and cultural isolation of the Malays, Chinese and Indians educated in their own language, and the emergence of a cosmopolitan, modernizing group drawn in varying proportions from the three traditional communities whose common bond was English.... English education tended to create a new division within each group so that, for example, social differences appeared between the English educated Chinese and the Chinese-educated Chinese, vernacular-educated Indians and Malays. (Chai 1977, 27)

This polarisation, partly based around the English language, reproduced existing inequalities within Malaysia. It also created a hankering for an education abroad among elite Malays. More and more young Tengku's and Raja Muda's were sent first to English language schools then to colleges and universities in England. The most famous of these being Tengku Abdul Rahman, who became Malaysia's first prime minister.

English and the Nation-Building Project in Malaysia

English enjoyed a dominant status in the early colonial era, but this changed with the movement toward Merdeka in 1957. The political arrangements up to and directly after the emergence of Malaysian independence saw several broad policy changes that reoriented the legal status of English relative to the national language of Malaysia, Bahasa Malaysia. These changes saw the replacement of English with Bahasa Malaysia as part of Malaysia's nation-building project. The first of these changes emerged in response to the demands of Malay nationalists in the 1950s. The 1950 Barnes Commission's enquiry into the education system recognised the marginalisation of Malays and recommended that they should occupy their place in relation to other communal groups and to assist in the formation of a united nation.

The Commission recommended that the government should establish primary schools open to all ethnic groups and staffed by qualified teachers from all ethnic communities. Providing free education for children between 6–12 years, these schools promoted bilingual literacy in Bahasa Malaysia and Bahasa Ingerris. They also provided a pathway to English medium secondary schools. The status of English was reinforced with the Fenn-Wu Report that recommended English be made the business language for all ethnic groups in Malaya and thus taught to all students. It recommended that English be introduced and taught as the second official language from the third year of primary school onwards. These colonial policies formalised and legitimated the dominant role of English even as independence appeared inevitable.

The Razak Report (Malay (Federation) 1958) was the first committee composed largely of locals having been commissioned by the pre-independence Government of the Federation of Malaya. It was chaired by a future prime minister the late Tun Abdul Razak, then the education minister. The Razak Committee studied the implications of the Barnes and Fenn-Wu reports and proved to be influential in determining language education and policy in Malaysia.

The Razak Report combined the ideas from the Barnes Committee and the Fenn-Wu Report, recommending schools continuing use of all four languages—Bahasa Malaysia, English, Mandarin, and Tamil. However, the report made it clear that Bahasa Malaysia should be implemented as the national language. As a consequence school students were encouraged to learn both Bahasa Malaysia and English. Bahasa Malaysia would be taught in Romanised script, although the Perso-Arabic script (or Jawi) would continue to be taught to Malay pupils. Recognising the sensitivities in the period leading up to independence, the Razak Report recommended Chinese and Tamil children continue to be taught their respective vernacular.

A key recommendation was to implement Bahasa Malaysia and English as the nation's official languages for the first ten years after Merdeka. English continued to be taught as the second language after this period but the national language was Bahasa Malaysia. By 1967 English became the second language for peninsular Malaysia and for Sabah in 1973. For Sarawak the state legislative assembly delayed the relegation of English to a second language until 1985. The Razak Report was an important attempt to develop political consensus around language education in the lead up to independence:

> The recommendations of the Razak Report regarding language education indicate that decisions were made based on social factors and ignored any linguistic considerations. Difficulties that might arise from learning different scripts were ignored. English has to be taught but how effectively it is taught remains an important issue. (Gaudart 1987, 26)

After Merdeka the Rahman Talib Report 1960 (Malaysia (Kementerian Pendidikan) 1971) recommended that Bahasa Malaysia gradually replace English as the medium of instruction in primary schools, and that in secondary schools instruction be in both Bahasa Malaysia and English. Eventually Bahasa Malaysia would become the sole medium of instruction with English being taught as a separate subject. By 1968 English was phased out as the medium of instruction in primary and secondary schools, being replaced by Bahasa Malaysia. Although English lost its status as the nation's official language, it remained important because of its value in higher education, commerce, and international affairs. The Third Malaysia Plan (1976–1980) assigned English the role of keeping the nation abreast of scientific and technological knowledge and participation in international trade and commerce:

> While the Government will implement vigorously the teaching of Bahasa Malaysia, measures will be taken to ensure that English is taught as a strong second language. This is important if Malaysia is to keep abreast of scientific and technological developments in the world and participate meaningfully in international trade and commerce. (Malaysian Government, Third Malaysian Plan 1976, 334)

After Malaysia gained independence in 1957 several tensions emerged over the role and status of English relative to Bahasa Malaysia. For a multiethnic, multireligious, and multicultural nation divided along racially structured class lines by a long history of English colonial exploitation the need for unifying nation-building activities occupied a crucial role. Bahasa Malaysia or more accurately Bahasa (Maleyu) was constitutionally identified as the national language and significant efforts had been directed to reaffirming its status. Most efforts were directed at the teaching of Bahasa Malaysia in primary and secondary schools and expanding its use within the communities where it was not previously spoken.

While Bahasa Malaysia occupied a key role in the nation-building project, English became the language of higher education, commerce, and making linkages with the global economy. This change in status was formalised in 1985 by a committee chaired by the then deputy prime minister, Dr. Mahathir Mohamad. The Mahathir Committee accorded English the status of a second language with specific aims. These included enabling students to use English in their work for specific activities and to improve their knowledge of English for use in higher education. This ensured that English would be taught in universities and that students would need to achieve a certain level of English language proficiency to participate in university.

To help implement these recommendations the Curriculum Development Centre (CDC) was established to ensure the training of sufficient teachers and the development of national curricula in all subjects except technical, Islamic, and health studies. The multidimensional task of reaffirming the use and broadening the scope of Bahasa Malaysia, the production of materials for language instruction, and the training of teachers to undertake Bahasa Malaysia teaching in all schools across Malaysia was an ambitious task for this new nation. In addition major reforms and expansions in the teaching of English in higher education placed extraordinary demands on the resources available within the school system and in the preparation of teachers. Not surprisingly the sise of the challenge resulted in significant gaps in teachers' English language proficiency:

> The upgrading of teachers' proficiency in the teaching of English as a second language will be intensified through in-service courses at the Maktab Perguruan Bahasa and Faculty of Education and Language Centre of Universiti Malaya. This promise of a massive thrust in in-service teacher education has yet to be seen. (Gaudart 1987, 31)

The ELT Market in Malaysia: Speed Bumps in the Superhighway

Two key trends emerged in the late 1990s that have had an increasing impact on the role and character of English in the nation-building project of Malaysia, namely the increasing privatisation of education and the rise of new technologies. The privatisation of higher education in Malaysia is occurring through the corporatisation of public universities and their internationalisation through the development of offshore partnerships, articulation agreements, and twinning arrangements (Lee 1998). In the period of the New Economic Policy the government sought to reshape Malaysian society by expanding opportunities for *Bumiputra* students to undertake tertiary education. The dimensions of this increase can be seen in the growth of student enrolment in higher education that grew from 86,330 in 1985 to 189,020 in 1995 (Lee 1999, 66). By the Seventh Malaysian Plan (Malaysian Government 1996) the budget for higher education was $3 billion Ringgit.

These increases have stretched the capacity of the national budget to continue to fund such expansions at a time when the Malaysian government was under increasing pressure to provide skills training to supply an increasingly globalised workforce associated with the K-Economy. There were increasing debates over the quotas imposed by the New Economic Policy, as sections of the Chinese-Malaysian communities were being denied educational opportunities in areas of unmet demand. In response to these tensions the Education Act (Malaysia 1996) facilitated the corporatisation of public universities, the centralisation of planning and accreditation, and the introduction of private and overseas education and training providers in Malaysia. The Act worked in tandem with the Higher Educational Institutions Act (Malaysia 1996) that made provision for the establishment of private universities, university colleges, branch campuses of foreign universities, as well as the upgrading of existing colleges and universities. The National Accreditation Board Act 1996 (Malaysia 1999) also established a qualifications authority which removed the monopoly of universities in accrediting courses. These developments have seen a dramatic rise in the number of private education and training institutions from 56 in 1992 to 354 in 1996 (Lee 1999, 37). Even before these legislative changes 367,214 or 37.7 percent of Malaysian students were enrolled in fee-paying private institutions.

These legislative changes also facilitated a number of key developments associated with the reaffirmation of English as Malaysia's second language. Perhaps more importantly the involvement of overseas ELT providers has had a significant impact on the role and status of English in Malaysia. As many of these ELT providers are overseas institutions, the restrictions concerning the use of Bahasa Malaysia as the language of instruction have been relaxed with English now being used by many private institutions. Many of these have incorporated English language instruction through the employment of expatriate teachers, a mechanism that has not been available to public institutions. These private institutions are also very different in their ethnic composition with participation being 90 percent non-*Bumiputra* students from urban middle-class communities. While these legislative changes were designed to diversify the public education system, the activities of the market have contradicted these aspirations (Lee 1999). These changes have ensured that the Malaysian market is very competitive with a large number of private ELT providers working in consortia with local partners. These developments have been described in the following terms:

> We see the more advanced countries wanting to export their institutions and programmes of higher learning on the one hand and developing countries being prepared to franchise these arrangements with their foreign counterparts on the other. This leads to higher degree programmes and institutional diversity in the private sector which will allow greater student choice but at a price in terms of some cultural fragmentation and incoherence. (Lee 1999, 56)

Part of the growth in private ELT provision has been the penetration into the Malaysian higher education system by listed companies with diversified business interests. This has ensured that the major growth in Malaysia has been in the emerging new hybrid enterprises that combine overseas partners, private providers, and listed corporations. Table 2 provides some examples of the type of organisational arrangements that typify hydrid education and training enterprises in Malaysia.

The Malaysian education and training market is typified and characterised by a range of creative options for students. As noted previously, consortia involving international providers generally offer twinning or split degrees, expressed as 2+1. International providers in partnerships with local operators offer two years of a degree program in Malaysia and the final year in overseas locations. These twinning programmes generally operate with the following arrangements:

Table 2: A Selection of Hybrid ELT Enterprises Operating in Malaysia

Hybrid Enterprise Name Location	**Partners**	**Qualifications**	**International Partners**
International College/ Kolej Anarabangsa (Bukit Jambal Penang) www.jaring.my	IJM Corporation Berhad (private) Penang Development Corporation (public)	* Intensive & Academic English. * BBA (Multimedia) * BIT(Information Technology * Higher School Certificate & matriculation. * TAFE Diplomas in business, commerce & IT	* Sydney University * Universiti Telekom Malaysia * NSW Dept of School Education * NSW Dept of TAFE

Continued on next page

Table 2 (Continued)

Sunway College (Petaling Jaya) http://www.sunwayk .edu.my	Sunway City Berhad Corporation (has interests in property developments, building, tourism, and resorts) (private)	* Intensive & academic English * Canadian & Australian matriculation * University Foundation year * Degree & Diploma in law, commerce, computer science, economics, tourism & mathematics	* Monash University * Victoria University of Technology * Wiakato University * Western Michigan * University of Western Sydney * London Guildhall University
Disted Stamford College (Penang) http://disted.edu.ay	Yip Chor Ee Charitable Trust Fund (private) Penang Development Corporation (public)	* Intensive & academic English * Australian matriculation * Certificate/Diploma in Hospitality * Bachelor of Computer Science * Diploma of Higher Engineering	* Universiti Sains Malaysia * Deakin University * University of Staffordshire * University of Aberdeen Dundee
Informatics Holdings (Singapore, Penang) www.informaticsgro up.com	Informatics Group Pty Ltd Singapore has 245 franchises in 27 countries. Owns Thames Business School (private)	* Operates TOEFL on-line. Uses "purple train" Web site to deliver: * Advanced Diploma/Diploma Courses in IT & Business (in Mandarin and English) * BSc courses * MBA level courses	* RMIT University * Curtin University of Technology * University of Surrey * University of Wales * Thames Valley University * University of Sunderland
INTI College (Kuala Lumpur, Penang, Kuching, Sarawak, Kota Kinabalu, Sabah) www.inti.edu.my	IJM Management (Inti Group of Colleges) (private)	* American University Program (AUP) in computer science, business, social science, liberal arts, engineering & applied science * Diplomas of Commerce	* 14 American universities * Queensland University of Technology * University of Adelaide * University of Otago * Lincoln University

- "Capping" partner's qualification with an overseas qualification.

This is generally done by offering an additional year for a degree beyond a diploma level course conducted by the Malaysian provider.

- "Articulation" or "direct entry" into a fully accredited program through a qualifying program that generally includes an English language component.
- "Advanced standing" operates where preferential entry and accreditation is extended to graduates of partner institutions on the basis of study undertaken in Malaysia.
- "Joint programmes" where partners offer a combined qualification based on the completion of parts of a course with each of the partners. Most often this occurs in postgraduate studies.

All these partnership arrangements are subject to agreements that specify assessment requirements, moderation procedures, course equivalents, curriculum, roles and responsibilities, fees, and support services. While there have been few instances of prosecution by government, some of the creative articulation and credit transfer arrangements between local and overseas partners are viewed with suspicion due to inadequate quality assurance procedures (Lee 1999). Some of these new providers are seen as highlighting problems about the quality of ELT in Malaysia. These anxieties concerning the quality and nature of English also surround England's national flagship provider the British Council.

Flagging English Interests in Malaysia

While the British Council has had a long-term presence in Malaysia which pre-dates independence, England's national flagship has not been immune from the sweeping changes that have typified Malaysian education. The British Council is one of the largest ELT providers in Malaysia. Its offices in Penang and Kuala Lumpur are centres for a countrywide presence involving a budget of £2.5 million. Since the 1980s the British Council has been required to secure 50 percent of its operational funds from non-government sources making it another competitor amongst other ELT providers in Malaysia. However, the very special nature of the British Council's relationship with England's Foreign Office and its ability to act as a link between national governments ensures that it has a distinct advantage in promoting (the) English. In the new knowledge economy the internationalisation of education sees countries like England and Australia exporting their educational programmes to countries like Malaysia that establish franchising arrangements with these exporters (Lee 1998).

The changes in the British Council's operations in Malaysia reflect a number of features of globalisation that are not exclusive to that country. These key themes include the changing nature of the relationships between England and Malaysia in the postcolonial era; the changing nature of English as a globalised language; and the reorientation of language education in response to developments in new technology, science, and engineering. The British Council conducts many of the functions traditionally associated with its global operations but developments in Malaysia's economy ensures that it has customised its operations to meet regional priorities.

The British Council has benefited in recent years from a reversal of the situation where English is a second language that accords with Malaysian government policy. The reversal of this policy in 1997 revitalised England's participation in Malaysian economic and educational developments. There are at present over 100 links between English universities and Malaysian colleges for split or twinned courses. There are also over sixty research links between English universities and Malaysia's nine state universities. Collaboration with English institutions is actively sought by Malaysia's private sector in order to establish new private universities or to upgrade existing colleges to university status.

Each year the Malaysian offices of the Council process over 75,000 applications for study in England, administers one million pounds worth of scholarships, conducts 15,000 IELTS examinations, and provides 8,000 courses of 30 hours. In addition the Council is active in the training of English language teachers, providing opportunities for Malaysian teachers to complete post-graduate qualifications in the field at six nominated universities in England.

Its range of ELT programmes is comprehensive spanning age groups 6–15 years; academic preparation, business, workplace, and industry English as well as examination preparation. Programmes are generally affordable with the popular 20-hour modules in the Muzzy children's programmes costing $320 Ringgit. Business English courses range from

$280–450 Ringgit. The Malaysian University English Test (MUET) preparation course is costed at $450 Ringgit.

These programmes exhibit all the aspects of ELT programmes in a competitive transnational environment, but the British Council has two distinct advantages. The Council has the prestige of being an accrediting agency and a provider of ELT. It owns the internationally recognised IELTS examination system and the Cambridge exam system. Further the Council is able to secure market advantage because English is seen as, and made to be seen as, the "natural" property of the Council. In these terms British English is British Council English. This relationship enables the Council to capitalise on the nostalgia for cultural heritage English and the enduring legacies of networks made during the period of the English empire.

However, the British Council is not complacent about its position. Rather than just conduct ELT classes, the Council has recognised the need for research and innovation, moving beyond the current demands of the market to reshape the way in which "English" products and services are defined, utilised, and sold. The Council uses the prestige of cultural heritage English and the advantage of being a government subsidised provider to leapfrog other national flagships and to minimise competition from hybrid ELT enterprises. The Malaysian operation of the Council represents a distinctive dialogue concerning English that is linked to the ambivalent project of globalising English, especially through the new digital technologies.

The Council has recognised several features associated with the project of globalising of English and has incorporated these into its operations in South East Asia. At one level the Council acknowledges the leading role that English gained through the new technologies. Given that 80 percent of global communication using the technologies is in English, it is working to use this to provide a market advantage. Whereas in the previous era, ELT was centred on cultural heritage English (e.g., English literature), ELT in Malaysia has moved into business programmes and information technology. Building on the now defunct technical support programmes to government, the British Council has initiated programmes in mathematics and science curriculum development and teacher education. This is a very strategic move because these are the disciplines used to service innovation in the new technologies. In addition to providing training in public administration the Council's main pro-grammes are in information technology, regional and institutional collaborations, and capacity building.

A Memorandum of Understanding (The British Council, Malaysia 1999) was signed between the British Council and the Malaysian Public Services Division for a three-year project for the Malaysian Civil Service, in collaboration with the Malaysian Institute of Public Administration (INTAN). The aims of the programme include the development of the English Language Assessment System (ELPA) to assess the English proficiency of officers of the Malaysian Administrative and Diplomatic Services. The programme will also assist in the development of Public Service Training through the use of multimedia case studies to be delivered via distance learning. For the programme to meet its objective of increasing staff expertise its linkages with multimedia ELT are indicative of the Council's new directions. Further evidence of the Council's efforts to capitalise on the complementarity of new technology and ELT can be found in its curriculum development involving the creation of a learning culture and teaching methodologies using new technologies in English. This programme is being conducted with the Curriculum Development Centre, Ministry of Education Malaysia and is designed to meet the needs of rural and isolated schools and their students. Conducted with the co-operation of the Malaysian government these programmes provide the Council a clear advantage in determining the nature and character of ELT products to be used in the future.

The British Council is also acutely aware of the emergence of localised Englishes in the Asia Pacific region and that English is no longer the exclusive property of the English. Council officials have initiated regional projects that explore the future of English and the implications of multi-vocal Englishes. One of the research projects undertaken to provide advice to the Council involved an Internet forum on the future of English conducted by David Graddol (1999). This forum helped to construct scenarios that explore the future of English as an expression and a consequence of globalisation. Arising from the forums conducted in Malaysia the Council sees the development of a globally independent, politically free language that provides a framework for international comprehension. The Council recognises the importance of a framework that enables international comprehensibility and the maintenance of localised connections. This provides an important reframing of language issues in postcolonial times and an important key to repositioning the Council's work in the context of new technology and the emergence of multivocal Englishes.

This emphasis on new technology is no mere whim; Malaysia has ambitious national plans in this regard. Since the 1970s, when the first computers were used at the Universiti of Malaya, Malaysia has moved to embrace digital technologies through the government's 2020 Vision statement. The 2020 Vision (Ahmad 1993) assigns a vital role to new technology in securing national economic development and an inclusive society. The Vision includes the development of regional areas reserved for the production, research, and innovation of new technologies. One such development, the Multimedia Super Corridor (MSC), exists between Kuala Lumpur and Port Klang. The MSC concept was launched in 1988, and being underwritten by the government it aims to attract foreign investments to enhance the export possibilities of Malaysian industry.

The basic features of the MSC have been replicated in Penang and at Sungai Patani in neighbouring Kedah state where hardware and component manufacture are clustered. Corporations such as Sharp and Siemens have selected Malaysia as the centre for their Asia Pacific operations. Malaysia's popularity for the manufacture of computer hardware is evident in the location of Apple computers there. Workforce skills and investment policy are important in attracting these new "K-Economy" industries. The government has identified deficiencies in the quantity and quality of English language proficiency among workers as an impediment to attaining economic success. The Malaysian Government's aspiration of creating a knowledge society is beginning with the education of schoolchildren through its computer literacy and Smart Schools programmes. The Government aim is to produce more computer literate students who have initiative and are intelligent, creative and independent. It is by these means that the Government plans for Malaysian students to learn English. The hope is that they will benefit from the language that presently dominates the world's digital technologies.

The Smart School project, one of the seven flagship applications of the

Multimedia Super Corridor, was initially conceptualised by the Ministry of Education in January 1997 (Smart Schools Project Team 1997). Since then 90 pilot smart schools have been running test programmes as the nucleus for the eventual nationwide implementation of Smart School teaching pedagogies, materials, skills, and technologies. These developments suggest that there is a future for English in Malaysia that will see the continuing expansion of ELT products, services, providers, and consumers. Nevertheless, there are significant dilemmas surrounding aspects of English in Malaysia, with anxieties about the quality of Malay-sian English, the English proficiency of teachers, and the relationship between Bahasa Malaysia and Bahasa Ingerris.

Speaking of Risks: The Politics of Language in Malaysia

Malaysia and neighbouring Singapore frequently engage in public debates concerning the standard of English and English language teaching. In Singapore headlines in *The Straits Times* foreshadow "Moves to Prevent the Erosion of English" with statements that "Singaporeans need to command a good standard of English to plug themselves into the global economy" (*The Straits Times* 29th October 1999, 1). Although many students can use standardised English, the concern is that this situation is likely to decline if there is no intervention by governments and bilingual education specialists. The public debate over the standard of English is linked to national economic performance and the ability to participate in the global economy.

In Malaysia these debates have centred on the "poor performance" of students in the Penilaian Menengah Rendah (PMR) Examinations. The PMR tests student performance across 11 subjects including English and Bahasa Malaysia. In 2000 the number of students passing English decreased by 3.8 percent, prompting the director general of education, Datuk Seri Abdul Shukor Abdullah, to explain that the apparent decline in passes was mainly caused by an increase of up to 25 percent in the critical thinking questions. Shukor also attributed the decline in passes to students' limited exposure to English in rural areas (*The Sun* 21st December 2000, 7). Students in urban areas recorded a 72.8 percent pass rate whereas only 49.6 percent of students in regional and rural areas recorded passes. The poor performance associated with English was also attributed to changes in the teaching techniques employed in schools. The new Kurikulum Baru Sekolah Menengah (KBSM: English) (the New Secondary School Syllabus) is a sensible attempt by the Malaysian education authorities to provide a holistic approach to English language education. It moves beyond the limitations of grammar translation methods and addresses the differences between the English language as used by Malaysians and that in the school curriculum. Now the test makers have to catch up with these innovative developments.

The KBSM supported by CDC is designed to provide a new curriculum structure that is not dependent on rote learning and is more student centred and technology oriented (see Figure 1). Importantly the KBSM connects the everyday language of students' life experiences to provide an integrated approach across Malaysia's four main languages.

The KBSM provides a curriculum structure that emphasises a communicative approach to language learning rather than the dated and limited focus on grammar. The KBSM also takes into account the position and role of the English language in Malaysia and its need at the national and international levels. Despite their very recent introduction these curriculum innovations, which are intended to address the specific nature of Malaysia's multilingual context, have been subject to significant criticism and even blamed for the decline in "standards."

The tensions associated with examination performance have been heightened by comments from teacher union officials concerning the poor standard of English teaching. The secretary of the Perak branch of the National Union of the Teaching Profession (NUTP), Mr. S. Sundralingam, attributed the poor examination performance to the mastering of the language's grammar being replaced by an emphasis on critical thinking. In a curious statement, he also said that many teachers were uncomfortable with English and that the emphasis on Bahasa Malaysia was responsible for the decline in English standards. This union official argued for better teacher education and suggested reform of teachers' work. The press statement highlighted situations where many untrained teachers were required to teach English or where those who are trained to teach English are allocated to other subjects (*The Sun* 22nd December 2000, 4). While concerns over English preoccupied the media and the government,

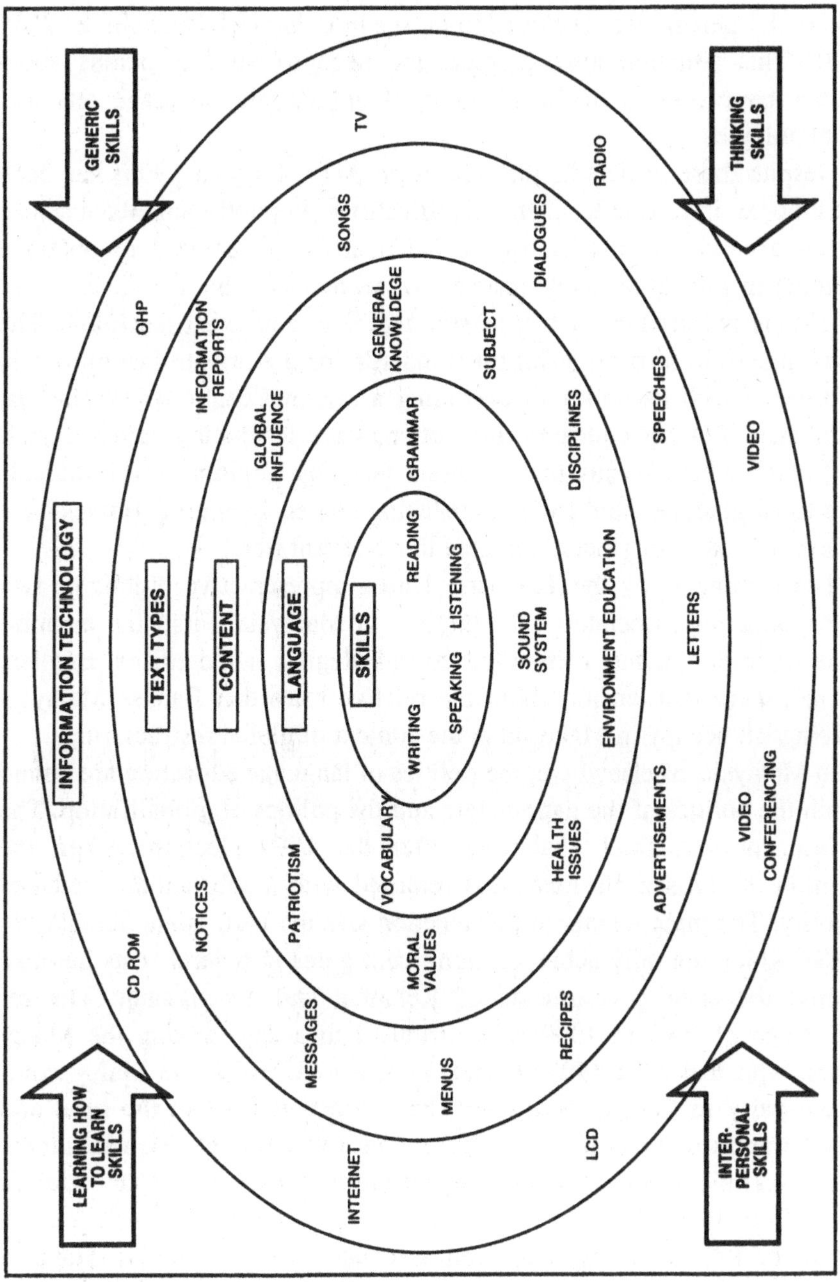

Figure 1: English Immersion in Information Technology Curriculum

little was said about the decline in the performance in Bahasa Malaysia. A drop of 1.1 percent was recorded in passes in Bahasa Malaysia in the 2000 PMR. This situation also suggests the need to raise questions about teacher education in the application of appropriate language teaching methodologies.

Despite these criticisms the Education Act (Malaysia 1996) has been instrumental in raising teachers' qualifications. In public schools, teachers of primary school students (aged 7–12) are now required to obtain a Diploma in Education while teachers of secondary school students (aged 13–18) are required to have at least a degree in a relevant discipline. The government has also set stringent standards for the private institutions in accordance with its policy of becoming a regional centre of educational excellence. Teacher education institutions have to employ suitably qualified staff, which means that lecturers teaching Diploma level students have to be graduates and lecturers teaching degree level programmes have to have a Masters or Doctoral degree in a relevant field.

The comments by the Teachers' Union representative highlights two major anxieties associated with English in Malaysia. First, the examination regime remains committed to privileging standardised English. Second, there is a tension about the relative roles that Bahasa Malaysia and English occupy in Malaysia in the context of global restructuring.

In Malaysia, as elsewhere, the politics of language education are bound within the politics of the nation-state and the politics of globalisation. The government was finely balanced after the 1999 elections when the coalition of Barisan Nasional was returned with a substantially reduced majority. The main winner in this election was the Parti Islam Semalaysia (PAS), which not only achieved significant gains in federal seats but also secured the state governments of Kelantan and Terengganu The re-emergence of PAS in 1999 was attributed to a split among the Malay voters, who had until 1999 remained loyal to UMNO, the Malay component party in Barisan Nasional. The success of PAS in the rural and regional areas of eastern peninsula Malaysia was due to disenchantment with economic inequalities and the negative consequences of "globalisation from above."

Part of PAS's success has been associated with the mobilisation of Islam to emphasise a return to the values and practices of the Koran. More importantly PAS was successful in harnessing resistance to US/American globalisation at the same time as appealing to the globalisation of Islam which has gained renewed impetus since the 1970s. While it is unfair to portray PAS as a religious fundamentalist party, its policies do embrace conservative interpretations of Islamic values, behaviour, and practices as a means of resisting American cultural and economic imperialism. Whilst Malaysia is a secular country, the success of PAS in linking politics and religion has been a powerful force in putting the government on the defensive in areas such as language education. PAS's success has also unleashed a tide of nationalism including demands for the reaffirmation of the national language, Bahasa Malaysia. There are also related demands for English to be removed from the public spheres of Malaysian life. Some construct reliance on English as "unpatriotic."

The status of Bahasa Malaysia relative to English is a particularly sensitive issue. The role of Bahasa Malaysia is enshrined in the Malaysian constitution as an important instrument in the country's nation-building project. Since 1998 public debates concerning the nation's languages have surfaced in the context of the rise of PAS, the economic future of Malaysia, and the problems created by "globalisation from above."

In a New Year statement for 2001 Prime Minister Mahathir said speaking English was not unpatriotic, and that those who spoke English were not "kafirs" or infidels (*The New Straits Times* 3rd January 2001, 3). While the press was able to lampoon the issue and ridicule aspects of these claims, the struggle between Bahasa Malaysia and English continues to be a point of tension. Educators have argued that the two languages can co-exist and that multilingualism is a market advantage in the context of globalisation.

The newly appointed vice-chancellor of the Universiti of Sains Malaysia Professor Dzulkifli Abdul Razak argues that globalisation demands multiple specialisations including the capability to span various cultural and linguistic contexts (*New Sunday Times* 11th December 2000, 27). The core of the issue for Professor Dzulkifli is to resolve the domains in which each language is used The national language has social value in fostering national unity while English is the language for knowledge production and international relations. The vice-chancellor does not see this as an either/or situation but suggests that the issue demands an approach where people are as comfortable crossing disciplines as they are crossing cultures. He argues that terms such as "either/or" should give away to "both/and" in this fast emerging borderless world economy.

The tensions arising from the threat of globalising English to kill off other languages will continue to be a feature of political debates in Malaysia, as too will be the issue of the legitimation of Malaysian English. These debates are framed around national concern over declining standards in language proficiency and the need to reverse this through systemic reforms. In a few respects the debates in Malaysia bear some resemblance to the attacks on public education which surface periodically in Australia, New Zealand, UK, and the United States (Apple 1996). Recipes touted as solutions for this situation are quite familiar: devolved school administration, greater central planning, and improved teacher qualifications. The Education Act (Malaysia 1996) was a response to these issues, providing a policy framework that gave form to the Smart Schools initiative.

However, Malaysia's problems have another layer of complexity because of the linguistic diversity which sees local English juxtaposed against models of standardised English. In many respects this polarisation is artificial because everyday communication in Malaysia is typified by code switching and the integration of elements from a variety of languages. In multilingual communities it is normal for Malaysians to use two to three different languages in a single interaction to ensure that a conversation can be easily understood. In a multicultural environment hybridities in linguistic communication are normal. However, for students of English this polarisation creates specific dilemmas over the policing of usage.

"Hey, you going where ah?" is a greeting one might hear between teenagers but one that would cause monolingual, Anglophone teachers of standardised English to express frustration. But this question is a direct translation from the Bahasa Malaysia: "Awak nak ke mana?" While this student can also use standardised English, here he/she is using local Malaysian English, and not "Where are you going?" There are many other similar uses of Malaysian English that are purposely used to put listeners at ease. The important point is that communication has taken place. So it does not matter if Malaysian or standardised British English is used, so long as both parties understand the content of the exchange and the relationship involved.

The question of which type of English should be used is a vital one. When and where is the use of Malaysian English acceptable in society? Malaysian English is quite popular among teenagers, among whom phrases like, "Come on lah!" or "Don't want lah" or "Relax lah!" can be commonly heard. The debate among language educators and the media is driven by concerns over the use of Malaysian English and efforts to standardise spoken and written English among students.

That colonialist English has been localised is emphasised by popular series such as "Kopitiam," "Life's a Pitch," "One 2 Some," and the award-winning Singaporean television program "Phua Chu Kang." The characters in these series adopt a language that is undeniably English but one that is appealing and known to local viewers. For instance, "Aiya, Chu, why you so like that one?" has been spiced up with Chinese-English. Radio DJs use Malaysian English to put the listeners at ease. This is because what they actually say is not important. The meaning is what matters and grammar has to be manipulated to give effect to these utterances.

A distinguished Singaporean speaker let slip "Got problem one!" in front of language teachers whose duty in life is to teach correct and error free languages. Surprisingly, the audience laughed because the speech was delivered in a light tone. The aim was to put everyone at ease and the phrase helped. The teachers did not scoff at such use because they understood the meaning and context in which the phrase was used.

Despite the use of Malaysian English throughout the country, efforts are being made to inculcate the use of standardised English in formal settings such as political speeches, the education system, print media, and lectures. However, the more practical, comprehensible, and teenager-friendly language is Malaysian English. Nevertheless, distinctions are made between speakers of Malaysian English and those who speak standardised English, privileging the latter as socially acceptable, professional, and educated. This scenario is different from the use of the national language, Bahasa Malaysia.

Much has been said and done about Bahasa Baku, the standard and correct pronunciation of the language. But in reality the horizons of its usage is limited to academic and political domains among the more educated sectors of society. Hence, the basic principle of language being communicative is challenged as one has to continually discipline the tongue, restricting the spontaneity and joy of talking, and accepting rigidity in pronunciation. Therefore, the basic communication tool is stretched to the point of losing its value in nonchalant free, enjoyable conversations.

The English language has developed strong roots in Malaysia since the end of the English colonial rule. Elites during that era claim to have used standardised English, but the resources for the mass education of today's generation suffer from a lack of communitarian support. While the rules of English grammar are taught in school, community resistance to the language means it does not go much further than that. The few hours of classroom instruction in English each week is made more difficult because many teachers do not have sufficient proficiency in the language.

What can we expect from a trainee who speaks a smattering of English, undergoes three years of teacher training mainly focussing on theories and techniques of pedagogy, hardly reads any English materials in a week, and who has not the slightest interest to expand her/his horizons? Nothing much is passed onto the students who are then made to feel inferior when put in a group of fluent English speakers.

A group of trainee teachers in a physical education session highlight some of these dilemmas. Upon hearing that they were English majors their lecturer enthusiastically suggested that the session be run in English. A chorus of resistant groans greeted the lecturer, "We've had five hours of English already. My mouth is hurting! Please use Malay!" With this kind of resistance to globalising English among prospective teachers it is not surprising that little of the standardised language is passed on to students.

The teaching of English in National Secondary schools is under strong criticism, particularly in the rural areas along the east coast of Peninsular Malaysia. Many students entering higher education are unable to construct a grammatically correct sentence in English. Has community resistance won out against all those English lessons in school? Is it possible that an undergraduate who can achieve good grades in all subjects performs badly in English? Does this signify a widespread resistance? Does this mean that the politics of language in Malaysia is impacting on students' learning?

The resistance to English language education among undergraduate students is discouraging for those dedicated to the project of globalising English. There is a certain regressive imperialism among those who lament the withdrawal of the English after Malaysian independence.

This recession and spread of English is balanced by two similar phenomena affecting Bahasa Malaysia. In the colonial period, Malay as a medium of instruction was confined only to the Malay schools of which the great majority was located in the rural areas. It was only an optional subject in the English-medium schools. The Chinese vernacular school used Mandarin as the medium of instruction and the Tamil vernacular school used Tamil for teaching purposes. From 1971 Bahasa Malaysia had become, by and large, the main medium of education in all government and government-aided schools. This meant that the level of proficiency in Bahasa Malaysia amongst the Tamil and Chinese Malays arose (Omar 1982, 11).

Recognising the hybridisation of English through mass education and resistance to it among the young, various combative measures have been taken to overcome this opposition. Among them is the move to revamp the unpopular English Literature Paper at Form 6 (Kementerian Pendidikan Malaysia 1999). Only those who have been carefully trained to read English literature and have the luxury of growing up in a monolingual English-speaking family benefit from this paper. Recognising the Anglocentrism of the paper, which is predominantly British in content, more Asian literature has been included. Students now begin to study English literature in Form 1. They read poems like "The Dead Crow" by A. Samad Said, "The Lake Isle of Innisfree" by W.B Yeats and "Life's brief candle" by William Shakespeare. They also study short stories like "Of Bunga Telur and Bally Shoes" by Che Husna Azahari, which has a local Malaysian flavour. Thus the CDC hopes that the inclusion of local English literature would make students feel more at home using the language. English might very well become just another Malaysian language and not an alien culture from England.

For a long time in Malaysia, English has been criticised because of the expectation that one has "to think like an Englishman to speak good English." With the new KBSM syllabus (Kementerian Pendidikan Malaysia 1999) the CDC hopes to overcome such fallacies. Teachers are encouraged to use English language resource materials created locally. English language newspapers are constantly recommended as a rich but relatively inexpensive source of materials for lessons. Most of the English dailies include special pullout sections devoted to the teaching of English in the classroom. It is hoped by localising the teaching of English students will be able to identify with the language and learn to make it their own.

The Malaysian government is acutely aware that in its drive to integrate the country into the global knowledge economy it must have a population that is proficient in English since, for the moment at least, English is the lingua franca of the information age. Government ministers and intellectuals exhort the population to take English seriously since it is purportedly the language of success. In a recent editorial in the *Berita Harian*, a Malaysian daily newspaper, Malaysians were strongly encouraged to take up and excel in the English language because their tardiness in doing so has resulted in the average citizen being disadvantaged (*Berita Harian* 11th November 1999, 6).

Conclusion

The challenges for ELT businesses in Malaysia are profound. Proficiency in English has been identified as a national priority in securing Malaysia's economic future. The status of English in Malaysian society has been subject to significant cycles of acceptance and resistance in its history as both a colony and an independent nation. English has never had nationwide coverage or acceptance, as it was largely limited to the Malaysian elite in the English colonial era to the benefit of that regime. After Merdeka English was relegated to a second language in Malaysia in favour of Bahasa Malaysia, which became the national language The future of English, however, was guaranteed through Malaysia's commitment to pursuing a globalised economy based on the new digital technologies. This commitment to the K-Economy and society in the 1990s saw a revival in English as a key language at all levels of Malaysian education.

Malaysia is an expanding ELT market. The entry of new ELT providers has created an explosion in educational opportunities for fee-paying students. These private institutions and international universities offer creative accreditation and articulation arrangements. While this expansion of educational opportunities has benefited urban middle-class students capable of paying high fees, there are concerns that this market-based regulation of education by the Malaysian government has produced a new level of educational inequality. One outcome of these developments is to incorporate ELT within courses eliminating the need for preparatory studies.

Concurrently the Malaysian government has sought to reshape the curriculum in the public sector to improve English language provision. This has generated attempts to incorporate more of the localised Englishes and to release the curriculum from the rigidities of grammar translation teaching methods. These initiatives have been frustrated by teacher proficiency in English, and contradictions between curriculum reforms based on broader views of English and an examination regime anchored in models of standardised English and grounded in the culture of England. The performance of students in English is viewed as reaching undesirably low levels that will not assist Malaysia attain its contradictory economic and social goals.

These developments centre on a series of complex risks associated with the changing political landscape in Malaysia. English is at one point essential for national survival and at another a language that works against the national interest. These contradictions are magnified by uncertainties created by a reluctance to recognise the rich linguistic diversity present in Malaysian society and the possibilities that exist in the hybridisation of its languages. Views about the deficiencies in students' English language proficiency are framed around outdated and static views of English constructed in a period prior to the digital information age. As a nation with a strong economic and political commitment to new technologies, Malaysia requires curriculum, teaching methodologies and practices with the dynamic qualities needed to embrace the flexibilities of the cyber age.

Malaysia is a quite successful example of a multicultural, multiracial and multireligious nation. For the government of Malaysia economic stability, prosperity, and racial harmony are linked. Part of Malaysia's future economic success will be determined by its ability to tap into globalisation through superior English skills. While this may oversimplify globalisation and the dilemmas associated with the role of English in Malaysia, it does highlight some of the political and economic risks at the local level.

CHAPTER 7

Australia's Globalisation Crisis: Contradictions and Dilemmas

> The evil of racism, an unhealthy self satisfaction, mental insularity, an exaggerated view of our influence on world affairs, an over cautious appraoch to immigration, a nostalgic desire for Australia to remain Anglo American and a reluctance to abandon trade protectionsim, all still linger in the Australian community to our national disadvantage. (Woolcott 2000, 15)

Melbourne, Australia's second largest city, has deliberately positioned itself in the vanguard of developments in education, technology, and computing. It has marketed itself as one of the world's most livable cities with new technologies at its heart. The commitment to the cyber revolution was demonstrated in 2000 with the opening of the Super Computer Centre in the city. Besides banking and finance inner city suburbs are dominated by educational institutions. The northern edge of the central business district is dotted with educational providers and the industries that service the business of learning. Clustered around this educational precinct are travel agents, cheap eats, bookshops, computer retailers, and stationery suppliers. Modern, high rise residential apartments have also been built to revive a previously drab city perimeter. This revitalisation of the inner city can be attributed to an influx of a large student population, many from overseas, and many of whom are attending the English language schools and academies that are scattered within the inner city education precinct. Melbourne, more than any other Australian city, has also profiled itself as having a cosmopolitan, multicultural atmosphere, an outcome of the waves of migration from southern Europe, the Middle

East, and more recently Asia. The physical appearance of the city and its residents suggests that Melbourne is a city that has a strong Asian presence. It is part of the new Australia that seems to have outgrown the legacies of White Australia politics, although its remnants are amply evident to those who care to look.

In many respects these appearances are deceptive. There are fundamental contradictions in Australia's responses and contributions to globalisation. The enthusiastic rhetoric competes with a deep resistance and anxiety about what globalisation might mean for the power and privilege of Anglo-fundamentalists and their culture of White Australia politics. The Australian response to globalisation is conditioned by the legacies of the White Australia politics that undermine its attempts to remake its engagement with Asia. On the one hand, Australian governments are pushing for flexibility and exposure to foreign involvement by international business, but on the other their openness to transnational migration, desire for a closer engagement with Asia, and a recognition that Australia is a South East Asian nation are frequently questioned.

There is stark evidence of Australia's rejection of closer engagement with Asia preferring to retreat from the region in the hope that its future lies with/in the United States. The inciting of distrust and fear of Asia seeks to position Australia as absolutely separate and detached from South East Asia. These sentiments have been expressed in the regressive parochialism of the "One Nation/White Nation/English-only" movement which has directly influenced the policy settings of the major Australian political parties since 1996.

The enduring legacy of White Australia politics has meant that Australia has a contradictory position toward globalisation. This ambiguous position is characterised by simultaneous government promotion of "globalisation from above" and a hysterical rejection of this neo-liberal political project that mistakenly targets Indigenous and Asian Australians as the cause of Anglo-fundamentalist disaffection. This ambiguity sees both the advocacy of isolationist views about Asia and enthusiasm for trade with Asia. The contradiction in this position suggests that Australia can engage in economic globalisation without altering the social practices and cultural behaviours integral to White Australian politics.

This chapter explores Australia's response to the internationalisation of education through developments in the ELT industry. It looks at how ELT policy settings, organisational responses, markets, and teaching practices have been influenced by and contributed to Australia's response to globalisation. The contradictions and uncertainties evident in Australia's engagement with globalisation are especially evident in the business of ELT.

Higher education, and the ELT industry in particular, represent a large foreign earning sector in the Australian economy with A$1.56 billion in fees and A$1.52 billion in goods and services in 1999. The sise of the education precinct in Melbourne is indicative of the investment capital that this sector attracts. Yet the industry is subject to significant instability even though it is seen as a boon. Some of this uncertainty is attributed to the normal business crises associated with international trade such as the financial crisis (1997), but it is mostly sustained by the criticism of international education from within Australia. While the internationalisation of education is applauded as an export industry by the politicians who have forced this development on public education institutions, the probity of many ELT providers and the multiple motives of many international students coming to Australia have been subject to significant attack. After political leaders created the economic conditions and compliance regime to subject the public education system to the regulatory force of the international marketplace, the debate then shifted to demands for greater regulation and restrictions on the activities of ELT providers. These criticisms about the probity of ELT providers and the complex motives of international students revive much of the old racist rhetoric of White Australia politics disguised under the modernist banner of quality assurance. However, these criticisms are contradictory to the policy imperatives in ELT that insist on a zealous adherence to neo-liberal tenets of regulation via market driven forces. The next section discusses these issues in relation to the nature and character of ELT providers in Melbourne.

Creating a Neo-liberal Economic Model of ELT

Australia has enthusiastically embraced the internationalisation of education but in a very different fashion to Malaysia where the state has reserved a strong role for itself. Up until the 1980s Australian governments occupied the dominant role in determining the nation's social, economic, and educational security. Since the mid-1980s Australian education has been subject to a wave of increasingly radical neo-liberal changes that emphasise consumer choice and market regulation. Previous commitments to an education system directed to providing socio-economic security and facilitating nation building have been replaced by resituating education as a tradable commodity to be sold in a transnational marketplace. The state has adopted a residual role in the provision of public educational security opting instead to being responsible for controlling the distribution of resources within the framework of market competition and support for the priveleged few. The relationship between the state and educational institutions has been redefined to that of "provider" and "purchaser" within a commodity exchange relationship.

This has ensured that private and public ELT providers have to compete for taxpayers' funds through a process euphemistically termed the "open education and training market." Australian policymakers have embraced with great enthusiasm the radical neo-liberal use of market forces as the mechanism for reorganising the education and training sector. One of the first areas to be affected by these changes was the ELT industry. The impact of the regulatory force of market has meant that long established providers of ELT, such as the Adult Multicultural Education Service (AMES) previously funded through recurrent state budget allocations, have been forced to compete with private and public providers to secure the tenders needed for their core funding.

AMES was established in 1951 to provide ELT free as a public service for the post–World War II European migrant labor recruited as part of the nation-building project sponsored by the state. Previously it was known as the Adult Migration Education Service, which was once funded as an arm of the federal government's immigration program. In the context of a competitive market environment AMES has been forced to diversify its client base to include industry and corporations, and to operate as a commercial provider. AMES, like many other Australian ELT providers, operates as a corporation along commercial lines with a range of partnerships. One outcome of market regulation and the internationalisation of Australian education has been a growing diversity of ELT providers and a diversification of their operations. The virtual monopoly that AMES held during the period 1951 to the 1980s has been challenged by competitors emerging from universities, TAFE, and private providers including many overseas businesses. This diversification of ELT pro-viders has also been accompanied by an increase in the range of programmes and services now on offer to meet a broader field of clients. This internal diversification is an attempt to capture "niche" markets that have been created in response to the globalisation of the Australian economy, the multicultural context of the Australian community, and policy settings in governing competition for education and training funds. These changes are well illustrated in the range of AMES programmes that have emerged from its previous role as one of Australia's national flagship ELT providers. These changes are consistent with the survival strategies employed by organisations confronted with the market forces imposed by successive Australian governments.

AMES no longer just provides English language services to newly arrived migrants as it did in the past. The new range of services include communication packages for workplaces and a business enterprise centre, all highlighting the policy imperatives that have re-oriented ELT toward small businesses and enterprise level training. Consistent with this business orientation, AMES operates as a consultancy with the capacity to provide endorsed and accredited vocational education packages in such areas as small business management. This means that AMES programmes and services have a dual function in providing English communication courses and vocational learning outcomes and qualifications. Accompanying this vocationalisation of ELT has been an explosion of industry specific courses that can be broadly described as English for Business and English for Technology. The course materials, methodologies, teaching practices, and assessment techniques are also strongly influenced by vocational education methodologies which include a competency-based approach to learning with an emphasis on demonstrating these in an industry context.

Accompanying the popularisation of vocational education is the adoption of the new technologies of learning by ELT providers. AMES has developed a Virtual Independent Learning Centre (Virtual ILC) which is marketed as a unique program offering the competencies contained in the Certificates of Spoken and Written English. The Virtual ILC uses the

Internet in association with online work with a moderator. The Virtual ILC is designed as a "fee for service" site that is targeted at both English language learners and professionals. In addition to this initiative AMES is also linked to the TAFE Online 2001 and conducts the Computer Literacy Centre (CliC) which runs Virtual ILC and develops resources.

While AMES occupies the role of a national flagship, the Melbourne ELT market has a large number hybrid enterprises. Many look like independent shopfront operations but most are franchises in business chains that span the globe. They have varying levels of affiliation and integration. For example, Global Educational Opportunities and Services has 30 branches across the world including eight in Australia and New Zealand.

Melbourne's Embassy CES operates as part of the worldwide Study Group International (SGI) with another arm being the British *The Daily Mail* newspaper. Embassy CES like many other ELT providers has been through successive identity changes, moving from being Acacia College to Taylor's College prior to being bought by Study Group International. In Australia SGI has branches in Sydney, Perth, the Gold Coast, Brisbane, and Cairns, and has international partners in the United States and Britain. Its integration into SGI has dramatically expanded and diversified the operations of Embassy CES with a broader range of markets, products, and services emerging for Asian, European and Latin American students. Among the more popular ELT programmes in Melbourne are the High School Preparation Programmes, and the General English and Cambridge Examination Preparation courses, which are usually 30 hours a week and cost between $270 and $300 per week. In general courses of one semester duration of 10–13 weeks cost between $2,700–$3,240 with the college year programmes costing $7,990 for 34 weeks. Other courses include vocational programmes such as English for Hotel and Tourism, English for Business Purposes, as well as English for Executives priced at $270 per week.

While Embassy caters for academic study, SGI's franchises in other Australian locations enable students to combine tourism with their English language studies. Students coordinate their study program with surfing or other sporting events, or treks to the outback by moving between the SGI branches. Tourist opportunities feature strongly in the glossy full colour marketing material with images of the Sydney Opera House and views of the Great Barrier Reef and the Gold Coast beaches boosting the holiday feel of Embassy offerings. This interface with tourism is marketed as the holistic experience where enjoyable and productive language studies are coupled with fun, sports, excursions and the making of new friends.

The potential for students to move from one location to another is enhanced by SGI's use of a uniform curriculum that is used in all its branches. This trend may be attributed to SGI's links with the publishing interests of the owners, *The Daily Mail* newspaper.

Melbourne is also well represented with independent shopfront operators of small to medium sise. The Cambridge Language Centre located in central Melbourne has the distinct advantage of having the same name as the famous English university and the language test, a fact which must give the organisation some market leverage. Cambridge is an example of an international hybrid initially operating out of Vancouver, Canada, and expanded into Taiwan and then to Melbourne, where it now has some 300 students. Its international students are mostly from Asia, with some 30 percent from the Indian subcontinent. Cambridge has recognised that the English language market has reached saturation point and offers English along with other vocationally oriented studies in parallel to enable year-round enrolment. The English language component of these parallel courses is "front ended" with award courses in marketing, business, and new technology at the certificate and diploma levels. Cambridge has negotiated an articulation agreement with Swinburne University of Technology for the recognition of its Diploma of Technology (Interactive Media) and Certificate IV courses. Like Embassy CES popular offerings include Diploma courses in Business and Management along with Certificates in hospitality and tourism. The fee structures for courses in English are in the same range as Embassy but the award courses cost up to $5,500 per year with two-year Diplomas costing up to $11,000.

These medium-sized private colleges also obtain funds by providing a range of associated services to ELT clients and students including accommodation, transport, medical insurance, and airport transfers. Institutions like Embassy CES and Cambridge have created integrated educational packages that sustain a diverse range of service industries in the city. These hybrid enterprises operate in medium-sized premises in high value rental locations in the heart of the city. Their facilities are modern and include student services, computer laboratories, and recreation facilities.

By providing integrated and networked services through global franchises these hybrid ELT enterprises are challenging small shopfront operations. Small language schools providing "self improvement" classes for newly arrived migrants are diminishing as the large multinationals come to dominate the ELT industry with sophisticated marketing and generic packages. A few small ELT providers operate on the basis of established networks and maintain steady return business. City Studio of Languages is one of these shopfront operations which has small premises where classes meet in a homely "kitchen table" atmosphere. It attracts a client base that is very different from the hybrid enterprises by offering customised programmes for hotel workers, travellers, and visiting executives. The personalised touch of the director provides an intimate learning environment.

Melbourne's diversity of private ELT businesses is complemented by a range of public ELT providers that target the international market. This includes universities and colleges of technical and further education (TAFE) which have established ELICOS centres as part of their response and contribution to internationalising education. Many of these centres operate as business arms of their parent organisations, including the RMIT University's Centre for English Language Learning (CELL) and the English Language Centre of the Northern Metropolitan Institute of TAFE. CELL operates as part of RMIT Training Pty Ltd which is a company wholly owned by RMIT University. Its inner city premises and its programmes are similar to those of hybrid enterprises offering a strong vocational orientation and preparation for university studies. Course offerings such as English for Art and Design, English for Aviation, and English for Hospitality Tourism, as well as English for Business indicate the linkage with RMIT's core award programmes in the technology, science, and business disciplines. In addition to these academic preparatory programs workplace language programmes and professional programmes also feature strongly in the menu of CELL's offerings. NMIT like AMES and CELL is another example of a public sector organisation that has shifted aspects of its English language provision offshore. Centres are emerging in countries such as China as front-end options to further study in either the offshore mode or eventual study in Australia. These offshore operations provide universities with the opportunity to secure brand loyalty and to provide customised learning pathways into their award courses. Increasingly Australian ELT providers are shifting their operations overseas. In 1999 there were over 26,600 students enrolled in Australian higher education institutions studying offshore; this was a 35 percent increase over the previous year. Four out of five of these students were studying either in Singapore (8,000), Hong Kong (8,000) or Malaysia (4,800).

In terms of program efficiencies there are imagined financial advantages in operating in countries with a lower rate of exchange and where lower labor, establishment, and operating costs offer ELT providers the promise of increased surpluses. With the compliance technologies associated with quality assurance becoming a more rigid feature of the education landscape offshore locations, in the short term, offer opportunity to avoid some of this calculative regime which is seriously inflating operational costs and displacing the focus from core business in Australia. For students avoiding the relocation costs and disruptions associated with overseas study, then study at their home country through an international provider offers a chance to escape some of its financial and personal pitfalls. It also avoids the tensions that some overseas students' experience with isolation, culture shock, and racism. Likewise, Australian ELT providers operating offshore can also avoid confronting these issues in any meaningful way. Offshore programmes promise a business opportunity that also avoids the White Australia politics of regressive parochialism that resurfaces throughout Australia from time to time. This movement offshore has created hybrid enterprises that feature strongly in the Malaysian market. Australian universities and ELT providers are active participants in twinning and capping programmes in Malaysia. Operations conducted by Australia's IDP replicate the national flagship mode of delivery conducted by the British Council. Part of the British Council's market share comes from its ability to combine ELT, technical programmes and cultural events that establish strong local alliances. Since the early 1990s Australia has played a mediation role in the Cambodian peace process sponsored by the United Nations. The 1993 elections in Cambodia were sponsored by the United Nations and administered by

Australia. General John Sanderson of the Australian Army and Foreign Minister Gareth Evans were recognised as being leading figures in assisting Cambodia move toward a resolution of the thirty-year-long civil war. During this time IDP Australia established an ELICOS centre for local and foreign aid workers in Phnom Penh.

Now called the Australian Centre for Education (ACE) it has some 2,000 students and over 100 staff providing a range of ELT services. ACE's operations in Cambodia extend to Battambong, Siem Reap Sihanoukville, and Kompong Cham. The popularity of the ELT programmes in Cambodia offered by ACE reflects the strong demand for capacity building and skill development in the country's reconstruction and the belief that English holds a key to its economic future. After the isolation of the Khmer Rouge era and the Vietnamese occupation there is substantial demand for English by Cambodians who see it as the medium for establishing economic and cultural relations with the rest of the world. ACE like other ELT providers has followed the trend of front ending its vocational programmes with ELT. Programmes that link English with accounting and management feature strongly in ACE's programmes. As part of IDP, ACE established strong local contacts that have capitalised on the goodwill that Australia accumulated from its government's peace-making efforts in the early 1990s. Like the British Council, ACE has a key role in maintaining government-to-government relations. Increasingly offshore operations are becoming a characteristic feature of Australian ELT provision, a trend that may be accelerated by political controversies in Australia surrounding broader debates about the internationalisation of education.

The Ghosts of the Past: White Australia Politics and ELT

The operation of Australian ELT providers on-shore has been the subject of continuing controversies about their probity, the quality of their programmes and the motives of overseas students. The ELT industry has been embroiled in a series of controversies about these issues that have links to the isolationist, racist culture of White Australia politics. In February 2000 press headlines carried news of "Sham Students Sent Home After Visa Rort" (MacDonald 2000, 17). The story described how

88 people had been deported after they entered Australia as students but were caught working as security guards in Sydney. While the newspaper article reported that "thousands of students are deported each year with their visas cancelled" official figures show that between 1989 and 1999 only 2,616 visas were cancelled. One in three applications from countries such as Sri Lanka, Vietnam, and China were rejected. Senator Kim Carr, the Australian Labor Party Secretary for Education, was reported to say:

> You have to ask yourself whether or not this scheme is being used to undermine the wages system in this country. It is not just security; it is in transport, taxis, hospitality and also in the sex industry. (*The Age* 12th February 2000, 17)

The press statement cited unnamed "overseas diplomatic sources" suggesting that "the lure of work, money and the Australian lifestyle meant they dropped out of university and worked full time, but few were monitored to ensure they were not working too many hours." While the story gave the impression of lax standards and poor monitoring by ELT providers and immigration officials, it also mentioned regular sweeps in the security industry, hospitality and fruit picking industries for visa breaches. Carr's statements made under parliamentary privilege strongly criticised the conduct of ELT providers and their policing of students. The Australian government's visa system and provider registration rules require that students have an endorsed and approved program with an 80 percent attendance rate. The report blurred the distinction between visa rejections and breaches of student visa provisions in Australia with questions about over-stayers and asylum seekers. The press report suggested that visa "breaches" are largely related to illegal labor, but most breaches relate to personal circumstances or course failure.

Carr's campaign extended to questioning the probity and bona fides of ELT providers. Newspaper reports alleged that many were fronts for illegal activities. These accusations also raised concerns about the way in which the new technologies of learning had created "the virus plague of creepy crawlies that are inhabiting cyberspace. I speak of those shonky, dubious and questionable creatures that have sprung up in cyberspace—those associated with the so-called Internet universities" (Carr 2000, 16126). In the colourful invective of the parliamentary arena Carr spoke about what he termed dubious ELT providers operating out of post office boxes, grog shops, and other retail outlets with names such as the

University of the Seven Rays, the University of Asia, the Australasian Institute, and Greenwich University. Carr not only questioned the veracity of the credentials of many ELT providers but also highlighted the failure of the Federal Howard Government to develop adequate quality assurance mechanisms to monitor educational standards, as if this mechanism for intensifying teachers' work directly addresses the causes of the problems such as government underfunding, privatisation, and regulation by market forces. Carr's comments in the Senate highlight the dilemmas associated with hybrid enterprises and the arrival of cyber-education:

> Suffice to say that it is appropriate for us to be looking at the quantum shift in the dissemination of knowledge and there is indeed a massive leap occurring within the education sector of this country. But the physical and corporate location of these proliferating entities create unprecedented challenges for those interested in education.... It is a serious problem when you have a government that is committed to privatisation and deregulation of so much government activity that when it comes to deal with an interface between the university establishment of the new corporate arms and new cyber entities, such as degree mills...it is likely government is not able to meet the challenges that need to be confronted by its own policy directions. (Carr 2000, 16127)

The issues of quality assurance and deregulation have implications across the Australian education sector generally but it is interesting that they should be raised in the context of the government-incited project of internationalising Australian public education. Issues of quality performance have implications for the reputation of Australia's education sector. The need for ELT providers to operate ethically is crucial in maintaining Australia's market share in an internationally competitive environment. However, there are concerns about slippages in this debate from concern about the effects of government-imposed privatisation, illegal immigration, crime rings, the sex industry, and visa over-stayers being used to intensify teachers' work through subjecting it to market regulation and surviellance audits. There is an orientalist linking of Asia and Asians with conspiracies and the sinister behaviour of gangs and their rackets. The suggestion that these rorts were the deliberate attempts to sabotage Australian wages revives the rhetoric and rationale of White Australia politics. These sentiments are contradicted by the fact that most overstayers are not Asians but Europeans and New Zealanders. Contrary to the myths about international students working illegally, most occupy jobs legally and their wages and conditions are identical to those of Australian workers.

ELT professionals see these debates as having a damaging impact on the reputation of Australia and its education. Australian ELT providers are anxious that their reputation is being tarnished by distorted and hysterical political campaigns. They argue that the misconduct of a minority of ELT providers is being portrayed as the industry norm and that this is having a devastating effect as overseas competitors seek to exploit Australia's vulnerability. This debate was used to incite fears about Asian im-migration which revealed just how precariously positioned Australia is in the new transnational education order.

Many ELT providers in Australia are predicting a boom in on-shore delivery but see government policy operating in an outdated paradigm associated with the "border guard" mentality. This is inconsistent with the competitive nature of transnational education. The current dilemmas associated with Chinese, Korean, and Indonesian students illustrate the extent to which the government has been trapped by White Australia politics.

In the late 1980s Australian policy shifted from government regulation and provision of public education to reliance on the regulatory force of the market where client-centred, ethical business practices were meant to substitute for government provision of public security. ELT providers were among the first to make an advantage of the new regime, quickly enrolling international fee-paying students. However, issues concerning the monitoring of student attendance and the quality of ELT programmes soon emerged. In 1989 the amnesty in the wake of the Tiananmen Square massacre ensured a large numbers of Chinese students in Australia gained permanent residence as refugees. The combination of the amnesty, debates over the "Asianisation" of Australia, and the problems with the lack of regulation of ELT providers led the Department of Immigration to increase its surveillance of Chinese students entering Australia.

Australian Immigration authorities divided the countries of origin into two categories, "gazetted" and "non-gazetted" countries, on the basis of the risk that students from countries in the latter category might overstay their visa. The non-gazetted countries were non-European countries such as India, Pakistan, China, all the South American nations, and the Gulf States. For many this division of the world into "gazetted" and "non-gazetted" countries had an uncanny resemblance to the administrative arrangements of White Australia politics that used the categories of European and non-European peoples to restrict immigration flows. The negative effects of these divisions for Australian ELT providers on recruitment and marketing were quite significant in those nations that were designated as "non-gazetted" countries. In terms of processing visa applications this meant that prospective students in "non-gazetted" countries experienced significant delays, were required to submit extensive documentation, and had to furnish financial guarantees.

These differences manifested themselves in the operations of IDP Australia, the country's peak student recruitment agent. For example, Singapore was a "gazetted" country, so students from there have easy access to Australia and are often processed at the IDP office within fifteen minutes. In China it took IDP Australia approximately six months to process each prospective student's application. This not only has an impact on their motivation but provides a window for competing nations to "poach" students who make multiple applications. As a consequence of the tardy Australian government practices in non-gazetted places, there was a significant leakage of students to New Zealand that has a faster system for processing student visas. The frustrations of ELT providers over the lengthy procedures resulted in a proposal by them to fund a position in the Department of Immigration in China in an effort to speed up the processing of visa applications.

In addition some of the financial guarantees demanded by the Australian government for potential students have also had counter-productive effects. There are cultural issues concerning the demonstration of wealth which presented difficulties in countries like China, Vietnam, and Cambodia as well as security anxieties about disclosing personal wealth. In these countries where there is a culture of converting savings to assets such as gold and gems there were difficulties in meeting the administrative requirements of the Australian government for bank account balances. To meet this requirement pro-fessional agents lent parents several thousand dollars to "park" in their bank account temporarily in order to enable the student's application to be successfully processed.

Countries experiencing labor shortages, particularly in the new technologies area, have adopted a very different approach to student visa requirements and over-stayers. In the UK, Germany, France, and the United States immigration requirements have been developed to make up for the shortfall in labor in these industries (*Newsweek* 24th July 2000, 20–23). An estimated 45,000 Chinese students are studying in the United States where labor shortages in the new technologies sector are seen as holding back economic development. After paying fees to study in US/ American universities many then gain residency so that they can add value to the economy with very little investment being required by the US government in their skills development.

Australia has failed to understand the factors that make the risks of overstay low relative to potential benefits. First, the majority of international students have no intention whatsoever of staying in Australia since many have strong familial and social ties to prompt their return at the conclusion of their studies. Moreover, Australia is not seen as the country of first preference for emigration. The United States is where jobs are plentiful, taxes are low, and the economy is large. Further, there are powerful incentives for overseas-trained professionals to return home. Salaries for senior professionals with overseas qualifications compare more than favourably with what they could earn in Australia.

The "risk" of overstaying their visa is not a matter of which country they come from, but is more closely related to the sectors in which students have selected to study. A student who was coming for a short course in Business English may or may not present a "risk" of overstaying, but somebody who is coming to Australia to undertake a higher degree by research is most unlikely to present such a "risk." To regard all students from a particular country as presenting a risk of overstaying is not appropriate. Students might be better placed into different "risk" categories according to the nature of the education program they have chosen irrespective of their country of origin. After much criticism this system was changed in July 2001 with visa process-ing now determined by a range of factors including country, length of course, English language proficiency, and place of residence.

The students with the highest risk of overstaying are those who come to Australia on short-term visas to study English at private colleges; no doubt the shortness of their visas contributes to them becoming over-stayers. Students who make a large investment through paying annual fees for higher education programmes present a much lower risk. This presents a major difficulty for many ELT providers that will be subject to increased pressures for more monitoring by government agencies, and the development of articulated pathways into longer courses.

The monitoring and assessment of students has emerged as a continuing source of debate in the internationalisation of Australian education and the marketisation of English. In early 2001 claims were made that differential and lowered assessment standards were being applied to fee-paying courses in Australian universities. These claims by a right-wing think tank sparked support from Senator Kim Carr who claimed to have evidence from academics of pressure to lower standards in fee-paying courses. While the initial claims were made in relation to domestic students, the issue soon escalated to include debate over the entry standards and English language proficiency of international students. In the "Cash for Degrees scandal" universities were taken to task over poor academic standards and lax entry requirements for English. Surprisingly the practice of front ending international students' programmes with English programmes, an entirely reasonable and sustainable educational practice, was criticised. In one story the issues were summarised as:

> The temptation for university authorities to lower English-language entry standards to maintain the swelling tide of fee-paying students is considerable. At least one university has skirted the issue by using the so called "direct entry" model to demonstrate English language proficiency for students coming from Thailand. (Noonan and Contractor 2001, 5)

The entry standards in most Australian universities were pegged at 6.5 IELTS and 580 on the American TOEFL. The allegations are that the language entry standards have been eroded as cost pressures produced by government disinvestment in higher education have created conditions necessitating the lowering of these standards. Comments by noted academics also highlighted the inadequacy of these tests as a predictor of student language proficiency in the "real" world of academic study.

The ELT industry in Australia operates within an aggressive market context with a diverse mix of providers competing for a differentiated clientele. While the ELT industry operates in the fast lane of the information superhighway, it regularly hits speed bumps, most notably the legacy of White Australia politics and the effects of the neo-liberal political project of creating an enterprise culture subject to global market forces. This highly politicised environment acts as an impediment to Australia's success as a participant in an increasingly competitive transnational education order.

A Policy for Internationalising Australians: English and a Second Language for All

Australia's international profile was lifted dramatically with the Sydney 2000 Olympics. These Olympic games, which profiled the cosmopolitan and multicultural character of Australia, were called the "best ever" by the president of the International Olympic Committee Juan Antonio Samaranch. The performances of athletes like Aboriginal gold medallist Catherine Freeman created an image of a nation unified around its ethnic and linguistic diversity. However, one incident reveals much about the status of English in Australia and efforts to use it to reaffirm an outdated sense of national identity.

One of many selection controversies for the Sydney Games was the dropping of Melbourne-born Italian resident Silvana Trampuz from the Australian women's marathon team. Trampuz's dumping was puzzling because she was the first of the Australian runners in the 1998 World Championships in Seville and was ranked number three in Australia. In the selection for the 2000 Olympics the third position was given to Nickey Carroll, a relatively inexperienced runner who had failed to finish in two world championships and had withdrawn from the 1998 Commonwealth Games marathon. The controversy deepened when Carroll also failed to complete the Sydney 2000 marathon. Heather Turland heightened speculation about the non-selection of Trampuz. Turland, the 1998 Commonwealth Games marathon champion, commented in 1999 that "foreign runners" should not be selected for Australia:

> She [Trampuz] is not an Australian, she can hardly speak English and has no intention of living here, so why should she be considered for the Olympics? It is unfair and I am sure most Australians would agree with me. It should not be about medals and funding. It should be about Aussies and running for Australia and being proud of it. (*Fox Sport* 22nd January 1999)

Turland argued that "Australians" should not be put out by Trampuz's selection. These comments invoke the English-only dogma of White Australia politics. Other Australian athletes refuted these remarks, including Steve Moneghetti who was the Australian athletics team captain at the Olympics. However, the slur cast a shadow over the workings of Athletics Australia. Criticisms over the failure by Athletics Australia to nominate Trampuz because she was a "non-Australian" athlete drew a terse response:

> The suggestion that Athletics Australia avoided nominating Silvana so as to appease those who believe she was not entitled to represent Australia is mischievous in the extreme.... The Olympics athletic team this year is likely to feature athletes from a multitude of ethnic backgrounds, from Sri Lanka to Syria and from Belarus to Ballarat. Silvana was eligible for nomination as any athlete and will remain so if she continues to make herself available. (Athletics Australia 8th June 2000)

There was a lingering suspicion that the Italian-Australian was selected and then dropped by the Athletics Australia Board because of concerns about the selection of an Australian who spoke little English. Her omission from the Olympics team suggested to many that English language abilities and residency were unspecified selection criteria. This vignette from one of the key moments in Australian popular sports culture highlights the strong link English-only politics has in residual constructions of the Whites-only Australian national identity. In 1991 the Australian Language and Literacy Policy (ALLP) recognised the importance of proficiency in English for the effective participation in all aspects of work, leisure, education, and training. It also recognised the importance of Australian languages othered through English (LOTE) including the need to support Aboriginal and Torres Strait Island community languages. The ALLP was modeled on the National Languages Policy and its four organisational goals: English for all, support for Indigenous languages, a language other than English for all, and equitable and widespread language services. The ALLP established a framework for equitable access to literacy and language services for some 700,000 bilingual Australians. The ALLP sought to reverse assimilationist English-only policies on language and literacy in recognition of Australian multiculturalism.

The arrival of the Howard Government in 1996 saw the erosion of policies designed to facilitate the development of an inclusive and multilingual society. Since the early 1970s bilingual education has operated as a foundation for education in Aboriginal communities in the Northern Territory. Bilingual education incorporated a philosophy that valued Indigenous languages, and used them as the basis for achieving English language proficiency and the development of inclusive bi-cultural experiences. The general approach to bilingual education involved the use of Indigenous languages in the early years of schooling followed by the progressive introduction of English. While this bilingual curriculum was seen as enhancing the possibilities for the survival of endangered Aboriginal languages, Harris (1990) argued that bilingual education is a vehicle for the unwitting destruction of Aboriginal languages and advocated Indigenous language education instead. However, the bilingual programmes never enjoyed the fulsome support of the Northern Territory Department of Education or the government. Their support came from Aboriginal communities concerned about the extinction of their languages, the loss of their knowledge, and the destruction of their identity. They saw the need to provide Indigenous language education for the rising generation through school and community interactions. Despite this resistance and associated structural disadvantages these programmes were also challenged for going against White Australia's strong monolingual, English-only politics. In 2000 the Northern Territory government set about abolishing bilingual education and introducing English-only instruction in all of its schools. The government attributed this move to poor English literacy standards among Indigenous students by conflating the issues of language and literacy performance. The abolition of the bilingual programmes was justified as a strategy designed to preserve English language standards. Jenni Herbert Nungarrayi an Aboriginal teacher explained the importance of differentiating between language and literacy needs in the context of preserving Aboriginal cultural identity:

> I believe the western notion of literacy to be limited when it comes to the maintenance of important to then maintenance of Walpiri knowledge. Literacy isn't all its cracked up to be! I'd like to extend the notion of literacy from a narrower view of literacy that writing is superior to oral forms. There are many things that successful Walpiri people need to know, very few of them are exclusively concerned with literacy. For example we need to know the about the correct useage of kinship terms, about the kinship system in general—without that we are no longer Walpiri people. (Nicholls and Nungarrayi 1995, 20)

Despite resistance, the Northern Territory Government is pursuing its "English-only" politics with the endorsement of the Federal Howard Government and closing bilingual education programmes in the remote Aboriginal communities. Once again colonising English has deemed

Indigenous languages outlaws and continued their path to extinction. However, in economically hard-pressed times, success in boosting exports and attracting foreign investment can depend on subtle factors, and the diverse languages spoken by Australians are now particularly important in the quest for worldwide trading opportunities. Statements and funding from "influential politicians and administrators" are necessary for creating both the resources and a "climate of opinion about the importance of [second] language learning" (Crystal 1997, 16).

The decay started in the mid-1990s with statements by the Minister for Education John Dawkins that "Australia is a nation of many cultures but Australia has but one national language English" (Moore 1995, 15). This deviation from the ALLP consigned many Australian's who do not write, read, or speak English to the status of a foreigner in their own country. Dawkins's statements shifted the debate to poor English skills as a national disadvantage in the context of global economic developments ignoring the significance of multilingualism in this changing environment. He also reshaped the strategy of LOTE teaching to shadow Australia's economic interests in North East Asia. This was followed by the Rudd Report (1994) which advocated the teaching of four Asian languages in order to enhance trade and economic opportunities in four East Asian countries. In this era English became the language of employment and the only other languages considered were those that had a role in regional commerce without any consideration of the role of diasporic communities in this new era of globalisation. While the teaching of languages rose marginally from 12 percent in 1987 to 19 percent by 1995 community languages were squeezed out of the education portfolio by budget cuts (Lo Bianco 1995; 1999).

Since 1996 there have been further cuts in the teaching of languages othered by English in universities and colleges throughout Australia that now threatens their very existence in higher education. Squeezed by government funding cuts and a policy bias toward courses in applied science and technology there has been a steady closure of programmes teaching all aspects of language education, from critical applied linguistics through to translation and interpreting. In Melbourne, an inter-university consortium struggles to offer a range of language courses, with students from one university accessing language courses offered by another institution. These closures are occurring at a time when the emphasis is on vocational courses in management, e-business, and international marketing. The brochures for these courses are liberally spread with glossy marketing hype about the emergence of these new technologies with the opportunities that globalisation offers, but there is a silence about the languages that this business will use. These courses seldom offer a language major. In the new e-business course the languages on offer have more to do with "cyber languages" than Asian languages. The assumption implicit in the new e-business courses is that English will rule commerce in all contexts and that there is very little to be gained from considering transnational multilingual markets. This mistaken assumption does not understand the rich diversity of international business contexts and the cultural and linguistic competencies required to successfully participate in them.

This reaffirmation of English-only pedagogy is a significant departure from the National Languages Policy of the late 1980s when there was a funding priority on teaching Asian languages. The funding was allocated on the basis of Australia's economic interests, albeit regionally rather than globally conceived, but this ensured that education in Japanese, Mandarin, Indonesian, and Korean enjoyed a brief but intense period of government security. While the National Languages Policy identified these languages as a priority, its implementation in schools suffered from a lack of planning, inadequate teacher education, and limited curriculum resources. In the early 1990s the Queensland government introduced the requirement for compulsory LOTE at the primary school level and allocated extra funds to educate LOTE teachers; this was at a time when the minister for education anticipated a surplus in generalist teachers. Neither the increase in LOTE teacher graduates nor attempts to retrain surplus teachers could address the problem of providing sufficient LOTE teachers in primary schools across Queensland. The shortage of educated LOTE teachers and the resistance of school administrators, teachers, parents, and students to this important initiative ensured that by the mid-1990s LOTE had slipped from compulsory to optional status. These insights into language politics in schools and higher education highlight the culture of institutional resistance in Australia to languages othered through English. While the durability of White Australia politics destabilises attempts to broaden the language heritage and competence of Anglo-Australians, the triumphalism associated with the global dominance of English reinforces complacency.

Melbourne's ELT industry is booming, fuelled by the city's status as a centre for educational excellence and its accelerated participation in the new transnational education order. To meet this growing demand the recruitment and preparation of teachers to work in the ELT industry is key to maintaining its viability and buoyancy. The education of English language teachers has exhibited two tandem but contradictory developments. The first involves the continuing erosion and shrinkage of education and research in public universities as a direct result of government disinvestment in a range of public security provisions. The second involves the continuing education of language teachers through ELT providers. This is a potentially significant market with links to employers and job opportunities providing a significant advantage for graduates. Training through ELT providers is characterised by an integration of teaching products, services, and examination that bears striking similarities to franchise arrangements.

The shrinkage in government-funded university places for the education of English language teachers can be attributed to the introduction of full fees for Australian post-graduate courses in 1989, the deregulation of course work places by the Howard Government in 1996, and its cutbacks to the funding of research higher degree students that began in 2001. Between 1996 and 1999 there was a decline of 7.5 percent in all post-graduate course work students across Australian universities. The slide is more apparent in some disciplines and vocations than others. Only business and information technology has recorded modest increases, with equivalent full-time students in education courses falling by 17 percent (DETYA 2000). This decline is in marked contrast to the promises of the federal minister for education that the "user pays" system would result in an 83 percent increase in post-graduate course work (Riddell 2000, 3). The impact of this decline has necessitated the closure of many courses that have traditionally provided teacher education and research for the ELT industry, which cannot afford to fund these itself.

A survey of five universities conducted by the New South Wales Advisory Council on the Quality of Teaching reported that there was a decline of 38.2 percent of post-graduate enrolments in teacher education in recent years. While Sydney University recorded a modest increase, the University of Western Sydney recorded a drop of 58 percent (Riddell 2000, 3). The impact on the ELT industry is particularly significant because it is characterised by part-time and sessional work. The introduction of fees for people wanting to work in an uncertain occupational setting has been a major disincentive for practitioners to pursue post-graduate studies. In the context of these changes, where a master's degree costs around $A10,000 a year, prospective ELT teachers are choosing to undertake shorter, cheaper courses with guaranteed employment on completion. This trend has ensured that short courses, such as the four-week-long Cambridge Certificate of English Language Teaching to Adults (CELTA), have continued to be a popular entry point for teachers into a market where labor is in demand. Several providers in Melbourne offer CELTA training that is marketed as a qualification for teachers with little or no experience in teaching English. Private providers such as Embassy CES and the Melbourne College of English run a regular cycle of RSA and CELTA training. The emerging arrangement is for Universities' private companies to offer the Cambridge or RSA courses, although there is no training of ELT teachers in the faculty responsible for teacher education. This structural arrangement, where teacher training is lodged with the university's private company, is indicative of the emerging pattern of subcontracting core functions to hybrid enterprises. It reflects a shift of language teaching from an academic concern to the emerging enterprises of fast capitalism which streamline teacher preparation to meet the demands of the buoyant ELT industry.

The ELT market is typified by a shortage with providers conducting courses with a view to inducting and recruiting teachers who are known to and familiar with the operations of the provider. The market extends internationally with Australian teachers being recruited by overseas ELT providers. In any weekend newspaper in Asian cities advertisements for teachers are quite common. Such advertisements capitalise on the low pay, poor conditions, as well as, uncertain future that many Australian teachers are facing in an era of diminished government commitment to securing the nation's education. Offshore employers or their agents offer relatively attractive packages that include airfares, subsidised accommodation, medical insurance, and high wages. The attraction of working in exotic locations and the promise of additional fringe benefits on top of wages in the range of $4,000–$10,000 per month provide a considerable incentive for teachers to go offshore.

The demand for Australian teachers is so great that even those without qualifications are recruited in different countries throughout Asia. This recruitment of unqualified and inexperienced foreign "teachers" is a significant phenomenon in an increasingly competitive market. It raises questions about the motivation of such risky recruitment strategies in countries where there are multilingual speakers who have the requisite English language teaching skills. The answer lies in the attraction to ELT providers and their clients of using "native speakers" as teachers. "Native speakers" are seen as coming from the former White, Anglo-ethnic dominions of the English empire clustered around Canada, South Africa, New Zealand, the United States, the UK, and Australia. The concept of "native speakers" is a racist position that exclusively identifies the notion of "native speaker" status with "Whiteness." There is a racialisation of the ELT industry that identifies "Whiteness" as a marker of superior linguistic and teaching skills (Pennycook 1998). Providers argue that the market demands native speakers because they have greater credibility with students. The logic applied by ELT providers is that "native speakers" are automatically better than non-native, non-White teachers. This suggests that the ELT industry is involved in protectionism; its closed shop policy is based on racist assumptions that identify Anglo-ethnics as superior speakers and teachers of English.

This racialisation of the employment of "native speaking" English language teachers is indicative of Australia's ambiguous responses and contributions to globalisation. The state promotes the rhetoric of flexibility, government deregulation, and the use of market forces as evidence of its openness and engagement with the world. Australia also promotes itself as a successful multicultural society accepting of linguistic and cultural diversity. Australian's are keen to remind the world that they have outgrown the legacy of White Australia politics. Yet its responses to the internationalisation of education suggests considerable ambivalences over these changes. While the ELT industry competes in a buoyant market, its business is conducted within a political climate that contradicts the promise of a more than tolerant Australia.

The public debates over transnational education and ELT in Australia are occurring in the context of protectionism, now reworked in the guise of concerns about quality of both ELT providers and students. Campaigns ostensibly designed to protect the image of Australia tend to reaffirm anxieties about the continuing legacy of White Australia politics. These inquisitions do little to address the problem of the diminishing commitment by the state to ensure the nation's educational security and sends a message that regressive parochialism and racism are alive and well in Australia. Since the mid-1990s government policy in Australia has seen a revival of monolingual, assimilationist views about the teaching of English. The brief period when inclusive policies of bilingual education and the teaching of other languages flourished now seems to be coming to an end as efforts are made to reestablish an English-only Australia. This regressive politics has been masked and obscured by a fetish for new technologies and their power to sell cyber-English. There is, contrary to the reality of English being diverse and dynamic, capable of new forms of adaptation and interaction through technology. Yet this has arisen at a time when the conduct of the government, the profession, and the market suggests a retreat to and popularisation of English-only pedagogy. Its also suggests that some teaching practices do little to support the promise of flexibility, openness, and acceptance of diverse and inclusive views of language and language teaching.

CHAPTER 8

Teaching English in a Globalised Marketplace

> For professionals working in the field the employment of unqualified people to teach English is a tremendous insult considering the time they have invested in their studies. In Bali ELT operators typically get several such enquiries per day. People wander in off the beach in their shorts and thongs to ask for a job teaching English. Professional ELT providers say, "What are your English language teaching qualifications? None? Why don't you wander down to the hospital and see if you can get a job as a doctor?" (English language teacher 2000)

The work of English language teachers has been profoundly altered by the combined influence of the globalised market in education and training; the new hybridised organisations which employ them, and the emergence of new technologies of human interaction, knowledge production, and reflection. These factors are relentlessly reshaping the nature of teachers' work, the pedagogy of teaching, and the relationship between teachers and their students. The ELT industry is typified by a "just in time" culture where time and space are compressed by the demands of the globalised market. This "just in time" culture and the differentiated ELT market has created a range of contradictory challenges for English language teachers. These have heightened concerns about proficiency, quality assurance, and unrelenting pressure for flexibility in responding to client demands. ELT teachers are in a period of expanding employment opportunities but are experiencing casualisation and de-professionalisation.

New uncertainties for English language teachers include the increasing integration of ELT with vocational education using new technology. There is an irony about the levels of uncertainty in the ELT industry.

Employers are experiencing difficulties in recruiting and maintaining multi-skilled teachers who are capable of meeting the diverse demands of the ELT market. This need for multi-skilled teachers of English appears at a time when employment patterns and the arrival of new technologies point to uncertain career opportunities. The changes in the work of English language teachers provides a valuable insight into the impact of educational markets and the diversification of knowledge that are now a feature of teaching more generally. A comparison of the work of Australian English language teachers in the nation-building era when migrant educational services were at their zenith with the present day sees a dramatically changed scenario.

Old Classrooms, New Cyber-learning: Contrasting Scenarios of Work

When ELT was part of Australia's nation-building project it was conducted around an emphasis on its civic and communal roles. The state funded education programmes employed teachers and organised a formal curriculum that integrated the teaching of English and citizenship. The formal curriculum established standards for English speech, reading, and writing that emphasised grammar and syntax. The modes of instruction were generally teacher-centred classroom delivery using "lessons" where competence was mandated through a graduated hierarchy of complexity. This graduated competence was formalised around "textbooks" for teachers and "workbooks" used by students that were designed using the situational method. The teachers' dominating role was prescribed as:

> The course is for use in the classroom. The matching Students' Books are not intended for self-study without a teacher. The course presents an aural/oral approach. (Department of Education 1975, xi)

The course materials were public property and carried the warning that "this book must not be sold." The situational English method that dominated postwar English teaching in Australia prepared migrant students for English language competence. This methodology was a departure from the literature-based, grammar translation method but did not recognise the differentiated and diverse contexts for using English. The emphasis was on the social use of language and generic situational contexts including "An [Anglo]Australian in London" and "Please tell me about the film" and "On holiday" (Department of Education 1975). Drilling and presentation were the dominant modes of instruction. Teachers were instructed on how drills should be conducted in individual, chorus, and class modes. The emphasis was on the tone and rhythm needed to attain standardised English pronunciations. These pedagogies once typified the dominant teaching styles used by the national ELT providers such as the Adult Migrant English Service (AMES). These flagship enterprises provided career paths for teachers and educational managers under the umbrella of public service conditions.

In many circumstances these postwar teaching and learning techniques are still used in many public schools in countries such as Malaysia. Current teaching practice seems rooted in the past, with the teaching methodologies having a huge emphasis on rote learning drill, written grammar, and standardised pronunciation. The endurance of such methods has been determined by limited national budgets, an examination regime, and the shadow of English colonialism. The only minor concessions to contemporary contexts are the addition of educational television and film. Malaysian concerns about teacher proficiency can be partly attributed to the persistent use of redundant teaching methodologies (and therefore limited and inadequate teacher professional development) at a time when many students and the community generally are actively engaged with the Englishes of popular culture. Teachers' capacity to productively engage contemporary manifestations of English in new technology, films, and popular culture is not helped by an examination regime dominated by standardised English. Resistance by students, parents, and some teachers to engage in English compound questions about teacher proficiency in Malaysia. This creates dilemmas in a system where the curriculum is driven by exams on reading and writing in English.

At one level some transnational ELT providers use teaching practices which featured in past eras and at another there is a radically different practice which is shaped by the market. The consensus about traditional ELT practices has been challenged by the workings of the new transnational education markets. The changing methodologies of teaching reflect a response to the unrelenting pressure of market-based education. The commodification of education and training ensures that the work of all teachers is subject to profound pressures and the uncertainties of continuous change; the globalised nature of the ELT industry has accelerated these trends in English language teachers' work. Marketisation has increased demands for teachers to not simply be a "classroom" teacher, but also a skilled broker capable of negotiating the sale and delivery of ELT products and services. The new ELT industry now demands of teachers skills in marketing negotiation, networking, project management, and the preparation of customised "deliverables." These new roles have not replaced but extended the traditional expectations of teaching. They have been "bolted" onto teachers' existing roles. This intensification of teachers' work has been overlayed with the widespread use of the new technologies of human interaction, reflection, and knowledge production.

In practical terms this means contemporary English language teachers are increasingly working in an environment where ELT is integrated into vocational courses in business using new technologies. Otherwise ELT may be "front ending" an academic course or offered as a short-term autonomous course designed to provide specialist language skills to a business enterprise. Additional complexities are arising for English language teachers as their curriculum and assessment practices and vocational education requirements are being merged into new "learning packages." All of this means that teachers need to have the capabilities to juggle the demands of competency-based training curriculum, workplace assessment, English language education, and new cyber-pedagogies. The dimensions of this complexity are heightened as participation in differentiated markets mean that each client or group of students requires customised delivery to meet their individual or enterprise needs. The program cycles are increasingly truncated to enable a rolling cycle of enrolment-teaching-graduation with no "dead times" in the teaching calendar. English language teachers now require a new skills set to manage these compressed cycles and to adjust individual student programs to these cycles.

English language teaching techniques are now more likely to be in "mixed mode," using a repertoire of classroom instruction, workplace-based learning, and the new technologies of computer-based learning. For the moment this reliance on computer-based learning has reoriented ELT away from oral and aural forms of English toward multimedia texts. These new literacies ensure that teachers will be working with programmes such as *Planet English* and *Encarta* as well as sophisticated electronic language laboratories and simulated "real world" learning environments. Those making the best use of this media are using it in very different ways to textbook and test-based pedagogies because they provide opportunities to customise offerings and for students to select their own non-linear programmes. The new technologies of learning in combination with the dynamics of the market are facilitating a shift from classroom teaching to student-centred individualised learning. It is not true to suggest that the new technologies have wholly replaced classroom teaching but rather that they have added an additional layer of complexity and diversity to the existing workloads of English language teachers. The multiple modes of teaching and the constant switching from individual and group learning with varied teaching materials and assessment techniques makes for an environment characterised by negative stresses and unwarranted anxieties.

This anxiety is amplified by the employment of teachers being reshaped by the transnational education market. The emergence of transnational hybrid ELT enterprises has in some cases created inequitable employment arrangements. Some in the private sector are owned by listed companies involved in diverse commercial activities and operating ELT programmes as subsidiaries. In order to maximise flexibility there is a reliance on the use of contract and part-time English language teachers. This trend is also evident in the public sector where organisations are experiencing a contraction in government investment in the public's educational security. ELT providers in corporatised universities are operated as commercial subsidiaries. With the objective of maintaining a "lean and mean" infrastructure where salaries are generally about 80 percent of overall costs, these new hybrid ELT enterprises seek flexibility by resorting to a casualised workforce (Kell 1997; Davis, Hirschl, and Stack 1997).

The careers of English language teachers are now typified by "serial" employment across multiple employers. Even in a buoyant period the use of contracted staff means there is an annual cycle of contract renegotiation that sees an increasingly nomadic teaching force migrate to the best paid jobs. In this environment issues of corporate loyalty, commercial confidentiality, and the difficulty of maintaining a strategic long-term corporate memory in specialist areas assume a problematic role in endeavours to secure market share. In a market where return business is dependent on a personal touch, ELT providers are particularly vulnerable to "poaching" by competitors and the loss of key employees. In the highly competitive markets salary packages are sometimes supplemented with lucrative incentives and benefits of a financial and in-kind basis (Kell, Balatti, Muspratt, and Hill 1997).

Increasingly the repertoire of skills required by English language teachers includes the capacity to effectively participate in transnational education markets. Now English language teachers need skills that are carefully oriented toward their fee-paying clients. They must be very user-friendly to their students, be able to listen, provide students with support in their business or information technology studies, be computer literate, multilingual, and need to have had offshore experience.

Since access to markets is so often shaped by individual networks and professional contacts, many ELT workers have to adopt the behaviour of a sales representative seeking to make the "big deal." This is new territory for most English language teachers and requires capabilities and skills for which they have not been prepared. ELT preparation and professional development has been almost exclusively confined to the skilling of teachers in language teaching methods. However, the demands of the market suggests there is now a need to incorporate opportunities for them to learn about the prevailing economic model of education, the compliance regime used to enforce it, and the associated elaboration of a culture of entrepreneurialism. While many teachers find this to be in conflict with the social and cultural role of teaching, or even an affront to their professionalism, it is an outcome of the marketisation and commodification of ELT.

These skills and capabilities are not new since teachers have traditionally required strong networking and political skills to survive in the bureaucratic maze that typifies many of the large public education systems. These skills now have to be refined for the growing network of transnational corporations in the ELT business. However, as the competitive ELT market reshapes teaching and learning into a more commodified exchange relationship, there is the danger of neglecting the social and cultural role of teachers' work.

The Proletarianisation of English Language Teachers' Work

With the advent of transnational markets in education, English language teaching has shifted from being exclusively classroom based to having a more diverse and broader entrepreneurial role. This change parallels the shift in the steering role of the nation-state to its use of the globalised education market to effect change and control. It is unwise and unwarranted to nostalgically portray the former era of ELT teaching as a period of certainty and stability. On the contrary *Appropriating English* argues that this era and the teaching methodologies reflected colonial arrangements which did little to empower students and address the politics of the project of globalising English. In many cases it was a period of uncertainty and marginalisation for bilingual students.

For some English language teachers the transnational market creates new and fulfilling opportunities to combine travel and teaching with the added incentive of flexible employment conditions. Indeed these benefits contrast with the confining conditions of teachers' work in bureaucratic state-run organisations. Some teachers relish the challenge of the market and have made new opportunities for their professional lives. For others lacking experience with change, unable to change, afraid of change, these developments are dismissed for their potential to reconstitute teachers' work.

These new roles have been referred to uncritically as "facilitators" and "knowledge navigators" (Lepani 1995; 1996). These terms recognise the broadening of teachers' roles and the changes to what is regarded as valuable knowledge and learning experiences where teachers' new work includes networking and coordinating knowledge and learning resources rather than just presenting information (Kell 1998). These reinterpretations of teachers' work concentrate on the functional role and do little to examine the extent to which there are changed relationships between teachers and knowledge; teachers, and students, teachers with each other, and most importantly teachers and the new technologies of learning.

The unrelenting press to internationalise education and the key role of

English in the neo-liberal project of globalism means that there is no turning back. Nostalgic views of a "golden era" where language curriculum was predictable and teachers "in control" provides little sanctuary from the new realities. While there is some "inevitability" surrounding the trends and relationships evident in the internationalisation of ELT, this does not mean that there cannot be a critical engagement with these contemporary developments with the objective of challenging and even reversing some of the disempowering practices that *Appropriating English* has highlighted.

It is important to address these issues through reconsidering English language teachers' work as a point for resisting the disempowering aspects of globalising English in the transnational markets while working to make the internationalisation of education humanly possible. This involves unpacking key aspects of the market on education and the construction of an agenda for global ethics. This will prompt awareness for the need to develop more inclusive models of teaching which do not recycle colonising and colonialist English. Teachers have a role to play in actively shaping the future of the ELT industry rather than as passive bystanders. This agenda does not succumb to deterministic views about the onslaught of neo-liberal globalism, the erosion of democratic norms, the homogenisation of cultural life, or the death of a public sphere. There are still opportunities to develop transnational frameworks for innovations that provide for democratic, equitable and socially useful forms of English language teaching.

In order for a framework to be developed it is essential that the trends and relationships in ELT and the notion of change be contextualised. This requires a political and economic analysis that interprets the changing conditions of ELT work as a trend involving the proletarianisation of teachers. This involves the steady de-professionalisation in teaching:

> In the first instance teachers are relegated to the instrumental tasks that limit possibilities for oppositional discourse and social practices. Pedagogy in this case is reduced to the implementation of taxonomies that sub-ordinate knowledge to forms of methodological reification, while theories of teaching are increasingly technicised and standardised in the quest for efficiency and the control of discrete forms of knowledge. (Aronowitz and Giroux 1993, 34)

This proletarianisation of English language teaching involves a rationality that separates the conception of activity from its execution and standardises practices and outcomes with a view to enhancing the interests of those managing and controlling the process of knowledge production. New technologies are seen as crucial instruments in this process. A key feature of this is a rationalisation that justifies the need for heightened levels of prediction and control in productive processes. These are seen as essential elements in the attainment of uniform and standardised outcomes. These outcomes are reduced to the calculative logic of performance indicators that are creatively constructed using audit management tools. These measures obscure their frail origins and contradictory operations to present an overriding message that social and cultural values are not important.

The temptation to standardise teaching practices and materials has significant advantages to transnational corporations participating in the ELT industry. They are anxious to avoid the need to offer a different range of products to dispersed and diverse clients. Standardised services introduce economic efficiencies as well as prove valuable for monitoring the relative performance of branches in franchised ELT organisations.

The accelerated tendency toward the proletarianisation of teachers' work can also be attributed to the technologisation of this work. This technicisation of teaching is seen in the steady erosion of the view that teaching is a social and cultural practice, so that it is now depicted as a technical activity requiring a technological fix. This repositions complex social and cultural, curriculum and pedagogical issues as a problem of managerialism and the deployment of the new technologies to auditing and the press for standardised outcomes.

This removes educational experiences from the social and cultural realm and collapses language teaching into questions about getting the right combination of management. ELT is fitted into a metaphor of production where teachers are responsible for the execution of a standardised program that minimises their opportunities to make meaningful interactions and interventions on behalf of students. Teachers' professional judgments are sidelined and made secondary to the directions advanced by the designers of instructional technologies. Teachers occupy a peripheral support role in the design and development of ELT programmes. Their role is almost exclusively restricted to monitoring progress and ensuring that students are "on track." This passive support role is represented as being that of a "learning facilitator." This is reinforced by shifts in the design and development of ELT materials that accompanied the marketisation of education, the corporatisation of curriculum development, and the rise of digital technologies. Rather than providing an expansive opportunity for teachers there is a reconstruction and contraction of teachers' options in relating to the task of learning and a challenge to their legitimacy in managing learning (Apple 1996).

Contributing to the proletarianisation of English language teachers is the growing popularity of pre-programmed ELT curricula where teachers are consigned to a subordinate monitoring role. The growth in pre-packaged technology-based curricula is evident in the prevalence of mastery learning schemes and the proliferation of competency-based teaching. The growth of these types of programmes can be attributed to the belief amongst corporate managers that these programmes reduce preparation time, offer a more economical program, and provide uniform sequencing and progression in the learning tasks. These packages defuse debates about learning objectives and learning theory. Paradoxically, while the ELT market has promised greater choice to consumers, these packages, which are often reliant on "lock step" and "time on task" behaviourist pedagogy, actually limit the options for learners (Aronowitz and Giroux 1993). The ELT industry has always been characterised by this type of package and in many respects these developments represent the use of new technology to reproduce these dated methods. However, there are significant changes that arise from the integration of vocational education with ELT through the use of new technologies.

New Technologies of Learning: Cutting-Edge Dilemmas

An integral part of the growth of transnational education markets has been the accelerating use of the new technologies of student interaction, reflection, and knowledge production. There has been a movement away from exclusive classroom delivery as multimedia, online learning technologies have become available. The ELT industry is one area of education where the use of computer-based learning has experienced substantial growth. This development can also be attributed to the rise of the hybrid ELT enterprises that see alliances between educational institutions, publishing companies, media corporations, and telecom-munications businesses (Kenway 1995). There is, however, an ambiguous quality about the use of this new technology. On the one hand, it has advantages in the functional capabilities it provides for expanding and diversifying curriculum packages. However, this appeal is seductive because while this new technology provides teachers with options for curriculum and opportunities to connect to the new Englishes of cyberspace, there is a downside. The generic nature of some ELT packages, often designed without new pedagogical expertise, contributes to the deskilling and proletarianisation of teachers. In many of the computer-based packages the "technical manuals" position teachers as support and "helpers." There is also a failure of these packages to engage with new pedagogical theories and practices and to repeat linear, "click and drag" testing techniques rather than exploring the full potential for open associative approaches to learning. Many of these online material developments repeat the pedagogical mistakes and inadequacies of the past but are sanctioned as "innovations" because of their use in new digital technologies. Some ELT packages tend to reproduce pen-and-paper testing procedures rather than explore multimedia opportunities that digital technologies can offer. Outdated drills and cloze exercises are all too often reproduced using new technology.

While ELT providers are hyperactive about the use of technologically based packages, their enthusiasm is not matched by all of their students. There is the expectation created by intense marketing that ELT will offer cultural and personal engagement. Consumer resistance is encountered when the new learning technologies become a screen-based substitute for this. Sitting for hours on end at a computer terminal to learn a language is not something that ELT clients are demanding. Teachers are now caught in a dilemma being required by their employers to become adept and efficient at the use of the new technologies, while their students desire learning experiences that maximise opportunities for social engagement. These dilemmas are heightened by the fragility of technological infrastructure, the lack of software reliability, and limited robustness of networks which cause cost-conscious operators to question their use. The contradictions between the demands by employers for cost efficiencies in teaching through the use of technology and the demands of clients for embodied learning experiences is an ever-present feature of teachers' work.

Added to these contradictory demands are also the growing inequities that emerge from the digital divide. There is an emerging polarisation in the ELT industry between large hybridised enterprises with integrated corporate ownership, small operators, and the public sector. This polarisation is defined by the access to clusters of technologies that sustain transnational teaching. Lacking capital, investment infrastructure, and experiencing diminished commitment by governments to secure their citizen's education, public ELT providers are being downgraded to second rate systems to improve the competitive climate for private providers. There is also a failure to provide professional development and training to teachers in the new technologies of learning. The access to these new learning platforms and the ability to use them professionally creates a new level of crisis among teachers anxious to embrace the opportunities of new technology but denied both the tools and the training to use them. The skills for using the new technology are learned on the job in an uncritical way. This just-in-time learning, with patched up hardware and software programmes, has implications for the quality of English language teaching. These quality concerns are compounded by the growing vocationalisation of ELT.

Putting English to Work: Vocationalising English Language Teaching

Many of the ELT products being developed in Australia are either part of vocational education programmes or "front end" these programmes. This is one of the growing areas in Australia's international education profile and sees the large state-run system of Technical and Further Education (TAFE) offering ELT courses in onshore and offshore modes. TAFE courses range from entry level training to Diploma courses. Over two million Australian students study in the Vocational Education and Training (VET) system. Since the late 1980s the VET system has operated a competency-based curriculum (CBT) to provide better links between training and industry practice. The CBT system involves the development of industry standard competencies as the basis for all VET programmes. The assessment and licensing of students for trades and para-professional occupations involves establishing the ability of students to perform specific competencies with an industrial setting. The arrival of CBT was accompanied by radical changes in the VET sector to provide greater flexibility in the training system and to ensure relevance to industry, particularly small businesses. Recognising that the state and corporate origins of these reforms to VET were not serving the training needs of small to medium enterprises the Australian government moved to develop training packages to meet their needs. The cluster of CBT and pre-packaged training packages with ELT programmes in offshore and on-shore settings introduces a range of dilemmas for ELT teachers. The use of CBT and training packages is consistent with moves toward text-based teaching materials, which raises questions about the effectiveness of this mode of learning in flexible, self-paced delivery. There are also questions about the suitability of self-paced ELT packages where the competence of students in English reading and writing skills is assumed.

Training packages, which are varied in their quality and effectiveness, incorporate many of the worst aspects of programmed learning. The industrial competencies developed in Australia feature narrow, reductionist, and instrumental views of work tasks. They do little more than offer a collection of decontextualised generic descriptors and specifications about tasks and outcomes that are limited in their transportability. Worse still they maintain the pretence of value-free objective task analysis of occupations. On the contrary, they provide value-laden views of work, workplaces, and how people work. The individualised nature of competency-based training is incompatible with more collective views of the workplace in Australia and elsewhere (Kell 1998). The nature of work is uncritically represented. For instance, the gendered culture of the workplace is ignored and so too is the fact that many workplaces in Asia are family workplaces. The relevance of workplace competencies in business packages which feature topics on "360 degree appraisal" and "team work" could very well be irrelevant in Asian family businesses. The failure to contextualise these training packages is evident in a forestry training package which fails to differentiate between the task of felling large-scale timber in native forests and pruning trees in a suburban garden.

Competency-based training methodologies and associated training packages have been a major factor contributing to the deskilling and proletarianisation of Australian teachers. While it would be incorrect to suggest all training packages are of a poor quality, since some have broken new barriers in curriculum development, their variable quality creates dilemmas for English language teachers.

Indeed the whole question of integrating ELT with VET creates dilemmas for teachers who are required to come to grips with the specialist culture of the occupations and industrial tasks incorporated in the new programmes as well as teach English. More worrying is the export of a teaching and learning methodology that Australian experience has found to be flawed. Given the dilemmas of CBT and training packages in Australia their export to an unsuspecting region sets new standards in "trade dumping." There is a danger that the quality of ELT materials and processes is typified by a process of "dumbing down," something that an Australian export industry can ill afford.

Re-professionalising Teaching: Teaching the Teachers to Teach in New Times

Recapturing a professional agenda for ELT is a key challenge for the future, and requires linking the preparation of teachers to the new ways of working in the ELT industry. In Australia the decline in university courses and the positioning of ELT in subsidiary companies has eroded the link between the industry, research, and teaching. In countries such as Malaysia there is a shortage of English language teachers giving rise to concerns about the proficiency of those being trained and the teacher education system. In this vacuum the Royal Society of the Arts (RSA) Certificate and Diploma in Teaching English as a Foreign Language remain the industry "gold standard." Some employers are now requesting post-graduate qualifications in Teaching English as a Second Language in addition to the RSA.

Some industry figures recognise the inadequacy of the RSA course in view of the diversified nature of the transnational market and the rise of multivocal Englishes. They are questioning the durability and utility of such short programmes and their relevance to the contemporary ELT industry. There is a view that a four-week-long "one sise fits all" course which concentrates on dated functional language teaching methods is inadequate. Methods of teacher education that stress the "golden rules of teaching" fail to account for the new multiliteracies associated with English and are inadequate for the complexities of ELT. Increasingly ELT providers are seeking teachers who are entrepreneurial, can work in multilingual contexts, and are capable of working with the new technologies of learning. Existing short courses do not account for these changing needs.

There are now demands for ELT courses that allow an exploration of principles that can inform practice to meet the contemporary challenges of globalising English. In changing ELT qualifications and broadening teacher education courses the nexus between qualifications and examination creates a privileged situation for the British-based Cambridge IELT system. There are international ELT competitors which are exploiting the inadequacies in the education of English language teachers with alternative programmes. In Australia there is the possibility for a national consortia of universities working with IDP to develop such a qualification. The objective of this is not only to renew teacher education but to provide alternatives to a narrow and rigid English system and respond to the demands of the Asia Pacific region. The education of teachers in Asia is a key priority that the British Council has strategically responded to with a 3+1 program in training 200 English language teachers involving five English universities. As well as this the Council is sponsoring the Institute of Foreign Language Education through the South East Asian Ministers of Education Organisation (SEAMEO) in Singapore. These ambitious plans for training and professional develop-ment suggest that the English are working to preserve their influence on teaching methodologies in ways that move beyond short courses.

Opportunities exist for the development of ELT courses and programmes that integrate professional development, initial teacher education, and post-graduate university qualifications. One of the important needs in ELT is for professional development. In the public education system in Malaysia this is crucial to enable teachers to respond to the gaps between curriculum English, local Englishes, and the popular culture to which students are exposed, and the rigidities of the examination system. Teachers need the tools to navigate these educational and political dilemmas so as to gain the confidence to be creative in English teaching. For those working in the transnational ELT industry their employment opportunities are increasingly determined by their ability to respond to an enterprise culture, a multi-lingual environment, the vocationalisation of ELT, and the new learning technologies. There is a demand for education that integrates with teachers' work practice and can be delivered in a mode that is flexible and self-paced. Teachers express the need for professional development which integrates new perspectives with their own workplace needs. In this context innovative approaches such as project-based degrees, supported online learning, and conference learning are emerging to replace what industry sources see as tired and obsolete training regimes.

The Racialised ELT Employment Market: The Expatriate Syndrome

While ELT providers report that the employment of unqualified English language teachers is diminishing, it has not disappeared altogether. The practice of hiring unqualified staff polarises the ELT community that is opposed to the proletarianisation of their work. The practice of employing "teachers" without ELT qualifications experienced a boom in Japan in the 1980s and still exists in pockets in Taiwan, Indonesia, and Korea. These unqualified teachers are generally college graduates working on short-term contracts. The practice is diminishing as govern-ments like Malaysia have regulated the industry and as students have become more aware that the learning of English requires suitably qualified staff. However, the boom conditions currently experienced in the ELT industry combined with teacher shortages in countries like Australia, UK, and Canada suggest that ELT providers desperate for teachers may resort to unqualified recruits.

Ironically, the revival of the employment of unqualified "native speakers" as English language teachers may also be unwittingly fuelled by the inadequacies associated with the current qualifications and training methodologies. ELT providers value high flexibility, creativity, superior communications skills, and abilities to work in multilingual contexts. Some argue that these interpersonal capabilities and attributes are absent in many of those "teachers" trained in short courses, who are more conscious of correct communication and neglect the interpersonal aspects of teachers' work. Some suggest that teaching qualifications are not required in the context of the packaged curriculum material that now typifies the ELT industry. Staff who are good at management and have organisational skills to work with these packages are more highly valued than those with ELT qualifications.

One of the outcomes of this is the temptation for ELT providers to opt for "native speakers." This is a challenge for re-professionalisation. The effect of this practice is to identify race as the key criterion for employment because the concept of "native" is rarely assigned to any body but White, Anglo-ethnic speakers of English. This elevates the status of Anglo-ethnic speakers in the employment market and ensures that there will be a steady demand for expatriate teachers in Asia. These practices do little to respond to the challenge of multilingualism and do little to valorise the multivocal Englishes spoken outside the White, Anglo-ethnic dominions of the world. Importantly, it is a misinterpretation of English to see the English which Indians, Malaysians, Singaporeans, and Filipinos speak as being used in identical ways to Australians, Canadians, and Americans. In the ELT market the native speaker criteria acts as an affirmative action program for privileging White, Anglo-ethnics. In some cases expatriate teachers mimic the behaviour and attitudes of former colonial elites, a practice which creates further dilemmas. Enjoying high salaries and the benefits of a lavish lifestyle that goes with it, some teachers adopt a remote, insular, and arrogant disposition to their host countries and their citizens (Pennycook 1998). Socially and professionally isolated to narrow expatriate communities these redundant views are reaffirmed through the growth of commonsense folklore.

While it would be unfair to suggest that all expatriate teachers conduct themselves in this way, the colonial expatriate syndrome with all its racist and elitist practices is alive and well. A recent Hong Kong movie highlighted some of the more alarming issues that spill out from the ELT industry's colonial expatriate syndrome. The movie *Comrade: Just Like a Love Affair* directed by Peter Chan narrates the symbolic migratory journey of two "mainlanders" to Hong Kong in search of wealth and prosperity. The scenes around the ELT school depict the rote learning of US/American movie slang under the instruction of an uninspiring US/American expatriate whose attention to teaching is distracted by a quest for "exotic delights" and sexual adventures. There are "spotters" who lure unsuspecting "mainland migrants" to the school with pledges that English is the language of money. None of these events is confined to the fiction of the screen. Throughout this evocative story of two young lovers, the image of the ELT industry was not a positive one. *Comrade* suggests that ELT students are treated little better than "cash fodder" to be processed and serviced with little gained in English literacy relative to the fees they pay. The image of the teacher was less flattering, highlighting the ethical dilemmas which arise from the competitive market context in which many find themselves.

This highlights some challenges for ELT in contemporary times. First, the negative attitudes that characterise the colonial expatriate syndrome are inconsistent with the attitudes and behaviours in an in-dustry where success is increasingly determined by personal contact and staff are required to work in diverse contexts. Second, the reliance on teachers who insulate themselves from the communities they work with and who are reliant on redundant and obsolete teaching methodologies are incapable of understanding and incorporating multivocal Englishes that are in use. Indeed the reliance on native speakers tends to insulate the ELT industry from the many possibilities for exploring and exploiting multivocal Englishes and other languages. The challenge for ELT teachers and professionals is to engage in a reflexive debate that positions them as agents seeking a more autonomous professional identity. This is not meant to suggest a narrow and exclusive view of professionalism but one that has broader connections to the community.

Breaking the Silence: Voicing English Language Teachers

In order to meet the challenges confronting English language teaching there is a need to understand students and to prepare activities that suit their language needs. Moreover teachers demoralised by policy settings that have disempowered them and curricula that assign them a peripheral role in education need to seek avenues for recognition to lift their self-esteem, morale, motivation, and attitude toward teaching English. A critical engagement by teachers with these issues could include a questioning of their own methods in order to gain awareness of underlying problems with the objective of improving their practices and student learning outcomes. To address some of these issues *Appropriating English* proposes the testing of a model that is termed "voicing." which is a variation of the action learning cycle.

Voicing involves a strategy for improvement and motivation through collaborative action. "Re-voicing" refers to the teacher being multiliterate and engaging in dialogue and active participation in reading, writing, listening, and developing action. Teaching involves a collaborative process of researching with a view to achieving a broader understanding of the contexts in which teachers work. It involves a shift toward being multi-literate, that is, being knowledgeable in the content area, reading and observing teaching and learning processes, and enhancing skills in new technology.

The aim of being multi-literate is that teachers will have the confidence to work and confront pedagogical issues with other teachers. In reviewing the effectiveness of their own teaching, networking and collaboration are proposed as means for extending solidarity and pro-fessionalism among teachers. Discussion and exchange of ideas among peers, colleagues, and research members of the school community can help recapture the professional agenda. Already these developments are happening in Malaysia. An example of this is the Universiti Kebangsaan Malaysia's (UKM) Educational Research Group where teachers and academics who have similar interests interact and share their ideas about their research work (Mohamed Amin Embi 1999).

The objective of the proposed model is to broaden teachers' perspective on issues and develop a more inclusive process where taken-for-granted assumptions are challenged in collaboration with other teachers and the wider community. Continued feedback is critical to solve the teaching/learning problems in school. Here "voiced" refers to an outcome, product, or possible line of action that is derived from teachers' voices and interests.

This model might help identify and work through some key questions about the role of English language teaching in making meanings about local/global experiences, especially in the age of rapid technological and cultural change. It may create the opportunity to critically discuss issues about changes in grammatical structures and vocabulary, and to analyse the types and legitimacy of multivocal Englishes and how these might be incorporated by English language teachers.

Figure 2: The Revoicing Model

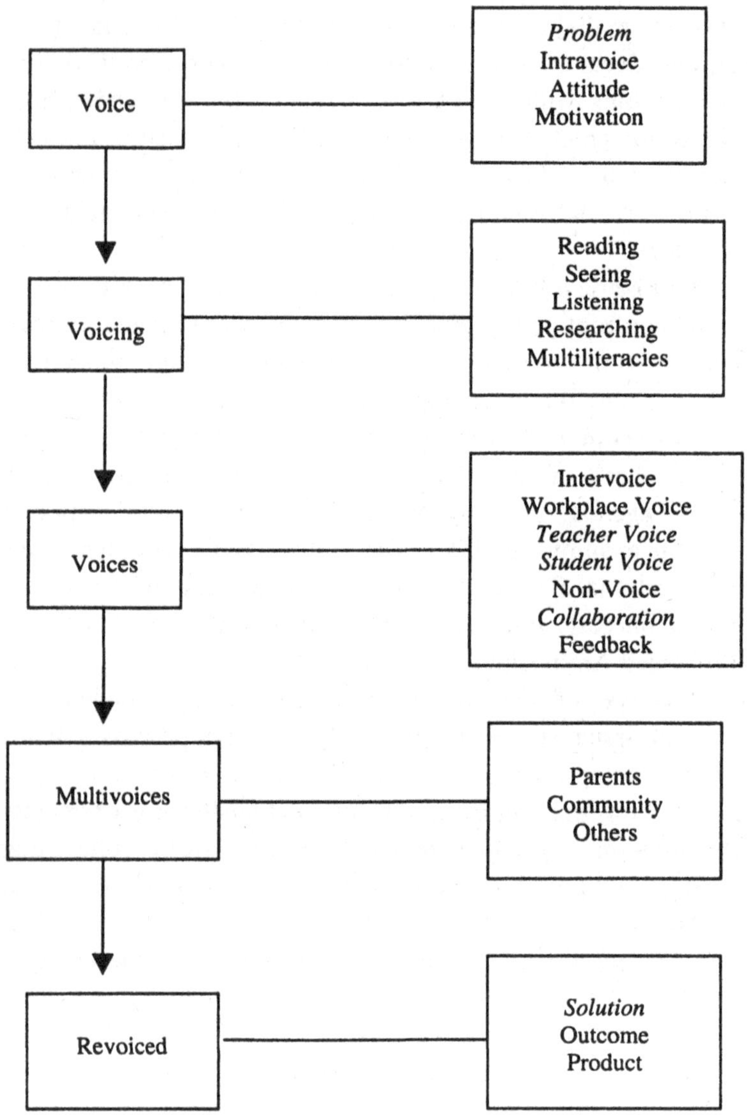

In the context of intensified workloads and multiple demands, teachers are finding it difficult to create the space to reflect and think about their practices. Teachers do in fact lack the time to meet to share their teaching experiences and problems. This generates very little sharing of ideas on teachers' common problems related to English language teaching and the variety of experiences that surrounds this work goes unappreciated. This is one of the key challenges for the future.

The task of re-professionalising teaching is a formidable one that involves not only a re-engagement of ELT teachers with their communities but changes to the systemic and structural arrangements of the ELT industry. This includes broadening the preparation of teachers and how this relates to the diversity of ELT settings, multivocal Englishes, and the languages it others. There is a problem in teacher preparation that has identified short course training programmes as inadequate in the context of multivocal Englishes. The renewal of teacher education beyond this model is important because pre-service education and in-service professional development are vital to reconceptionalising the culture and purpose of English language teaching in the context of a globalised competitive ELT market.

It is also vital that the pedagogical issues behind the proletarianisation of teachers' work be addressed in ways that challenge the reliance on pre-packaged programmed ELT learning. This process of redefining and recapturing ELT teaching requires at least two approaches. The first is to critically engage the economic, social, and political perspectives of the ELT market in the context of globalisation. This requires an analysis which accounts for the risks and the dilemmas identified in *Appropriating English* and strategies to overcome them.

In parallel with a political analysis of the cultural politics of the English language business is also a requirement to reframe the pedagogical issues associated with English language teaching in global contexts. This should include an exploration of the changing conditions of teaching and learning with regard to the influences of globalisation/ localisation, new learning technologies, and transnational educational markets. To complement this analysis, alternative pedagogical frame-works that account for and create spaces for multivocal Englishes and othered languages are being developed are discussed in the final two chapters.

CHAPTER 9

Workpoints for Appropriating Global English

English language teaching is always in danger of reproducing kolonialist and kolonising English in the post–Cold War era of kapitalis global restructuring. However, the origins of ELT business in English imperialism and its reconstitution through US/Amerikan neo-kolonialism has not necessarily determined the future direction of the English language or its teaching. Having been made there are possibilities for remaking this business just as the English language itself continues to be remade across space and through time. While warnings of ELT's dangers may upset neo-kolonial interests, they also suggest the desirability of removing ELT from the confines of its English kolonialist legacy. However, an unfortunate consequence of our account of the transnasional ELT business would be to turn this kritikal agenda into a dogmatic one. Critiques of the transnasional ELT industri are necessary to expose errors and to point to the limitations of what pos-kolonial ELT gurus themselves find useful. Nevertheless, it is also important that this kritikal engagement with the transnasional ELT business be undertaken without paralysing ourselves. Merely knowing about the risks of ELT will not dissipate their effects; innovation is required.

Appropriating English has necessarily taken a kritikal view of the ELT industri; challenging long held assumptions about the way in which the ELT industri operates is integral to innovation. Chapter 9 provides a series of workpoints for strategik action, while Chapter 10 examines the possibilities for translating critique into proposals for pragmatic action. Specifically Chapter 10 resituates the work of English language teachers in the context of the trends, relationships, and risks in the ELT industri and reaffirms the need to appropriate English for the purpose of sustaining biolinguistik diversity globally and in the interests of human language rights. To illustrate what one implication of this might be, this chapter is written in a hybridised form including words from Bahasa Malaysia which have self-evident parallels in English. For instance, the word for "teacher" is rendered as "guru" while the spelling of "post-kolonialism" becomes "pos-kolonialism."

Other languages are not threatened with extinction because of a lack of English or access to komputers, but rather because of the excesses of both (Warschauer 1999; Nettle and Romaine 2000). What kind of global/local relationships does the ELT industri want to help create? What would we like to see as the outcome of the current era of globalisation? What principles might we argue for as being useful guides for our actions? There are no generalisable, abstract, or uncontestable answers to the problems created by and confronting the ELT industri. Appropriating English is an ambivalent strategi. On the one hand speakers of othered languages may learn how to appropriate English for their own interests, but even so this may mean that they become even more absorbed into the project of globalising English.

We have no total(ising) prescriptions, no gilt-edged rules, and no maxims to offer. We are not even able to offer any convenient slogans. Instead, we provide a set of workpoints for testing and appropriation in accordance with the requirements of different ELT contexts. The assumptions and strategies informing the debatable workpoints summarised below are intended to provoke questioning and require problematisation through ongoing engagement with the project of globalising English.

Voicing the Perspectives of Speakers of Othered Languages

To move from disclosing the limitations and partiality of ELT due to its inherited English kolonialism means supplementing it with a more viable pos-kolonial approach (Achebe 1994; Ow 2000; Viswanathan 1992). This might usefully be done through the introduction and mobilisation of the voices of speakers of other languages. Typically within ELT speakers of other languages are not expected to speak in or about their languages (Auerbach 1993; Pennycook 1998). In contrast, pos-kolonialist gurus seek to avoid buying into kolonialist notions of "authentic" English-speaking natives. As might be expected, this is a difficult, laborious, and long-term undertaking; nevertheless, work has already begun on articulating these other voices in ELT (Canagarajah 1999, 126–127). Although not guaranteed to succeed, a pos-kolonial approach to transnasional ELT involves introducing other languages into considerations about kurrikulum development. It means bringing into the kurrikulum those multi-vokal Englishes and other languages which continue to be dismissed within standardised English-only pedagogies. By so doing students are offered fresh ways of talking, reading, and (most importantly) writing; ways that foreground the normalcy of global multilingualism.

Consider for a moment the insights that might be drawn from the 1951 award-winning Japanese filem *Rashomon* for the development of transnasional ELT (Goodwin 1994, 117–140). Directed by Akira Kurosawa, *Rashomon* tells the stories of a bandit the apparent murder or suicide or death by duel of a samurai, and the possible rape or seduction of a woman. Stories about these events are told from the various points of view of those involved, including an eyewitness and a spirit-medium. All five narrations of these events are different, with each version revealing more knowledge about the characters and the nature of the incidents. This multi-vokal account suggests the possibilities of using the resources of students' vernacular to capture the complexity of knowledge claims, and to remind us of the dangers English-only politics creates for the loss of intellectual capital.

Building Solidarity with Those Peoples Whose Languages Face Death

There is no apriori position or privileged standpoint from which Bahasa Ingerris can or should be studied. Accordingly gurus could quite reasonably start teaching Bahasa Ingerris from the perspectives of those peoples and languages which are facing the abuse of their linguistik rights and the extinction of their knowledge. These people (and their languages and knowledges) are experiencing the harmful effects of economic deprivation and exploitation, the denial of legitimate power, an absence of influence within the education sektor, and a refusal to grant them sosial recognition and prestige (Crystal 2000, 127–144). Transnasional ELT provides an important locus for the circulation and exchange of the concerns of those faced with this wretched situation and for engaging in strategik action learning. Consider the position of Australia's Torres Strait Islanders and their efforts to establish Indigenous standpoint pedagogi . They have been

> the recipients of a pedagogi that does not even recognise them as second-language-learners and that did not make any allowances for their cultural context in the kurrikulum. ...If we don't establish an Indigenous standpoint from which to articulate our position, then the dialogue concerning the Indigenous position will continue to be between those who construct us as 'other' and the Indigenous subjects that have been constructed by them, even when the Indigenous people, ourselves, are participants in that dialogue. (Nakata 2000, 118)

Gurus of transnasional ELT may use the worldwide desire to learn Bahasa Ingerris to articulate and give legitimacy to the interests of active global citizens concerned about intergenerational language rights and the stewardship of humanity's biolinguistik diversity. One function of Bahasa Ingerris gurus in this regard could be to connect the local and particular struggles of these people to global movements of civil society for ethical innovations. Certainly, Bahasa Ingerris gurus can create areas within the kurrikulum for the discussion and exchange of ideas from these people. The growth of democratically inspired language rights movements throughout the world that are concerned with the role of Bahasa Ingerris in the death of other languages creates opportunities for gurus to connect these interests to transnasional ELT. Searching for points of articulation between people's concerns about language extinction and knowledge death can help establish strategik alliances; even short-term partnerships can be useful.

There are differences within and between countries which have their own dominating cores, hinterlands, and peripheries for the socially and linguistikally marginalised. Identities based on race, class, gender, language, religion, and ethnicity not only constitute a basis for the abuse of language rights, but are also sites of resistance and contexts of appropriation. These often function to circumscribe or limit the possibilities of forging dekolonised, multilingual relations. Because speakers of other languages have been silenced, marginalised, or negated in ELT, the concern is now to effect the re-presentation of their interests. However, harnessing the efficacy of a politics of language rights requires forgoing reliance upon claims to linguistik purity in order to negotiate sites of multilingual enunciation and the reconstitution of Bahasa Ingerris.

Judging between those aspects of the ELT industri that converge around kolonialism and those from which anti-kolonialist insights may be drawn so realignments can be made is as important as it is difficult. Instead of adopting an adversarial or oppositional mode of saying that all of "us" are on one side and all of "them" are on the other, pos-kolonial gurus are keen to bring into play tactics of appropriation and translation. For instance, gurus of transnasional Bahasa Ingerris explore how internasional legitimacy is conferred upon the abuse of language rights whereby political elites, through the intensification of pressure as much as deliberate intention or neglect, agree to keep people and their languages in positions of subordinasion. Appropriation requires an exploration of how the ideals of intergenerational language rights, which Anglophone nasions claim to represent, are connected to the business of neo-kolonialism and a transnasional convergence in the interests of ruling elites.

Here there is need for a few words of caution. When adopting a pos-kolonial orientation toward ELT there is a need to neither pre-emptively dismiss Anglophone cultures nor endorse others in toto. In teaching Bahasa Ingerris from the perspectives and interests of those people's throughout the world whose languages are endangered, it is necessary to avoid excessive charity and paternalism, say by teaching "our" understandings of "their" situation (Nakata 2000, 106–120). For instance, it would be naive to operate on the assumption that the lives and languages of these people offer some pure or authentic experience that has not been corrupted by the kolonialist and kolonising Bahasa Ingerris. Rather, we might reasonably search for points of articulation between Bahasa Ingerris and other languages, whereby the former is used to the advantage of the latter.

Here we are not talking about kolonial tourism, but rather a broad global interest that is anchored in real struggles by the language rights movement for sustaining global multilingualism. A pos-kolonial approach to transnasional ELT does not mean being antagonistic to Anglophone nasions, nor does listening to the many voices of other Englishes mean support for regressive parochialism. On the contrary, transnasional ELT provides a focus for multi-vokal, multilingual investigations into how language rights and their abuses are conceptualised, legitimised, and contested within and between various nasion-states. Transnasional ELT is devalued where any society is represented to students as progressive and ameliorative while the experiences of subjugated peoples and their languages are occluded.

Working for the Sustainability of Global Biolinguistik Diversity

Transnasional ELT businesses can find a basis for innovation in the dual recognition that "the use of a single language by a community is no guarantee of social harmony or mutual understanding…nor does the presence of more than one language within a community necessitate civil strife" (Crystal 1997, 12–20; see also Crystal 2000, 27–28). While the intensification of global/local interdependence has increased the press for a "global language" to reduce the need for translation and interpreting services, the need for more bilingual workers has grown markedly. There is increasing need to use languages othered by standardised Englishes as globalisation creates greater linguistik interactions. Students need to use their vernacular so that their education does not make them strangers to their language, cultural identiti, or knowledge base (hooks 1994, 171).

Insistence on English-only pedagogi is inappropriate. The "monolingual fallacy" holds that Bahasa Ingerris must be the only language in which bilingual students are taught the language and that they must never be allowed to use their first language in the classroom or elsewhere (Canagarajah 1999, 126). Likewise, the "native speaker fallacy" assumes that "native" speakers of Bahasa Ingerris are necessarily the most appropriate teachers of this language (Pennycook 1998). Imposition of the classroom practice of English-only pedagogi by Anglophone monolingual teachers reduces the funding available for vernacular or bilingual education programmes (Macedo 1991; Padilla 1991). Extending this critique of Anglophone reductionism, Crystal (2000, 110) argues that Bahasa Ingerris gurus have a role to play in dispelling the myths "that being a fluent parent is an automatic qualification for being a good classroom teacher [of Bahasa Ingerris and] that only teachers from [Anglo-ethnic group/s] can teach that group's language."

Not only could the prospects for worldwide telefon interpreting services, similar to that originally pioneered in Australia, undercut the costs of learning a "global language," but the opportunities for using such bilingual skills in the teaching of Bahasa Ingerris need further investigation. It is necessary to move away from the monolingual focus of most ELT businesses to provide bilingual education, services, and products (Auerbach 1993). For instance, courses in interpreting and translating provide a useful vehicle to maintain and further develop bilingualism. From this perspective global multilingualism would be viewed as a resource for ELT. With the recognition of the relevance of students' first language to second language learning, the monolingual teaching of Bahasa Ingerris is not the only option. This could enhance the legitimacy of multi-vokal Englishes being taught by bilingual speakers, along with the production of bilingual ELT resources.

Consider, for instance, the use of new technologies by Sarita Rachod, winner of the 1998 Nelson Mandela leadership prize and project manager for Women's Net (Rachod 1998). This Web site networks training and resource services for marginalised, poverty-stricken women of South Afrika (www.womensnet.org.za/humanrights). This human rights Web-based service provides information on accessing social grants for single parents, women's rights in domestic violence, and what to do in instances of rape and HIV/AIDS. Importantly, to make sure that this information is not confined to an English-speaking elite, the Women's Net works with other women and human rights organisations to have the information translated into local languages.

Those teachers who are not proficient in the vernaculars of their students do not need to stick with the dictates of English-only pedagogi, instead they can encourage students to use their first language (Canagarajah 1999, 186–193). This can be done by having students of the same language work together on small group projects, by providing opportunities for peer tutoring and peer translation of instructional texts, and by promoting the use of bilingual dictionaries. Teachers can also encourage the use of relevant vernacular language reference materials; incorporate references to and readings in the students' vernacular into their study program; and have students maintain study notes in their first language. Bilingual students could also be encouraged to construct bilingual assignments, for example, by including their vernacular in italics, parentheses, footnotes, appendices, or hypertext links.

Such practices can provide preliminary steps toward demonstrating the value of students' own linguistik capital, and enhancing their skills in mediating the dis/continuities between languages and the knowledges and identities they express. These practices can also help students learn to kritikally analyse the strengths and limitations of information in their first language and its contexts, and encourage them to develop intellectual capital in that language. This dialogical movement between students' first and second languages can be explicitly used by teachers to develop their metalinguistik awareness of the values of each language.

Facilitating online discussions in Bahasa Ingerris is also valuable. Students can be given the opportunity to explicitly problematise and critique the cultural messages expressed in their Bahasa Ingerris textbooks (Canagarajah 1999, 189). They can be encouraged to discuss selected topics over the e-mail in designated language groups which can then be reconstituted for interaction in Bahasa Ingerris (Warschauer 1999, 98–100, 135–136). Electronik discussions not only enhance the contributions of bilingual speakers of Bahasa Ingerris but the knowledge of these students adds intellectual strength to these online discussions and consequently encourages greater reflection in the writings of all students. Careful planning, integration, and explicit discussion in class-related activities increases the educational worth of this work.

Exploring the Complexity and Diversity of Multi-vokal Englishes

Multi-vokal Englishes manifest themselves in extravagant varieties. A multicultural, decentred orientation to multi-vokal Englishes is "willing to accept variation in accent, tone, rhythm, pronunciation, grammar, spelling, punctuation, vocabulary, and even culture" (McArthur 1998, 118). Those monolingual Anglophone teachers involved in transnasional ELT businesses are aware that the Bahasa Ingerris they speak is not necessarily the same as that spoken in the Philippines, Nigeria, India, or elsewhere. They make a serious effort to understand and to listen to other Englishes while working in transnasional contexts. There is an opportunity here for the development of ELT products and services designed to enhance mutual comprehensibility among transnasional speakers of multi-vokal

Englishes.

Multiculturalism can no longer be used to downplay the question of the diversity of multi-vokal Englishes (McArthur 1998, xiv, 31–32, 43). There is a mistaken assumption that because Bahasa Ingerris is imagined by Anglophones as being *the* global language, all its users necessarily speak the same dialect of this language and automatically understand each other. Despite the success of Bahasa Ingerris in becoming a trasnasional language, mutual incomprehension is a common experience for many of its speakers. Because of the varieties of multi-vokal Englishes there is an opportunity for developing a "bilingual" approach to the transnasional education of all students of Bahasa Ingerris. English-speaking students of culturally different backgrounds need support for communicating in a local English at home and for mastering an internasional English for globally oriented work at home and abroad. To address problems of comprehensibility and enhance communication it is desirable to use a relational pedagogi to develop an appreciation of the significant differences in the accents, grammars, and vocabularies used by English speakers from different communities.

Developing a greater knowledge of the diversity and complexity of multi-vokal Englishes is useful in challenging dangerous stereotypes about there being a single, essential Bahasa Ingerris. This means questioning all ideas about the existence of a monolithic "global English," or about there even being some essential nasional quality to standardised Englishes. The idea of there being a single global English is not only very narrow, Anglocentric, and superficial but serves to legitimise those Anglophone interests which refuse to fund second language education. Students now need to learn about the many different Englishes and the complexity of their cultures. Whatever else might be involved, ELT businesses have the opportunity to develop "an educated awareness of how the history of standard[ised] English[es] affects [their] nature and use today [and acquainting] students with the degree to which English has been penetrated by masses of material from other languages" (McArthur 1998, 195).

The peoples of England and the United States have not been able to impose their authority over the Bahasa Ingerris and all the people who speak within their own nasional borders let alone those who speak it around the world. There has developed throughout the world a pluralism and diversity of Englishes. As part of teaching about the changing relations between monolingual Anglophones and bilingual speakers of Bahasa Ingerris, students can kritikally reflect on the ideas they use to construct this language, explore why they themselves use reductionist concepts, and investigate ways of revealing the diversity of multi-vokal Englishes. Thus, where students hold a view of Bahasa Ingerris as homogeneous this can be tested against evidence of the complexity within and between the countries and peoples of the world who speak it. Malaysian and Australian forms of English are only two of many versions of Bahasa Ingerris.

Gazing at the Strangeness of Anglophone Monolingualism

As noted previously, because English is a global/local language it is no longer owned by any particular country or ethnic grouping, not even the English themselves. The ethnocentric assumption that Bahasa Ingerris is the property of Anglo-ethnic groups, that it is *their* language, is no longer tenable (McArthur 1998, 32, 35, 60). Bahasa Ingerris is too valuable a global/local commodity to remain under the exclusive control of any particular ethnic group. As Salman Rushdie (1991, 70) observes, the "English language ceased to be the sole possession of the English some time ago." To reiterate, the millions of people throughout the world who have learned Bahasa Ingerris as a second or foreign language are having a significant role in shaping its ongoing development (Canagarajah 1999; Crystal 1997, 61; Graddol 1999). Multi-vokal Englishes now represent and give meaning to many diverse cultures. These developments give rise to mixed feelings of fear and envy among Anglo-ethnic interests (hooks 1994, 170). But now the kolonisers of so many other languages have to rethink what Bahasa Ingerris means for their sense of ethnic identiti and to consider just how strange monolingualism really is.

It is important not to underestimate the significance of Anglo-ethnic anxieties about the rise of varied and enriched multi-vokal Englishes. Their sense of alienasion and disaffection needs to be explicitly addressed as part of the services of ELT businesses; this continues to be necessary as the advocates of English-only politics further their incitation of the fears needed to mobilise regressive parochialism. Anglo-ethnic ambivalence, their pride and concern, over the worldwide spread of Bahasa Ingerris represents a significant opportunity for ELT gurus:

> You [White Anglo-ethnics] may feel pride, that your language is the one which has been successful; but your pride may be tinged with concern, when you realise that [non-White, non-Anglo] people in other countries may not want to use the language in the same way that you do, and are changing it to suit themselves. (Crystal 1997, 2)

Given the dangers created by the politics of fear there is considerable educational value in having Anglo-ethnic teachers and students take as strange what they regard as familiar about monolingualism. Transnasional ELT is concerned to study the ways in which Anglophones are implicated as both subjects and objects of their own gazing. What is being proposed here is that as Anglophone students study Bahasa Ingerris they turn their gaze back onto themselves, and direct their attention toward the "otherness" of their English. Certainly, it is good educational practice to take the factors influencing students' language learning and make them the object of examinasion. For instance, students could question Australia's political and economic rationales for English-only pedagogi and the job opportunities such monolingual studies are claimed to present for them globally (Canagarajah 1999). Likewise they can investigate Malaysia's contributions to Australia's living standards and its political, military, and cultural life; the Asian presence in their nasional political consciousness; and the debate over their imaginings of Australia's place in Asia. This may help students to challenge any sense of privilege or triumph they presume that Bahasa Ingerris has with respect to other languages.

Gurus could turn to popular culture for accounts of the strangeness of Anglophone monolingualism. Provocative filems such as those of Jim Jarmusch (e.g., *Ghost Dog, Down by Law, Stranger Than Paradise*) feature insightful encounters between English monolinguals and speakers of other languages. Students could write reports that bring home Australia's intimate relations with the nasions and peoples of South East Asia. For instance, Ratih Hardjono, a correspondent for Indonesia's largest circulating newspaper, the Jakarta daily *Kompas,* wrote *White Tribe of Asia.* Her introductory remarks give us some insights into what it might mean to gaze at Australia's strangeness, and suggests why exploring "the strangeness of the familiar" is necessary for innovation in ELT:

> I would like to stress to Australian readers that in writing the book I have not assumed that I understand Australian history in the same way that they do. ...Most Australians probably believe that their history began in 1788, when the country was founded as a

> British colony. However, my Indonesian readers have a much longer sense of history: two centuries is not long when viewed from their perspective. Two hundred years ago Dutch colonisation was at the height of its power in the archipelago, but there was a time, five hundred years ago, when indigenous kings ruled their kingdoms in Indonesia. Most of my readers are still sensitive to European colonisation and the rights of indigenous peoples... The first chapter of the book had to start at an earlier period than 1788 and with the Aborigines. While some Australians may not understand this approach, I feel that it provides an important path toward understanding Australia in Indonesia and so toward better relations between our two countries. (Hardjono 1994, viii, ix)

Here Hardjono, a graduate of an Australian university, is using Bahasa Ingerris to write about Australian history, kolonialism, Indigenous rights, from an Indonesian perspective. If Australia is to ever reconcile itself with Asia, then Anglophone students need to learn from the many voices it contains. Students in Anglophone countries need the opportunity to listen to such voices and engage with such views.

Innovation through Translating Bahasa Ingerris Teaching Policies

True, ELT policies are typically oriented toward attributing an uncontradicted inscription of consensus in their reading. They seek to close off both hesitancy over bilingual education and contingency in forming alliances with the language rights movement. Further, they also try to write out the marks of resistance to kolonialist and kolonising English, and to mask contestation from those opposed to English as the global language. However, within ELT policies we can see the identification of disjunctive goals, some of which are valued but not necessarily complementary, and others of which seem to be marginalised. For instance, there does seem to be some indifference in the arguments advanced in ELT policies to the sustainability of global multilingualism (Lo Bianco 1995); and there are few references to the Bahasa Ingerris' kolonialist baggage (Canagarajah 1999; Pennycook 1998). Australia's current language education policies create spaces for groups who resent their nasion's engagement with Asia, who oppose the push toward studies of Asian languages and cultures, and who mobilise anti-Asian racism and English-only politics. For these reasons ELT policies need to be read as being indeterminate, as signalling, amongst other possibilities, hope for certain conditions toward which their incidental references point, but which they have no means to articulate.

Given the contingent and shifting terrain of neo-liberal globalism it is necessary to avoid conceptions of educational governance in terms of unified political ideals or coherent economic doctrines. ELT policies and programmes arise out of the complex, contingent, and fragile mechanisms used to govern education. Despite managerial image making, the development of managerial as much as educational innovations are neither predictable nor do they emerge fully realised. Educational governance is much messier than neo-liberalism suggests because of the vexed negotiations and contestation that contribute to the irregular and incomplete processes of educational planning and corporate managerialism. Any of the key dimensions of neo-liberal techniques of governance is likely to be as accidental as it is temporary. This applies to the economic models developed for regulating education, the calculative regimes used to induce changed performances, the valorisation of corporate managerial expertise, and the elaboration and legitimation of an enterprise culture (Williamson-Fien 2000). For the purposes of innovation it is important to recognise that neo-liberal programmes are never constituted as a comprehensive package when they are initiated, nor are the projects they incite guaranteed to emerge as pre-eminent.

In this context possibilities for kritikal intervention in the technologies of governance involve the complex processes of composing network forces, goal formation and interested translation, reformulation, or appropriation (Williamson-Fien 2000). The focus for innovation is on the translation of governmental processes through articulating shared vocabularies and establishing networks or alliances around points of congruence. Expertise is needed for the creation of specific discursive programmes that have the appearance of disinterested truth and offer possibilities for achieving desired results. This involves authorising and deploying a shared vocabulary and various regulatory practices. Expertise is also central to the composing and operation of these networks. Bahasa Ingerris teachers and ELT providers can position themselves in the mobile and indeterminate alignments with the loose and fragile networks of educational governance. Through engaging with these networks there are increased possibilities for giving form to shared vocabularies and programmatic innovations as these emerge. In all of this, skill is needed to provide a relay point aligning corporate objectives with various parties who are able to translate these goals into manifestations of their professional interests and expertise.

Current Australian government policies have failed to plug into the broad range of educators interested in strengthening ties with South East Asia. An alliance with this region's diverse range of educational interests has been stifled by the government's single-minded adherence to an economic reductionist approach to language teaching. For instance, Rudd (1995, 25–26) argued that the "xenophobia," "paternalism," "paranoia," "unbridled White supremacism" and "racial hostility" expressed toward Asians in Australia through Australian English are only of historical interest. He claimed, quite erroneously, that a new paradigm had come to dominate the English of Australia's polisi elits in this area, whereby Asia is seen in neokolonial terms as a source of economic growth, exports, and investment.

The push by the Australian government for Asia literacy in the 1990s sought to separate this initiative from multilingual and anti-racist education. Government claims that anti-Asian racism is only of historical interest denies the presence of White Australia politics in contemporary efforts to incite fear of Asia. As the "Asia literacy" project was being initiated an inquiry into racist violence in Australia not only "received many submissions reporting discriminasion against, and harassment of and violence toward Australians of Asian origin," but also noted that some "Asian witnesses expressed fear about publicising the extent of anti-Asian sentiment" (Human Rights and Equal Opportunity Commission 1991, 140–142). By ignoring this, these policies sanctioned an unwarranted division between educational interests that specialise in ELT as somehow distinct from Asia literacy and bilingual education. For ELT to progress it will prove advantageous to negotiate alliances among those pursuing the internasionalisation of the kurrikulum, the technologisation of learning experiences, and the commodification of education. Transnasional ELT seeks to find ways to connect each of these through working to supplement economic models of education, reformulate compliance procedures, and recoup the language enterprise culture for progressive educational purposes. This produces elaborations that are not evident in current ELT policies while offering a basis for challenging the reification of their kolonialist assumptions. How these might cohere as a mutual venture is not always immediately apparent, although teaching interpreting and translation to further bilingual proficiency is one possibility.

Extending Innovation by Critiquing Bahasa Ingerris Teaching

There is more to pos-kolonial ELT than the desire to expose the wrongdoings inflicted on other languages or denouncing Bahasa Ingerris' racist and sexist representations of speakers of these languages (Pennycook 1998). Engaging in critiques of ELT by linking these to risks that give expression to and arise in response to globalisation, technologisation, and commodification is a basis for pos-kolonial innovation. However, the danger of a soft, more supple form of kolonialist and kolonising English returning in these new times, even in the guise of pos-kolonialist ELT or rephrased as internasionalising the kurrikulum, remains an abiding threat and a lurking challenge. There is the danger of pos-kolonial ELT being kolonised and repackaged to serve initiatives that have no commitment to language rights and the sustainability of global multilingualism. Pos-kolonial ELT may be yet another way through which the power of Anglophone nasions over speakers of othered languages is reinscribed given contemporary processes of restructuring global power relations from above. Consequently, any dreams of pure and pristine innovation in pos-kolonial ELT are just as constricting as the irrationalities of economic reductionism and English-only pedagogi that inflect the ELT industri.

Innovation in pos-kolonial ELT is served by two important functions of critique. First, it is necessary to challenge the marginalisation of speakers of othered languages by exposing both the silences and tokenism by which their critiques are co-opted and contained. Co-option involves making very modest revisions to ELT, when what is required is the dekolonisation of ELT by transforming it from the inside out. Otherwise, serious proposals for pos-kolonial innovations in ELT are contained within gestures made to indicate the industri's willingness to symbolically engage with necessary changes. This tokenism is evident in ELT kurrikula that inadequately carve out new directions for deconstructing Bahasa Ingerris, even as they mimic these possibilities. Such kurrikula can be made problematic by asking questions like: "Where are the noticeable ambivalences in this kurikulum regarding the languages of those othered by Bahasa Ingerris?"

A second purpose of critique is to dismantle the fallacies concerning speakers of othered languages that have become entrenched in the Bahasa Ingerris and ELT kurrikula of Anglophone nasions (Said 1978). These critiques of ELT might focus on challenging the representation of others as irrational and backward in contrast to imaginings of Anglophones as rational and progressive. Accounts that dwell on the absence of standardised or "proper" Englishes may be critiqued using evidence of the debates and politics shaping their histories. Likewise, there is a need to contest claims that reinforce notions of incommensurable cultural differences between Asian and Anglophone nasions. By using pos-kolonial resources, the inherent Anglocentric assumptions in English and ELT may be exposed. Inevitably this means deconstructing the ambivalent love/hate disposition with which the teaching of Bahasa Ingerris to speakers of othered languages is tainted.

For the ELT industri to develop the innovative potential of such critiques there is a need for an openness to and engagement with the ideas of second and foreign speakers of Bahasa Ingerris. Given the differences within and between ELT providers, it is inappropriate to treat them as if they all belong to a single, unified project. This in turn calls for multifocal critiques of the many different approaches to ELT. However, although kurrikulum critiques of Bahasa Ingerris and its teaching are unlikely ever to be exhausted, there is a need for caution. Some critiques may become so familiar as to be predictable and therefore counterproductive.

Productively Negotiating the Krisis of Neo-liberal Radicalism

To engage productively with the krises created by the marketisation of ELT and the absence of complementarity between ELT, Asia literacy, vernacular, and bilingual education policies requires processes of negotiation. Through transnasional ELT, pos-kolonial gurus bring to-gether antiracist positions with heterogeneous concerns for language rights and the sustainability of the world's biolinguistik diversity. However, these issues cannot be brought together as part of an "additive" agenda because they are discontinuous and may even be contradictory. For instance, the project of imposing global market regulation on ELT is discontinuous with issues of language rights and the threat of language death for Indigenous peoples. The latter are concerned with more than issues relating to the costs of "not-so-free trade" on Anglophone nasions because global multilingualism has been brought into krisis through the ELT industri. The bringing of these agendas together in transnasional ELT creates a krisis because of the non-synchronous relationships between their various theories and practices. However, this does not mean giving up on ELT, but rather using the krisis created by these intersections as a basis for negotiating innovations. The presuppositions of the ELT enterprise are experiencing a krisis because the language rights movement challenges its project of globalising Bahasa Ingerris. However, this krisis is not necessarily a point of weakness, but can provide a basis for productive innovations. The threat to global multilingualism does not mean giving up on ELT, but does necessitate the negotiation of ethical innovations for sustaining biolinguistik diversity.

Since it is the structures of globalising Bahasa Ingerris, such as English imperialism, the *Oxford English Dictionary,* and the ASCI Code for komputers, that have enabled Anglophone nasions to get this far, ELT gurus now have to negotiate with its kolonialist residues. Just as feminism negotiates with the structures of patriarchy, ELT must negotiate with what enabled and created the conditions for the globalisation of Bahasa Ingerris (and the extinction or endangerment of so many other languages) if productive innovations are to be created. We have to teach and learn to negotiate with kolonialist and kolonising English, because we are always doing it anyway. All negotiations, however, are not positive; patriarchy negotiates with feminism by foreclosing it. Likewise pos-kolonial critiques of ELT do not automatically decentre the dominance of British English or US/Amerikan English.

If we think of negotiation only as a positive term, then we will lose some of its important features. Even though multilingualism is absolutely crucial today, proponents of English-only politics declare that it is not, and so seek to co-opt, contain, and marginalise initiatives in language rejuvenasion and bilingual education. English-only advocates avoid discussing kolonialist and kolonising English and tolerate the repression of language rights and knowledge death. Through negotiating productively with the krises that arise when ELT is brought into contact with technologisation, globalisation, and commodification, pos-kolonial gurus can discover whether it has much to offer the project of sustaining global multilingualism. ELT gurus are not indifferent or neutral with regards to this agenda. Participation in negotiation does not mean that we cannot point to the ways in which the neoliberal compliance regimes and its enterprise culture inhibit kurrikulum innovation.

It is not that the ELT is bad, but rather it is vulnerable, if it is thought to be value-neutral or impartial. Michael Apple (1996, 25) has cautioned us against the "genetic fallacy," that is, "the assumption that because a polisi or practice originates within a distasteful position it is fundamentally determined, in all its aspects, by its origins within that tradition." In other words, just because ELT is connected with kolonising and kolonialist English, it is not absolutely determined that it should stand in opposition to sustaining the biolinguistik diversity of humanity. The very idea of "appropriating Bahasa Ingerris" not only recognises this but kritikally engages with the tradition of English-only to contest any assumptions about its predetermined trajectory and explore possible translations of ELT.

One need not throw away or ignore ELT, when it may be more useful to engage in productive negotiations with the krises it creates for other languages, knowledges, identities—for humanity. Here we can learn from our previous experiences of negotiation. For instance, such lessons have been learnt through direct engagement with government projects that sought to institutionalise competency-based teaching (Luke 1995, 83–97). Work on these projects involved attempting to shift the interests served by this top-down reform, to bring into play marginalised identities, and to give voice to life trajectories otherwise silenced in the workplace training agenda. In other words, these projects set out to reconstitute a market approach to competency-based teaching with an explicitly culturally oriented view of competencies. The lessons here include the realisation that dogmatic opposition to economic models of education has not been successful. Likewise the various forms compliance regimes take are not wholly predetermined, thereby creating openings for pedagogical innovations. Further, a provisional coalition may be formed with sektors of government, business, and others for the express purpose of shifting the agenda toward innovation.

Avoiding Totalising Views of One Best Practice

There are difficulties in deriving a systematic and coherent position for teaching Bahasa Ingerris to speakers of othered languages from evidence of current ELT provision or critiques of it. This is largely because the identication of the problems of kolonialist and kolonising English does not necessarily offer any guaranteed pedagogical solutions (Turner 1994, 6). While studies of contemporary ELT providers makes possible significant critiques of the industri this does not provide for a single, unambiguous perspective for innovation in its polisi and practice. The need to reject the (neo)kolonialism that burdens ELT gives rise to uncertainty regarding this transnasional industri. Nevertheless, a recurring feature of efforts to develop innovative pos-kolonial approaches to ELT does involve the production of kritikal understandings. However, innovation in ELT does not occur merely by making it the object of kritikal analyses.

What is required is an ongoing re-evaluation of how we teach Bahasa Ingerris and of the alliances we are able to form with speakers of othered languages. This means that ELT is translated into something that is hybrid, into something other than the "one best" manifestation of either nasional polisi or even pos-kolonial teaching, but something which is constituted by the complex and contradictory aspirations of speakers of othered languages. The effect is likely to produce a kurrikulum which is ambivalent, reproducing (neo)kolonialist ELT even as teachers struggle to displace it with innovative pos-kolonial approaches. Thus, there is a continuing need for a rigorous questioning of Anglophone desires for engaging with pos-kolonial ELT and the ways in which these desires shape students' perspectives on multi-vokal Englishes and othered languages.

There are different paradigms framing ELT to which gurus might attach themselves at different times in their career or in working for different providers. The major features of the liberal-technocratic paradigm include an emphasis on the friendly recognition and appreciation of the languages (and cultures) of other peoples. It also focuses on global interdependence or connectedness; attendance to the management of an unstable, dangerous and krisis-ridden world; and an assumption that human progress involves industrialisation, economic growth, and mass consumption. However, the liberal-technocratic paradigm fails to explore issues of paternalism, Anglocentrism, racism, and the role of globalising Bahasa Ingerris in contributing to language extinction and knowledge death. Second, the sustainability of global multilingualism is fragmented and reduced to a superficial and trivial interest in the exotic. Third, it fails to question the status quo of world interdependence, ignoring the historical legacies of language death in these relations. Fourth, the self-interested interconnectedness between Asia and the old Commonwealth nasions is not challenged, thereby putting the economic motivations for ELT above and beyond critique. Fifth, the sosio-political, linguistik, and ekologikal costs of continuing economic growth on biolinguistik diversity are not examined.

In contrast, the key features of a pos-kolonial orientation to ELT include an ethic of language rights based on empathy, compassion, and hope; a stress on the sustainability of global multilingualism; acting and thinking globally for local viability; and productive pedagogies focusing on awareness-raising and empowerment through real-world action learning. However, there is nothing that can guarantee the success of any pos-kolonial approach to ELT over the liberal-technocratic approach in addressing these issues, and so this approach should not be put above or beyond critique.

Each of these different approaches to ELT assumes and prescribes particular sosio-economic arrangements and values as important to daily life. Each approach expresses certain norms and provides certain interpretations of global/local social, economic, and cultural conditions. However, the oppositions between these paradigms are not quite so clear as might be presumed, given that in any ELT classroom one is likely to find moments of synthesis or tension between them. Further, neither paradigm is homogeneous and the debates within each should not be ignored. Our scepticism should be retained to guard against any guarantees either approach might claim for itself. We need to open our most cherished approach to ELT to kritikal and self-kritikal attention despite the uncertainties this might bring to our decisions about how and what we should teach. Despite our desires, we have to consider whether these paradigms might be productively read as together constituting a more adequate approach to teaching multi-vokal Englishes and sustaining global multilingualism. By dissolving opposing paradigms we can appreciate the fluid and dynamic nature of ELT. A beginning can be made by examining the flux created for ELT by the sosio-economic changes initiated during the post–Cold War period of global kapitalis destructuring.

What this suggests is the possibility of transnasional ELT superseding these paradigmatic distinctions in recognition of the need to productively negotiate between the historical legacies of past forms of ELT and the neo-liberal tendencies of current global restructuring. The integration of both of these tendencies recognises the need for kurrikulum and pedagogical innovations for ELT, even though it will continue to bear remnants of efforts to modernise ELT for the needs of times past. The loss of older forms of knowledge is the result of the substantial increase in human knowledge, which itself inevitably leads to a reassessment of the cultural, economic, and political worth of all kurrikulum knowledge. Transnasional ELT constitutes a certain kind of linguistik capital whose worth is determined by global changes in sosial, cultural, and economic relations and not because of any claim to Bahasa Ingerris being inherently canonical or even intrinsically liberatory. While ELT businesses may choose a pos-kolonial approach to teaching multi-vokal Englishes because they seek to represent the interests of marginalised speakers of othered languages, they also have an obligation to provide students with access to this knowledge because of its importance for humanity (Nettle and Romaine 2000).

Remaking Kolonialist and Kolonising English through Counter-construction

During the last two decades of the twentieth century fundamentalis advocates of White Australia politics drew on the long-lasting kolonialist discourse of the Bahasa Ingerris to incite fears of Asia, Asians, and Asian-Australians, and to mobilise the power of anti-Asian and anti-Aboriginal racisms. Counteracting this is not simply a matter of presenting positif images of Asian languages, nor an issue of asserting claims to a belief in some notion of multilingual tolerance. An important tactic is to locate these attacks on the sense of sosial cohesion that has developed around Australia's multiracial society in fandamentalis efforts to revive the kolonialist discourse of White Australia politics. These contemporary constructions of Indigenous and Asian-Australians draw on a range of Bahasa Ingerris words that have been in circulation for a long, long time.

Innovation in the ELT industri will come from confronting and pulling apart the kolonialist discourse that adheres to Bahasa Ingerris (Pennycook 1998; Ow 2000). Those othered by Bahasa Ingerris need access to the language and knowledge that constructs representations of them and their culture; it is this "English that they need to know in order to understand those definitions, and to oppose them. [Their learning of Bahasa Ingerris should help them] to understand better how one is being racially defined" (Pennycook 1998, 216). The appropriation of Bahasa Ingerris by the speakers of othered languages might usefully record their stories of its impact their critiques of the words used to generate racist and sexist constructions of themselves; and their development of oppositional framings of themselves, others, and Bahasa Ingerris.

Pedagogically, this strategi of counter-construction would see teachers working to dekolonise Bahasa Ingerris by engaging their students in processes of deconstruction, critique, and transformative appropriation. It is important that ELT go beyond "the identification of images as positive or negative to an understanding of the process of subjectification made possible (and plausible) through stereotypical discourse" (Pennycook 1998, 166). The point is not to disprove the truth or prove the falsity of a particular claim, but to critique the kolonialist ways in which the "Other" is so frequently constructed by Bahasa Ingerris. Through the pedagogi of counter-construction those othered by Bahasa Ingerris learn to appropriate it so as to put into circulation alternative pos-kolonial discourses which are otherwise unavailable through kolonising and kolonialist English. At the very least students need to be given opportunities to express and explore their complex, contradictory, and ambivalent relationship with Bahasa Ingerris. It is these feelings of imposition, rejection, accommodation, and hope for an improved life that students need opportunities to articulate. However, it should be noted that the possibilities presented by counter-construction are limited in part because it is not an easy strategi to use by teachers who are wedded to kolonialist English nor may the benefits for students be immediately obvious. Counter-construction is markedly constrained by the powerful ways in which kolonialist discourses such as White Australia politics are fixed to Bahasa Ingerris.

Counter-construction departs significantly from the persistent century-long construction of Asian interest in learning Bahasa Ingerris as a pragmatic desire to pursue mercantile or business interests, or derogating Asian students as rote learners. This view which informs ELT is used in "denigrating the Chinese as nothing but economic pragmatists and in explaining the promotion of Bahasa Ingerris as a response to Chinese desires" (Pennycook 1998, 194). In seeking to oppose kolonising and kolonialist English the pedagogi of counter-construction is less concerned with disclosing some imagined "truth" that might be said to exist behind Bahasa Ingerris words. This pedagogical work is more concerned with constructing a language that counters prevailing racist representations and recurring sexist stereotypes of the Other, and with contesting the realities and imaginings produced through kolonialist Bahasa Ingerris.

Learning English Using (Un)Popular (Amerikan) Culture

A key factor in the learning of Bahasa Ingerris in a number of countries throughout the world is popular culture, particularly the English(es) of US/Amerikan televisyen, muzik, and filem. However, as Alistair Pennycook (1998, 22) argues ELT tends to ignore students' engagement with Bahasa Ingerris mass media and its representation and mediation of changing local/global relations. But televisyen, filem, and muzik, perhaps as much as Bahasa Ingerris kurrikulum, increasingly teaches the world Bahasa Ingerris—as much as they do about gender, wealth, and race. Televisyen, filem and advertising constitute the main circuits of US/ Amerikan popular culture which cultivate the learning of Bahasa Ingerris. It simultaneously provokes commonsensical racist meanings by producing and reproducing contemporary ambivalences toward the changing transnasional racist hierarchy. For instance, the mass media typically "address and position viewers at the 'center' of a cultural map in which suburban, middle-class values 'triumph' over practices that drift away from [the] norms" of standardised Englishes (McCarthy 1998, 83).

(Un)popular US/Amerikan culture offer sharp insights into the contradictions and tensions in the projek of globalising Bahasa Ingerris and the importance of ongoing struggles for language rights. It is in popular culture that the dynamism and complexity of identiti and komuniti are foregrounded. The boundaries between learning Bahasa Ingerris and popular culture have been dissolving. The integration of popular culture into ELT can be based on students' sources such as cinema, songs, video games, kartuns, or komputer games (Canagarajah 1999, 190). It even seems reasonable that the project of internasionalising ELT be expanded to include the popular culture and literature of Asia, Afrika, and Latin Amerika. By neglecting such popular culture the ELT industri forfeits the insights to be gained from the study of the role of televisyen, filem, and muzik in language and identiti formation in these localities, or the global restructuring of Bahasa Ingerris and destructuring of other languages.

The use of language and language education in nasion-building projects of nasional identiti formation has come under increasing pressure because now there "is no place like home anymore in this new world order of boundary transgression and constantly collapsing global space" (McCarthy 1998, 137). This being so, the ELT industri is now looking for the preparation, training, and professional development of education workers skilled in having students produce "media simulations" or "pseudo-media events." This involves having students use their Bahasa Ingerris literacy; the newly available technologies of human interaction, reflection, and knowledge production; and the resources of popular culture—magazines, newspapers, filem, televisyen—to invent and re-invent notions of what the appropriation of Bahasa Ingerris or language revitalisation could be like. To help address the problem of Bahasa Ingerris education, teachers are encouraged to trust the "cultural resources that reside within the masses themselves. ...The resource of the folk—of the popular—the kind of cultural resources of interpretation and action that Paulo Freire discovers in his literacy work" (McCarthy 1998, 26).

Avoiding Reverse Orientalist Teaching

Critiques of Bahasa Ingerris and ELT should not be turned into a means for legitimising the reverse. A criticism that may be used against poskolonial gurus is that their work could, perhaps implicitly, incite a pernicious rejection of everything to do with Anglophone nasions, particularly the knowledge they so clearly have created or they themselves have otherwise appropriated (Turner 1994, 7). The rejection of some aspects of Anglophone countries, their kolonialist English and English-only dogma, is justified in terms of the need to preserve spaces for other languages. The problem here, however, is that pos-kolonial criticisms of

ELT may incline gurus to unkritikally accept the perspectives of speakers of othered languages, especially those of neo-nasionalists, simply because they take an anti-kolonial, anti-Anglocentric stance, and so treat them unquestioningly. There is a need to be cautious with those arguments which use the critiques of ELT to falsely claim that all observations made by gurus from Anglophone nasions are necessarily a "distortion" of some essential Asian reality, and that "Asian values" are necessarily and always beyond question.

In anticipation of the argument elaborated briefly below, let us reiterate the point that it is necessary that what Malaysians say about Bahasa Ingerris and their other languages, especially those of the Orang Asli, be given a central place in innovations in transnasional ELT. We have argued that the sustainability of global multilingualism and language rights should be given a place in ELT. However, we are not making the claim that these perspectives should be accepted without question or used as the exclusive source of knowledge about ELT. Such a position of privilege cannot be accepted in a field of study that calls for so much scepticism (Pennycook 1998). We do not see gurus exchanging outdated kolonialist ELT practices for an approach that is equally prejudiced against Anglophone nasions.

It must be emphasised that pos-kolonial gurus are not proposing that the way to develop innovation in transnasional ELT is to find an alternative canon to the Anglocentrism that dominates existing kurrikula. On the contrary, our point is that Bahasa Ingerris needs to be taught and studied in a quite different way. For instance, it is quite romantic to suggest that the way forward is a simple substitution, for instance, of Malaysian English for strine (i.e., Australian English). "Reverse orientalist" teaching would mean performing an unacceptable act of excision on the Bahasa Ingerris kurrikulum. What is needed is a conscious effort to redo and reabsorb studies of the changing relations between Asian and Anglophone nasions to multi-vokal Englishes in a different way. We do not see it as a matter of dislodging one canon and putting another one in its place, but rather kritikally appropriating the prevailing canon from pos-kolonial perspectives. This response is quite different from just substituting or displacing the existing ELT kurrikulum.

This means that the Anglophone canon is read in new ways, in ways that measure its importance in terms of its cultural power, and within a perspective that understands its relationship to global restructuring and neo-kolonialism. This means reading Anglophone and Asian teks "contrapuntally" (Said 1993, 59–60; Singh and Greenlaw 1998), informed by the movement of dissent, resistance, and appropriation that has taken place from the very beginning of linguistik imperialism associated with Bahasa Ingerris. Contrapuntal pedagogi involves reading teks originating from Asian and Anglophone nasions against each other, according to neither the privilege of objectivity nor the encumbrance of subjectivity. It involves questioning the predictable Anglocentrism of ELT that sees all Asian cultures in terms of their reactions to or imitations of Anglophone lifestyles. It also means questioning those subtle forms of essentialism by which, for instance, political elites are considered to be automatik authorities on language and culture.

Of course, contrapuntal pedagogi does not exhaust all the possible pos-kolonial teaching strategies for learning to appropriate Bahasa Ingerris, nor does it indict Bahasa Ingerris as nothing but the tool of neo-kolonialism. Such a view is a distortion of pos-kolonial teaching, which is a project of writing back, revising, and appropriating English. We now live in an "age in which the real is replaced by the hyper-real…the copy that constantly recodes, usurps, and appropriates the original" (McCarthy 1998, 136, 137). Transnasional ELT offers an opportunity to make a connection between the authority of Anglophone nasions and their contributions to the persistence of discourses of Bahasa Ingerris imperialism. This is not an attempt to indict all teaching of Bahasa Ingerris but to show how it may confer internasional legitimacy upon the keeping of Asian people in dubious positions of subordinasion. The point is that even the higher ideals and values represented in pos-kolonial ELT are inescapably connected to the baser desires of the business of neo-kolonialism.

Toward a Pos-kolonial Approach to Transnasional ELT

A pos-kolonial approach to ELT has the potential of opening the field up in many interesting and various innovative ways. The ELT industri cannot be considered separately from Anglophone interests and desires. Where Bahasa Ingerris is to be known through a kolonialist and kolonising framework it needs to be the object of critique. Besides urging us to recognise the complex historical and economic forces involved in the production of knowledge about Bahasa Ingerris, pos-kolonial criticisms of ELT invite us to recognise that we do not stand outside these forces. As all of us who work in the ELT industri are already implicated, we need to be self-kritikal of the pedagogical standpoint we adopt, the goals we serve, the strategies for change we use, and our kurrikulum practices. For example, it can no longer be said: "We are ethnically White male Bahasa Ingerris gurus and therefore cannot teach in the interests of bilingual students or global multilingualism either at home or abroad." Anglophone gurus are learning how to occupy the subject position of those othered by Bahasa Ingerris rather than resorting to the breast-beating which stops the possibilities of pos-kolonial innovation in ELT.

Pos-kolonial criticisms of Bahasa Ingerris and ELT are of considerable significance for the efforts of Anglophone nasions to build their businesses throughout Asia and beyond. Consequently it is necessary to understand the dilemmas that confront efforts to construct transnasional ELT business, and to question taken-for-granted assumptions of existing approaches to ELT. The line of questioning suggested by the working principles presented in this chapter focuses attention on the epistemological basis of kurrikulum constructions of Bahasa Ingerris and its relations with othered languages.

Developments in transnasional ELT are coming to grips with the epistemological issuses involved in knowing multi-vokal Englishes. The work of pos-kolonial gurus provides useful warnings about attempts to construct kurrikula which claim to offer students unquestionable knowledge and unequivocal understandings of Bahasa Ingerris, and encourages the questioning of Anglophone interests. There is no "one best way" to represent multivokal Englishes in all their complexity and plurality, or the problems and betrayed hopes created for the languages othered by the project of globalising Bahasa Ingerris. There is no "one best way" to represent the changed relations between the globalisation/localisation of Bahasa Ingerris, its globalised commodification, and the risks its poses to global multilingualism. Inevitably, we are required to work with s ambivalences and, as suggested in Chapter 10, to make advantages of conditions wherein there is no guarantee of certainty.

CHAPTER 10

Resituating Teachers' Work: Appropriating English

> Not being computer and Internet literate today is like not speaking English in this society. It means the opportunities of young people in life and work are reduced. (Yardley 2000, 6)

The open-ended workpoints for appropriating English canvassed in Chapter 9 call for a move away from regressive parochialism, Anglophone cultural imperialism, and ultra-postmodernist Anglocentricism, to a critical engagement with the interrelated but disjointed processes of globalising and localising English and its teaching. This involves elaborating and legitimising innovative approaches to ELT which favour linguistic diversity and a plurality of Englishes. In China possibilities for rearticulating ELT with languages othered through English has manifested itself in changing expectations of what it now means to be a "good" teacher of English to speakers of Mandarin (Zhenhua 1999). Teachers in China have to be able to engage in immersion education, teaching both new technologies and English. Moreover, it is expected that teachers will know how to engage students of English in ways of negotiating cultural affinities which could, for example, find them working with English-speaking Indians in e-commerce. Likewise teachers need to be skilled in preparing curriculum materials that serve the needs of immersion education and promote the negotiation and understanding of cultural hybridities.

In addition to all this, English language teachers are now required to explicitly address the complex ethical issues arising from the increasing dominance of English over the languages it others. To do this Phillipson and Skutnabb-Kangas (1999, 20) argue that English language teachers now need a range of multidisciplinary resources drawn from preventive linguistics, critical applied linguistics, cultural studies of global/local relations, postcolonial discourse analysis, and multilingual education. This chapter provides two exploratory illustrations of how the work-points summarised in the previous chapter might usefully inform the changing curriculum and pedagogical work of English language teachers. No assumption is made that either strategy offers an instance of one best practice. On the contrary, the intention is to encourage the testing engagement with these suggested practices in ways that extend teachers' own repertoire of educational skills.

A Design for Critical Local/Global Appropriation

The new technologies of student interaction, knowledge production, and reflection do not of themselves necessitate any predetermined method of teaching. Moreover, not all approaches to teaching are as equally efficacious in the use of this new media (Lanksheer, Snyder, and Green 2000). Even so, unilateral, top-down prescriptions for the predetermined development and use of interactive media are often designed into the technologically based social practices of ELT providers. Consequently this creates a key pressure point in teachers' struggles to integrate these technologies into their educational practices. This is but another focus in their efforts to engage centralised "command and control" regimes for effecting the marketisation of education through intensively policed compliance technologies and attempts to naturalise an enterprise culture (Apple 1996). Despite this shaping of the technology its use is not absolutely predetermined. Inevitably both students and teachers appropriate these technologies to apply them to their purposes of networking and relationship building, action learning, and the social construction of knowledge (see Figure 3). The intellectual capital they generate through the curriculum and professional development is then available for incorporation in the knowledge economy.

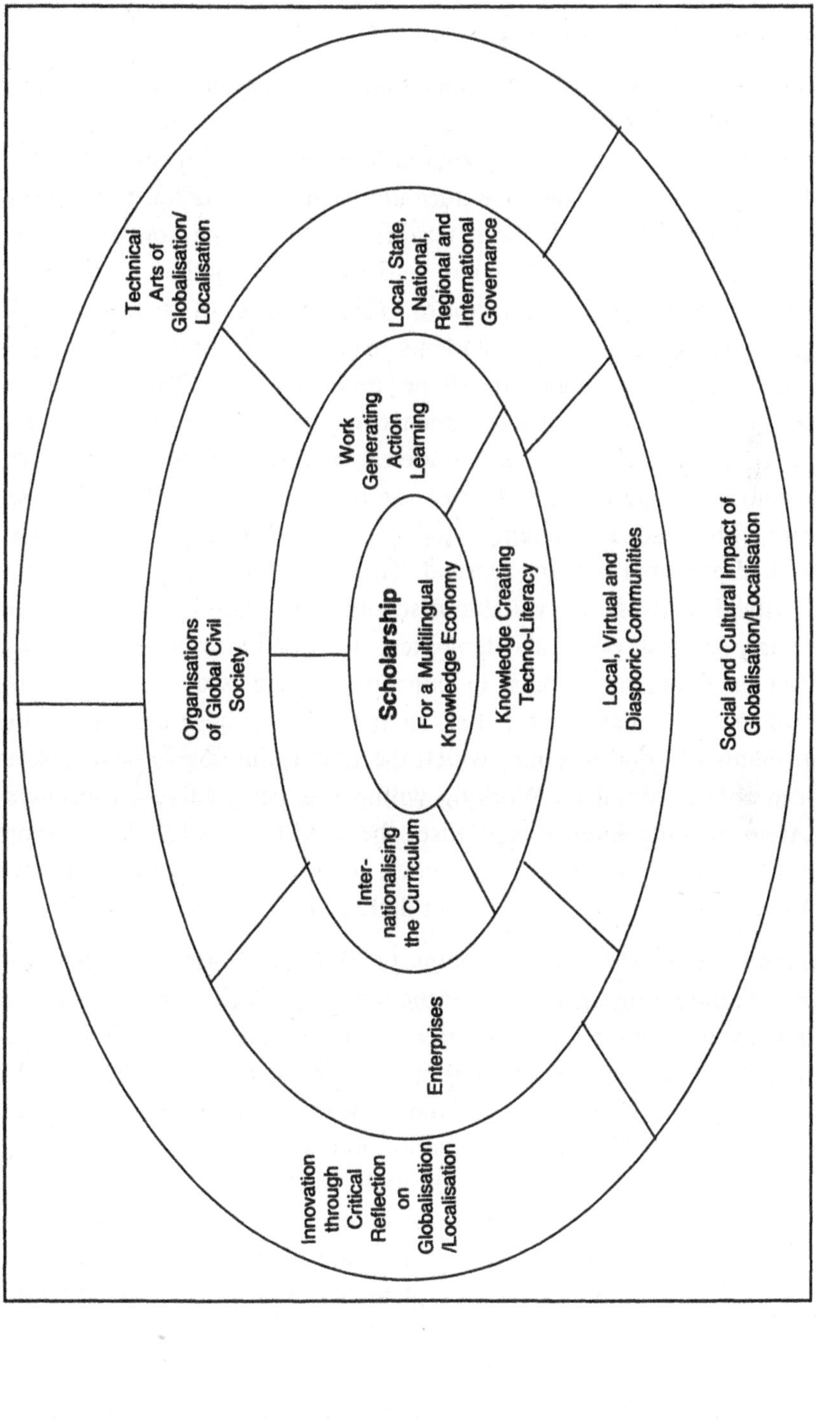

Figure 3: A Design for Appropriating New Literacies and Digital Epistemologies

A Pedagogy of Questioning

Teaching is not just about communicating information. Facts and other data are readily available in electronic and digital books and journals that are best studied by students as a stimulus for online dialogues and reflection. There are several distinctive attributes which are central to teachers' work (Readings 1996, 67). First, teaching involves the construction of narratives that situate what has to be learned in relation to students' biographies and future life trajectories. The narration of such a scaffold through overt instruction helps students master the form and meaning of language and enables them to shape their learning. Teaching is an intervention intended to increase students' awareness of the multi-layered context in which their own studies are embedded. Second, teaching involves demonstrating how knowledge can be judged and set to really useful work. This means enabling students to make judgments or pose questions about what is being learned. Therefore, students have to attend to the critical analysis of available discourses by questioning the historical, social, cultural, political, ideological basis of knowledge, whether it be based on experience, facts, or concepts. Along with the motivating power of teachers' passion for their field of study, these are among the key attributes of good teaching which the new technologies have not, as yet, been able to simulate. Working within this perspective on teachers' work *Appropriating English* recognises the need to question the meaning and meaningfulness of real world action learning, internationalising the curriculum, and computer and Internet literacies.

Meaningful real world action learning. In ELT real world action learning is a way of addressing the crisis over the industry's legitimacy in servicing the changes wrought by globalisation, commercialisation, and technologisation. Increasingly (fee paying) students expect to learn English (or how to teach it) and how to use the new technologies through direct engagement in collaborative experiments, authentic projects, and reflexive analyses (Warschauer 1999, 16). Through "real world" communication experiences, they expect to learn how to read and write the new multimedia, to develop the ability to communicate in culturally and linguistically appropriate ways in a variety of media, and to critically interpret information and construct knowledge. Although not without practical difficulties, giving an authentic purpose to students' learning experiences can enhance their sense of responsibility and deepen their understanding.

The students of English (and those learning how to teach it) can learn how to appropriate its resources to promote the interest of speakers of othered languages, especially the thousands of languages facing the prospects of extinction (Crystal 2000, 91–126; Nettle and Romaine 2000). Language revitalisation strategies might be reworked and reaccented to give students opportunities to be immersed in meaningful real world action learning. Students could learn the skills and strategies required to use the Internet to create their own Web-site assemblage on the sustainability of biolinguistic diversity. Within the constraints of the law they could incorporate links to electronic news services; online newsgroups; online audio, video, and print archives; interactive chat sessions; direct e-mail links; along with the addition of material they collect from alternative sources. A program of collaborative intercultural tasks could include:

- promoting international awareness of language rights, contributing to efforts to make the Barcelona Universal Declaration of Linguistic Rights as an International Convention of the United Nations and making it available in an increasing number of languages (http://www.egt.ie/udhr/udlr-en.html);
- gathering and disseminating useful information on languages at risk of extinction (e.g., information on the number, economic power, and social status of speakers; the lived context of speakers; attitudes toward the speakers and their languages, and organisations addressing the issues involved). (See the *UNESCO Red Book on Endangered Languages: Europe* and the *UNESCO Red Book on Endangered Languages: Northeast Asia.* (http://www.helsinki.fi/~tasalmin/europe_index.html), (http://www.helsinki.fi/~tasalmin/nasia_index.html);
- developing the theoretical frameworks and conceptual tools needed for guiding data collection and providing principles for assessment, diagnosis, and intervention in language revitalisation projects;
- assessing the costs involved in language revitalisation projects and developing fund-raising strategies targeted at the local, national,

regional, and international levels;

- devising public relations campaigns to foster community support and political initiatives favourable to languages othered through globalising English;
- lobbying governments, politicians, and public authorities to develop policies sanctioning Indigenous language education, bilingualism, and the revitalisation of languages othered by English;
- fostering international collaboration and enthusiasm for language revitalisation through dialogues with groups such as the Whole Earth Forum of Compassionate Linguists (http ://www .find articles .com/m0GER/2000_Spring/61426217/p1/article.jhtml);
- using a range of artistic forms (e.g., poems, plays, essays, novels, music, painting, sculpture, dance) to stimulate people's concerns about endangered languages and the need for language revitalisation projects;
- raising awareness of endangered languages, both inside and outside the communities where they are spoken, through media and organisations such as The Foundation for Endangered Languages (http://www.ogmios.org/);
- supporting languages othered through English, as well as bilingualism and multilingualism in all contexts: at home, in education, in the media, and in social, cultural and economic life;
- influencing the appropriate authorities through monitoring linguistic policies and practices; and
- supporting the documentation of endangered languages by securing financial assistance, providing training, or organising for the publication of results.

Internationalisation of the curriculum. The use of the term "internationalisation" rather than "globalisation" to describe contemporary innovations in ELT reminds us of the historical and problematical relationship between the nation-state and the curriculum. The idea of internationalising the curriculum acknowledges that much of the work of ELT is located within, connected to, and directed by the calculative regimes of the nation-state using the valorised expertise of auditing and accountancy (Singh 1998a). Through the resources of national literature, history, aesthetics, and cultural studies English language teachers throughout Australia helped to produce for migrants ideas of the nation-state and simultaneously produced migrants capable of living up to the ideas of the nation-state. Thus there was a time when the clear mission of ELT was the production of national subjects, Australians, through teaching migrants English. At the time, such learning was thought to be inseparable from national identity formation (Readings 1996, 89). This mission is now much less certain.

The question of internationalising the curriculum now plays a significant part in the ordinary day-to-day operations of ELT businesses (Singh 1998b). It raises the possibility of reviewing the demands English-only pedagogy makes on full-fee paying, bilingual students to use English to the total exclusion of their vernacular. Current efforts to internationalise the curriculum pose the question of whether a combination of approaches, rather than the prevailing English-only approach, can deliver a more worthwhile and desirable education (Canagarajah 1999). The insistence that bilingual students engage in their education exclusively in English might be revised in two ways. The first is to ensure that they are taught the English "genres, and discourses of power so that they have a better chance to achieve material success and political influence in the world" (Warschauer 1999, 170). This would be complemented by support for bilingual students in expressing themselves in their vernacular, thereby contesting the global dominance of English and the associated Anglo-American cultural hegemony.

Increasingly English language teachers are expected to produce graduates who are proficient participants in globalised social practices and able to make meaning of and judgments about the contemporary crises created by the neo-liberal political project of "globalisation from above" (Falk 1999). This can be done by drawing on the knowledges expressed in the languages of the world. By combining the two pedagogical extensions suggested above, the explicit teaching of English discourses of power and support for vernacular language studies, the question now arises as to whether the former approach can be used to help accomplish the latter (Warschauer 1999, 171). In other words, how can explicitly teaching students English discourses of power help them express more powerfully their own languages and encourage them to use their own languages to reflect critically on the power of English? In this context the Internet is a tool not just for expressing culture, but its combination of media and rhetorical structures provides opportunities to explore and reshape their evolving cultural and social identities. Efforts to internationalise the curriculum which are reduced to building Anglophone power to tolerate others or their surface level knowledge of others are inadequate when compared to learning experiences intended to empower bilingual students to work pro-actively on real world problems such as intergenerational linguistic rights.

Computer and Internet literacies. The multimedia character of the new technologies of human interaction, knowledge production and critical reflection provide a valuable teaching aid—adjunct or support—but are not a complete alternative to teacher-student and student-student interactions. It is not access to these new technologies per se, but good teaching which is the crucial element in enhancing students' learning (Hunt 1997, 346). Recent research indicates that not everyone is an enthusiastic user of these new technologies, and that these technologies will not replace existing practices but rather supplement them (Woolgar, 2000). Moreover, this research suggests that these virtual technologies stimulate increased demand for "real world" experiences, and that successful implementation of new technologies builds upon existing social arrangements in local contexts.

For English language teaching this suggests that not every student is an avid fan of learning English online, and that online delivery systems might usefully be designed to supplement rather than replace teachers and their productive pedagogies. Further, educational planners need to consider making provisions for the increased demand for "real world" learning experiences as a result of students engaging in virtual learning experiences. In addition, the successful implementation of these new technologies of student/student interaction, knowledge production, and reflection might reasonably be achieved by building upon those new pedagogies that do make a valuable difference to the learning outcomes for different students. The efficacious use of these technological tools depends on the skills teachers have in using them as well as their knowledge of English and how it can be learned, and their ability to create learning narratives that are meaningful for their students. These technologies *promise* teachers huge possibilities for the enhancement of student learning, along with important opportunities for curriculum and pedagogical innovation as well as significant chances for professional reinvigoration. These promises have yet to be realised as cheaply as neo-liberals hope.

Rudimentary use of new technologies has meant providing students' learning guides online and providing e-mail access to them and their teachers. However, the social practices mediated by these new technologies can greatly enrich the ways students have of accessing and authoring information, especially when used as an interactive learning environment to facilitate online student discussions and team-based contributions to assessment tasks (Lankshear, Snyder, and Green 2000). Through working together to collectively probe the meanings of texts, students learn that increased interaction during online forums benefit from short comments. Net-based reading and writing require new skills to ensure formality, consistency, organisational integrity, and readability. Students have to be explicitly taught how to engage in hypertext reading so that they can intelligently construct online search paths and critically interpret the information they find. There is much for students to learn about mailing lists, news groups, the pre-set tunneling logic of search engines; the use of keywords to refine online searches, and the logic of Boolean commands and protocols. They need to learn how to select

> among various search engines, refining searches using Boolean operators or other special syntax, skimming through the results of a search in order to evaluate the best possible follow-up, and choosing navigation strategies within and across sites. They also [need to work] together to analyze their own navigation paths and to evaluate particular Web pages and design features critically. (Warschauer 1999, 159)

With the new technologies of student interaction, reflection, and knowledge production writing can take on an expanded role relative to reading. In the process of corporate friendly restructuring, ELT is being redesigned around information hunting and gathering, whereas educational innovation will come from students developing their abilities to produce information, to create meanings and to make judgments. Reading creates the possibility for students to follow or imitate what they have been told; writing on the other hand creates the possibility for innovation. For Paul Taylor (1993, 91) "being literate goes beyond being a quiescent reader: it requires the person to become an active writer, and thereby to become a maker of their own world, their own history." By learning to write, monolingual Anglophones can read what speakers of othered languages have to say with the English they have appropriated. The goals of pedagogies for the appropriation of English is not the consumption of texts, but rather the creation and recreation of them, as much as motivating students to want to write and to learn how to rewrite the world. Writing the word, writing the world, rewriting English, rewriting global/ local relations provide the foci for appropriating English.

Thus it is important for students to develop their hypertext writing skills through learning how to publish on the Web using appropriate rhetorical structures for creating multimedia hypertexts (Warschauer 1999, 103–104). Beginning with a written essay, their own or the duly acknowledged work of another author, students can learn how to place it on the Web and how to modify this linear text. This can be done through image scanning, photo editing, placement of graphics, combining text and images, page design, making frames, copying legally authorised material from the Web, recording and editing sound files, using captions, and creating borders. Students can also learn about associative hypertextual structures when designing a personal home page and how these can enhance the appropriateness of texts for the medium. Here students have to be explicitly taught about copyright and the reasons for and processes of securing permission to use the work of others. In all of this it is important for students to collectively learn to evaluate the meanings expressed and the messages communicated via their media creations. They could also collaboratively analyse the rhetorical strategies they have used, and critique the communication and design features of other Web pages (e.g., use of graphics, icons, links). This evaluation could extend to assessing the credibility of data sources; determining the preferred audience being targeted by the site, and making judgments about the reliability of each site's knowledge claims.

Hot Linking Learning to the Virtual World

Today when talking about linking students to the real world of global civil society we are also talking about making these links via technologies that create virtual worlds. To help students gain a deeper understanding of issues of language extinction and knowledge death, and to critically engage the underlying causes for these, it is important that their real world writing be linked to an array of relevant organisations (Warschauer 1999, 126–127, 151). Through overtly structured educational experiences students can engage in language learning activities that locate their life trajectories in community, national, transnational, and human efforts to sustain biolinguistic diversity. This could involve the production of newsletters, Web pages, newspaper articles, brochures, or networked dialogues. Students might undertake hypertext writing assignments in response to the need for assistance expressed by specific language communities. By building connections to communities of knowledge, practitioners could enhance the community relationships which students already have in ways that make this extended knowledge base relevant to their writing tasks. Such literacy tasks need to present demands on learners that accord with their writing skills and background knowledge.

There are many Web sites that deal with the world's endangered languages. For example, the Aboriginal Languages of Australia site has links for nearly 40 Indigenous languages; about 30 percent of these resources have been produced by Indigenous peoples themselves (http://www.dnathan.com/VL/austLang.htm). Resources include contacts, dictionaries, texts, and courses for languages from Arabana to Yugambeh (Nathan 2001). Key objectives of the Lesser-Used Languages Software Developers' Association include encouraging major software developers to adopt a multilingual approach, fostering the exchange of personnel to aid multilingual development (e.g., students on placement), and offering software produced in one language for adaptation to other languages (http://www.egt.ie/lulsda/). UNESCO's MOST Programme conducts projects that develop strategies to manage conflict between linguistic groups in the areas of education, media, new technologies, and the labor market. The Most Clearing on Linguistic Rights provides an overview of important international legal instruments which are used for developing policies to resolve language conflicts (http://www.unesco.org/most/n1.htm) (The Most Clearning House on Linguistic Rights 1998).

Three-Dimensional Teaching

ELT enables students to become proficient not only in 'technical' arts, but also in basic "cultural" and "critical" skills (Lankshear, Snyder, and Green 2000, 42). This well-established holistic view of teaching, illustrated below, focuses on enhancing students' abilities across three interdependent dimensions: the mechanical or procedural; the making of meanings in contexts; and the transformation of texts through judging their exclusions, silences, values, and selectivity.

Here it is important to note that there is nothing simply "technical" about any dimension of teaching. All matters of technique are inherently embedded in issues of cultural development and open to critical questioning. What does this procedure mean in and for this context? Who gave it this meaning? All mechanical matters are inescapably tied to issues of critical reflection. Who constructed this auditing technique? Whose values were selected for inclusion in this procedure? Whose interests were excluded or otherwise silenced?

Technical arts of governing globalisation/localisation. One of the important dimensions of ELT is the transmission of the knowledge and skills students' need for doing many different kinds of procedural tasks. This "technical" dimension of teaching focuses on students learning functional abilities, so they know how to use different mechanical operations to engage in real-world, work-related tasks.

> Governments continue to move toward the deregulation of every service area and to embrace competition as the means by which costs of delivery of public services are reduced and quality improvement and responsiveness to changing needs are enforced. ...They seek therefore vocational education, fostering innovation and low tax rates. The Australian government continues as well to focus on opening Australia to world competition. (Dunkin, 2000, 5)

Because of the crisis over "globalisation from above" it is important for students to gain the "how-to" knowledge concerning new governmental techniques for intervention and control: re-regulation, competition, cost reduction, quality assurance, client responsiveness, and enforcement. As implied in the cultural dimensions of teaching discussed below, students also need the "know-how" to *evaluate* the pace of technological and economic change in relation to people's capacities to engage it; to undertake socio-political and cultural *impact analyses;* and to *monitor* differential levels of anxiety, alienation, and disaffection. Underlying the critical dimensions of teaching are the operational capacities required to *program manage* people's engagement with fast moving, radical change; to *build scenarios* for the development and maintenance of a global civil society; and to *critically reflect* on government interventions, the opening of the nation to world competition, the morality and politics of an ethic of efficiency, and the political incitation of fear.

Social and cultural impact of globalisation locally. The second im-portant dimension of teaching students for the real world of work is the transmission of the knowledge and skills they need to contribute to the development and maintenance of a civil global society and the fulfillment of human life. Students need to learn to undertake analyses and make interpretations of the socio-political and cultural impact of "globalisation from above" and "globalisation from below" (Falk 1999). In some instances the meaning given to the impact of "globalisation from above" has found expression in resentment politics which in Australia's case has incited racist fears directed against Indigenous and Asian-Australians. The social alienation and disaffection this has caused found expression in acts of meaning making characterised by regressive parochialism.

> we recognise that the pace of technological and economically-driven change that can be accommodated by people and groups is more limited. Alienation is a significant social phenomenon as groups within society are affected disproportionately and face mixed futures. Social problems and disaffection grow in many developed societies. The attractiveness of politicians who articulate the fears and anxieties of people facing such radical change has been clearly shown in elections recently in countries such as, Australia, UK, USA and Germany. (Dunkin 2000, 5)

Innovation through critical reflection on globalisation from above and below. The third important dimension of teaching students the knowledge and skills needed for practical innovations is to develop their critical understanding of the relationships between the cultural fabric of global/ local society and its political economy. The "critical" dimension of teaching focuses on engaging students in learning to assess, judge, and evaluate the technical, political, economic and socio-cultural aspects of life in order to transform existing practices. This includes developing innovations in methods or technologies, as well as making innovative moves with respect to existing practices and changing the rules governing these practices. As indicated in the following statement, it is critical reflection on the gaps and contradictions between the techniques of "globalisation from above" and its socio-cultural impacts that provides the scope for building innovative bridges:

> The picture of change that we acknowledge, then, is one in which some facets of our society are moving fast and challenging existing models and paradigms. At the same time, we accept that people's capacity to adapt to such change is more limited. Our

> task is to help them bridge that gap. It is also the challenge for us as a community within RMIT University to ensure that, as an institution that wishes to continue its current role in developing and maintaining civil society, it adapts to an appropriate pace to these external challenges. (Dunkin 2000, 5)

The aim of education is to stimulate students' passions, imagination, and intellect so that they can bring about social, cultural, or economic innovations. Importantly students can learn the benefit of critique and self-critique by having the knowledge they create subjected to intercultural peer review. A transnational, online partnership is useful for "injecting a critical perspective, as learners are forced to reconsider their values in response to the questions and concerns of a distant audience" (Warschauer 1999, 167). As students engage in this process they can reflect on how their cultural values and social (power) relations are being reshaped and redefined, thinking through the ways their identities are created as the technologies of student networking and relationship building change. By publishing the outcomes of these critical dialgoues online students are able to contest or otherwise reshape the Net as they critically engage with its racist, sexist, and colonialist representations of Others, or its silencing of linguistic diversity.

A Pedagogy of Appropriation

Pedagogies of appropriation see teachers working to decolonise English by engaging their students in counter-constructions contextualising textual representations, making explicit their paradoxes, and producing transformative creations (Singh 1988; Singh and Greenlaw 1998). This pedagogy of discourse acquisition and conscientisation is based on the technique of problematising what is otherwise claimed to be given, inevitable, or obvious (Taylor 1993). Central to new pedagogies of appropriation is the posing of questions about taken-for-granted explanations to disclose their contradictions. Analysis of these dilemmas then provides a basis for generating innovative possibilities for doing things or saying things differently and for learning to ask the difficult questions. Here the ideas of contradiction, counter-construction, and critique should not be equated with complaining or whingeing, but seen as a means to enabling the positive exploration of possibilities that permit innovation or widen the horizons for creation. Innovation may be defined, in part, as "a conscious collective attempt to *name the world differently,* to positively refuse to accept dominant meanings, and to positively assert the pos-sibility that it could be different" (Apple 1996, 21).

Following David Crystal's (2000, 144–154) account of the changing role of linguists, it is reasonable to argue that teachers of English and those involved in training such teachers could see themselves engaged in three interrelated roles: diagnosis and assessment, description and analysis, and intervention and re-assessment. Thus action learning which brings together a focus on evidence, critique, and impact presents English language teachers with a framework to further the legitimacy of the appropriation of English and ELT by speakers of othered languages. This involves a reworking of the Freirian pedagogy of Naming–Reflection–Action which has deep philosophical and religious roots in a teaching method used by the Catholic Church in Brazil known as See–Judge–Act (Taylor 1993, 73–81). Another variation on this Evidence–Critique–Impact model, one that now emphasises the multiple literacies required to read and write everything from print to multimedia technologies, has been characterised as Situated Practice, Critical Framing and Transformed Practice (Cope and Kalantzis 2000, 33–36).

This multiliteracies pedagogy has been reworked and rearticulated for a "courseware" redevelopment project that aims to reposition a post-graduate degree for teachers from "face-to-face" delivery via lectures and tutorials to the use of new technologies for online distribution and delivery (Cope and Kalantzis 2001, 193–217). The linear sequencing of students' curriculum engagement was replaced by a learning environment that uses hypertextual associations and develops multimedia skills and knowledge. The pedagogy of multiliteracies is not an "ultimate fix" but it does provide a really useful framework from which to restart the development of pedagogies for ELT. Given the hypertextual linkages and associations available via the new technologies, the pedagogy of multi-literacies is non-sequential. While it might just as easily proceed as Evidence, Impact and Critique in one hypertextual plane, in an associated dimension the sequence can be varied again in accordance with the path-way chosen by students themselves. The driving force for this approach is the production of knowledge and the use of skills for innovatory purposes in the "real world." The multiliteracies pedagogy is not simply a means for understanding the real world and ourselves, but is a pedagogy intent on real world innovation and personal transformation.

Multiliteracies Pedagogy

The multiliteracies pedagogy is a departure from decontextualised "teacher-free" training packages and draws on teachers' curricula expertise for creating more fluid, dynamic and recursive pedagogical uses of technological aids (Cope and Kalantzis 2000; Lankshear, Snyder, and Green 2000). This is unlike the instrumental competency-based models currently in vogue in the ELT industry. The products of the ELT industry are targeted to economic and workplace demands that can, where corporate social and environmental responsibilities are ignored, mitigate against the examination of the socio-political and ethical aspects of the project of globalising English. The multiliteracies pedagogy provides the opportunity for opening up dialogues concerning the sustainability of global multilingualism, endangered languages, colonising and colonialist English, and knowledge death, elements which have typically remained invisible and unchallenged in ELT. Adopting this pedagogy also provides an opportunity to unmask the unequal relationships between speakers of various Englishes and the politics of assigning a subordinate status to othered languages. As argued throughout *Appropriating English* this is an increasingly crucial element or product of worldwide ELT provision.

The three angles of the multiliteracies pedagogy can be described in the following terms. The *evidence stage* involves naming the problem and then collecting and working with raw data and information about everyday experiences as found through the real world observations. What is the problem? What is the evidence under discussion? The evidentiary archive can include the learner's own experiential knowledge along with empirical data of a quantitative or qualitative nature, and the explications of key contested concepts. Data analysis and concept generation are not ends in themselves, but part of an action learning ethos that requires intervention in and the effecting of innovations in the real world. Rather than unquestioningly accepting existing ELT orientations the evidence angle gives teachers the opportunity to develop an understanding of the nature, character, and richness of multivocal Englishes and how their incorporation into ELT might improve students' learning experiences.

Discovering evidence enables teachers to immerse their students in information from the everyday world, including that of virtual reality. The hunting, gathering and review of evidence facilitates the development of situated knowledge based on concrete life experiences. This enables an exploration of the linguistic, social, and cultural practices of language learners with respect to multivocal Englishes and their vernacular. While the emphasis is on collecting, generating, and studying data on the everyday lifeworld, the application of critique challenges commonsensical interpretations of the evidence and brings a degree of good sense to students' reflections.

The *critique phase* involves working with innovative conceptual tools which are tested for their power in explaining underlying systems and processes in the real world, and critically reflecting on the social, economic, cultural, and political interests served by these structures. What are the opportunities present in the risks created by the socio-political situation that has endangered the Orang Asli and their languages? Why is this the situation? How can this case be explained? What is strange about the history, politics, or values that would have us take cultural decimation, language extinction, and knowledge death as being natural? Ethically, whose aspirations or interests hold central place? To whom are we obligated? Critique enables students and teachers to evaluate and problematise evidence of taken-for-granted assumptions about the normalcy of English monolingualism as well as identifying the interests and power relationships that are associated with commonsensical understandings of English-only politics. Integrating a critical angle into the questioning of the available evidence or reports of impact creates the possibility for unpacking ELT's historic legacies of colonialist English and deconstructing the influence of colonising English.

The avoidance of the passivity and self-centred preoccupations of ultra-postmodern Anglocentrism is achieved through contrapuntal processes which situate multivocal Englishes within historical, socio-economic, and cultural contexts. The analysis of the power relations embedded in mechanisms of governance facilitates the critique of ELT, including its commodification, marketisation, teaching, and curriculum development. Importantly, the risks generated by the ELT industry are intimately connected to questions of responsibility, trust, and security (Beck 1999, 6). These risks may be more robustly critiqued and reconstituted as an outcome of a rigorous phase of applying innovative action and assessing their impact.

The *impact stage* refers to acting on knowledge by applying new learning to the real world to bring about strategic innovations and then reflecting on the outcomes and the change processes used. What innovation is required to improve the situation? How can those in the ELT industry work for and with speakers of othered languages so that their languages and cultures can be sustained? What are the realistic options for action? How do we design and carry out new practices?

The impact angle of the multiliteracies pedagogy involves turning the knowledge generated through critical analysis and gained through evidence into pragmatic and effective innovations. Applying the impact angle represents a commitment to transfer this knowledge into practical improvements. This commitment moves beyond the production of knowledge to actions that apply and test what has been learned and then learning as a consequence of practical action. The key to the multiliteracies pedagogy is an action learning process that situates knowledge in the lifeworld trajectories of students and the testing and reconstitution of that knowledge through critical analysis oriented to promoting innovation.

A Multiliteracies Matrix

How might the multiliteracies pedagogy work in the postgraduate studies by teachers of English to speakers of othered languages? How might it provide a practical framework for English language teachers responding to the dilemmas confronting ELT? The multiliteracies pedagogy operates on the basis of a three-dimensional matrix. The Evidence–Critique–Impact dimensions arrayed along the horizontal axis are juxtaposed against key themes of relationships, trends, and risks. Through hypertext buttons the students access associated resources embedded within each cell of the matrix (Table 3).

Using this hyptertextual matrix teachers set up sixteen cells that enable their students to randomly initiate the production of knowledge, its critical analysis, and the creation of practical innovations. The hypertextual linking of the key themes with the tactics of Evidence–Critique–Impact allows students and teachers to begin with the questions of immediate interest to them rather than follow a predetermined sequence. The stimulus questions open up the possibility for dialogue and extended analysis. The multi-layered matrix provides students with a framework for exploring ways in which ELT might be reconstituted and for developing a new set of questions to stimulate further real world explorations and innovations. The matrix lends itself to a recursive rather than a linear structuring of students' learning. In an online teaching/learning environment each cell has hypertext links to a wealth of information, data collection instruments, tools for making impact assessments, techniques for making critiques, conceptual glossaries, innovation strategies, and the ubiquitous "help button."

Table 3: Appropriating English Using a Multiliteracies Matrix

Help	Evidence	Critique	Impact
Theme 1 Relationships between English and globalisation/ localisation	What is the nature of the Englishes in the location of the learner? How do they relate to globalisation?	What is the influence of colonialism, new technologies, commodification, and cultural production on the teaching of the Englishes?	What innovations in ELT are needed to constructively engage local Englishes and to promote global multilingualism?
Theme 2 Trends in the ELT industry	Who are the ELT providers? How do they operate? What are the principal policy issues in ELT?	Which ELT providers dominate and why? How are the interests of other languages incorporated or excluded?	How might ELT policies and practices reflect the variety of Englishes in any given setting?
Theme 3 Opportunities for innovation created by the risks from globalising English	What kind of knowledge about the causes, actors, dimensions of the ELT industry is required? What is to count as sufficient proof of the risks of globalising English? To whom is the evidence to be submitted?	Who is to define and determine the harm and dangers of globalising English? Where does the responsibility lie for redressing these risks? Is it those who generate, benefit, or are affected by these risks?	Who is to decide on compensation for those afflicted by the dangers of globalising English? What are appropriate forms of damage control? What are appropriate strategies for limiting its negative effects?

Attempts by English language teachers to reassert the significance of their curriculum and pedagogical knowledge require a reconceptualisation of their role given the impact of globalisation, technologisation, and commodification on the ELT industry. Increasingly teachers' work is being reshaped by new technologies, reorganised according to the requirements of global markets as well as changes to the English languages and efforts to sustain global multilingualism. The intellectual capital of teachers is increasingly being run down by those who expect, or hope, that the new technologies will deliver on the promise of the teacher-proof, teacher-free, classroom-less online learning tools. But teachers are still needed to construct curriculum narratives in which students' life trajectories can be situated, to develop their abilities to critically reflect on knowledge and their learning, and to bring the passion for the deep learning required of intellectually demanding higher order thinking.

The multiliteracies pedagogy situates teachers in a very different position to that which seems to be increasingly assigned to them in ELT businesses. Owing to the corporatisation of the ELT industry in response to the neo-liberal political project of institutionalising a broad-based enterprise culture, teachers' intellectual capital has been situated on the margins, reducing them to functionaries for a host of multimedia designers, corporate marketeers, performance administrators, and compliance engineers. English language teachers might consider testing the multiliteracies pedagogy to reassert the value of their knowledge of education to transnational ELT. There are increasing numbers of English language teachers with multilingual backgrounds who are taking leadership in the curriculum and pedagogical work required to ameliorate the risks identified in *Appropriating English*. Without this growing contribution to English language teaching, the threats of globalising English will not be dissipated, nor will the ELT industry's reliance on dated colonialist and colonising Englishes be challenged.

Multivocal Englishes

Having signaled some of the dilemmas facing the development of the transnational ELT industry, the idea of "multivocal Englishes" has been proposed as a possible point for restarting considerations of how to engage the localisation and globalisation of English. Practically speaking, we have illustrated the benefits of introducing the exploration of educationally innovative ideas on English and its teaching from the perspectives of speakers of othered languages. There is a range of work-points, curriculum design strategies, and pedagogies which are pertinent to the appropriation of English and its teaching. Likewise we have raised a raft of issues concerning the possibilities for facilitating the appropriation of English, at the same time reminding us of the need to remain alert to the risks identified.

The identification of these uncertainties provides a basis for the sustained critical reflection needed to interrupt the familiar containment of multilingualism and the habitual domestication of postcolonial re-workings of ELT. Through analysis of these dilemmas, linguistic, cultural, and educational entrepreneurs in the ELT industry may illuminate the connections between the expectations of everyday teaching practices and a critical orientation to globalisation/localisation, ethical transnational ELT business development, and the opportunities the risks of language extinction and knowledge death present for innovation. In all of this, we have only just begun to confront the problematic situation of critiquing ELT and engaging in the appropriation of English and its teaching.

It is important to resist the idea of "appropriating ELT" as a finished project or one that can be coherently and comprehensively put into a single educational framework or entrepreneurial product. Likewise, we cannot tie our ideas about the transnational ELT industry unquestionably to the fetishes of the neo-liberal political ideology of economic globalism. The teaching of English as part of the economic project of Anglo-American engagement with Asia, Africa, Latin America, or Eastern Europe is not educationally worthwhile if it merely (re)produces neo-colonial relationships. Rather than providing a solid foundation or unchanging basis on which English language teachers can conduct their work, the tactical appropriation of English foreshadows innovative possibilities which will project us into unanticipated situations. Nevertheless, the contemporary technological prescriptions, market-driven imperatives, and programmes for globalising English by Anglophone nations do not exhaust all possibilities of what ELT businesses might do and what it is possible to do.

The commodification, globalisation, and technologisation of ELT impose marked limitations on what is possible, so we have to productively negotiate with these in order to secure any opportunities for the appropriation of English, the future development of postcolonial ELT, and the sustainability of global multilingualism. In this context, then, it is wrong to dogmatically condemn ELT businesses for their neo-liberal economic orientation, or their reproduction of colonialist and colonising English, or their belated attention to linguistic rights and endangered languages. Despite this they are the sites where colonialist and colonising ELT practices and policies can be critiqued and translated by tactics of appropriation. Certainly, there is some discomfort with the economic reductionist sentiments of the ELT industry and at times its rather self-conscious support for transnational capitalism. But the business of ELT can also be understood in a way that places this important educational work in a whole range of contested traditions. Not the least being that tradition which has appropriated English as a tactic of resistance to linguistic imperialism. This creates possibilities for considering how ELT has become attached to elite political and ideological functions across the nations of the world, and how ELT might be otherwise situated through its appropriation.

Bibliography

Abbott, G. "Understanding one another's Englishes." *World Language English* 1, 1 (1997): 1–4.

Achebe, C. "The African writer and the English language." In *Colonial Discourse and Post-colonial Theory,* edited by P. Williams and L. Chrisman New York: Columbia University Press, 1994.

Ahmad, S. *Malaysia's Vision 2020: Understanding the Concept, Implications and Challenges.* Kuala Lumpur: Pelanduk Publications, 1993.

Appadurai, A. *Modernity at Large: Cultural Dimensions of Globalisation.* Minneapolis: Universitiy of Minnesota Press, 1996.

Apple, M. *Cultural Politics and Education.* Buckingham: Open University Press, 1996.

———. *Educating the "Right" Way: Markets, Standards, God, and Inequality.* New York: Routledge Falmer, 2001.

Aronowitz, S. and H. Giroux. *Education Still Under Siege.* London: Bergin & Garvey, 1993.

Athletics Australia. *Information Release,* 8th June 2000.

Auerbach, E. "Reexamining English only in the ESL classroom." *TESOL Quarterly* 27, 1 (1993) http://www.ncbe.gwu.edu.

Axford, B. *The Global System: Economic, Politics and Culture.* Cambridge: Polity Press, 1995.

Bahhrin, S. and S. Wickham. *The Raja Bahrin Story.* Kuala Lumpur: Times, 1997.

Baker, M., J. Creedy and D. Johnson. *Financing and Effects of Internationalisation in Higher Education: An Australian Country Study.* Canberra: AGPS, 1995.

Baucom, I. *Out of Place: Englishness, Empire and the Locations of Identity.* Princeton (NJ): Princeton University Press, 1999.

Beck, U. *World Risk Society.* Cambridge: Polity Press, 1999.

Berita Harian: Editorial. 11th November 1999, p. 6.

Borrie, W. "Australia and the world in transition." In *A White Australia: Australia's Population Problem,* edited by W. Borrie, G. Cuthbert, G. Wood, H. Harris and A. Elkin. Sydney: Australian Publishing, 1947.

Brine, J. *Under Educating Women: Globalising Inequality.* Buckingham: Open University Press, 1999.

The British Council Malaysia. (a) *British Programmes in Malaysia—Education. Memorandum of Understanding 1999.* 14th May 2000 (updated) http://www.britishcouncil.org/malaysia/Education/ECS/FAQ/BPMal.htm. 13th June 1999 (visited).

"Calls to master English hailed." *The New Straits Times,* 3rd January 2001, p. 3.

Canagarajah, A. S. *Resisting Linguistic Imperialism in English Teaching.* Oxford: Oxford University Press, 1999.

Carr, K. *Commonwealth of Australia Parliamentary Debates Senate—2000 Archive.* 2nd March 2001 (updated). www.aph.gov.au/hansard/ hanssen.htm. 16th March 2001 (visited).

Case, W. "The Anwar Trial and Its Wider Implications." Paper presented as part of the 2nd Australia Malaysia Conference, Australian National University, Canberra, May, 2000.

Chai, H. C. *Education and Nation Building in Plural Societies: The West Malaysian Experience.* Canberra: Development Studies Centre, The Australian National University, 1977.

Chu, H. "Tian-ah! Kenny bei guagiao!" *The Age (Green Guide),* 4th January 2001, p. 9.

Colebrook, R. "Linguistic and cultural considerations of writing ELT texts for use in Asia." In *ESP in Southeast Asia,* edited by T. Crooks, 1–16. Melbourne: Defence Force Training Centre, 1996.

Conhaim, W. "The Internet: The digital divide." *Link-Up,* July/August (2000): 5–8.

Cope, B., and M. Kalantzis. "E-learning in higher education." In *Literacy Matters: Issues for New Times,* edited by M. Kalantzis and A. Pandian. Sydney: Common Ground, 2001.

———. eds. *Multiliteracies: Literacy Learning and the Design of Social Futures.* South Yarra (Vic): Macmillan Publishers Australia Pty Ltd, 2000.

Crystal, D. *English as a Global Language.* Cambridge: Cambridge University Press, 1997.

———. *Language Death.* Cambridge: Cambridge University Press, 2000.

Curriculum Development Centre. *Curriculum Specifications for Smart Schools. English KBSR-KBSM.* Kuala Lumpa: Ministry of Education, 1997.

Daly, M., and M. Logan. *Reconstructing Asia: The Economic Miracle That Never Was, The Future That Is.* Melbourne: RMIT Press, 1999.

Davis, J., T. Hirschl and M. Stack. *Cutting Edge: Technology, Information, Capitalism and Social Revolution.* New York: Verso, 1997.

Department of Education. *Situational English for Newcomers to Australia Part 3, Teachers Book.* Canberra: Australian Government Publishing Service, 1975.

DETYA. *Australian Education: International Overseas Student Statistics 1999.* Canberra: Commonwealth of Australia, 2000.

Dicker, S. "Ten official English-only arguments and counter-arguments." Unpublished manuscript, CUNY: Hostos Community College, 1996.

Dogancay-Aktuna, S. "The spread of English in Turkey and its current sociolinguistic profile." *Journal of Multilingual and Multicultural Development* 19, 1 (1998): 24–39.

duGay, P., S. Hall, L. James, H. Mackay, and Keith Negus. *Doing Cultural Studies: The Story of the Sony Walkman.* London: Sage, 1997.

Dunkin, R. "Introduction." In *Teaching and Learning Strategy: 2000–2002.* Melbourne: Office of the Pro-Vice Chancellor (Teaching and Learning), RMIT University, 2000.

2nd March 2001 (updated). www.Teaching.rmit.edu. au/#intro. 23rd March 2001 (visited).

Eggerton, H. *British Colonial Policy in the Twentieth Century*. London: Methuen, 1921.

Etchells, C. "Teaching Experience." *Green EFL*. (1995): 1.

Falk, R. *Predatory Globalisation: A Critique*. Cambridge: Polity Press, 1999.

Featherstone, M. *Undoing Culture: Globalisation, Postmodernism and Identity*. London: Sage, 1995.

Fitzgerald, S. *Is Australia an Asian Country? Can Australia Survive in an East Asian Future*. St. Leonards (NSW): Allen & Unwin, 1997.

Fox Sport. 22nd January 1999.

Francis, J. "A simple sorry may end big row down under," *The Sunday Star* 9th April 2000, p. 34.

Franklin, R. "When Bush speaks, the English language trembles," *The Sunday Age* 17th December 2000, p. 9.

Gaudart, H. "English language teaching in Malaysia: A historical account." *MELTA The English Teacher* 16th December (1987).

Giddens, A. Beyond Left and Right: The Future of Radical Politics. Cambridge: Polity Press, 1994.

Gill, S. (ed.). *Gramsci,Historical Materialism and International Relations: Cambridge Studies in International Relations: 26*. Cambridge: Cambridge University Press, 1993.

Golingai, P. "A particle from our past: The lingo tango," *The Star* 6th April 2000, pp. 3–4.

Goodwin, J. *Akira Kurosawa and Intertextual Cinema*. Baltimore: Johns Hopkins University Press, 1994.

Graddol, D. *The Future of English? A Guide for Forecasting the Popularity of the English Langauge in the 21st Century*. London: British Council, 1997.

———. "The decline of the native speaker." In *English in a Changing World*, edited by D. Graddol and U. Mienhof. Guildford (UK): Cathcline/AILA Review 13, 1999.

Hardjono, S. *White Tribe of Asia: An Indonesian View of Australia*. Melbourne: Hyland House, 1994.

Harrington, J., S. Palethorpe and C. Watson "Does the Queen speak the Queen's English?" *Nature* 408, 21, 28th December (2000): 927.

Harris, G., and G. Jarrett. *Educating Overseas Students in Australia: Who Benefits*. Sydney: Allen & Unwin, 1990.

Harris, S. *Two Way Aboriginal Schooling; Education and Cultural Survival*. Canberra: Aboriginal Studies Press, 1990.

Hobsbawm, E. *The Age of Extremes: A History of the World, 1914-1991*. New York: Pantheon, 1994.

hooks, b. (aka G. Watkins). *Teaching to Transgress: Education as the Practice of Freedom*. New York: Routledge, 1994.

"Howard moves to change racist laws." *New Straits Times* 11th April 2000, p. 18.

Human Rights Commission. *Bringing Them Home*. Canberra: AGPS, 1997.

Human Rights and Equal Opportunity Commission. *Racist Violence: Report of the National Inquiry into Racist Violence in Australia*. Canberra: AGPS, 1991.

Hunt, N. "Using technology to prepare teachers for the twenty-first century," *Asia-Pacific Journal of Teacher Education* 25, 3 (1997): 345–350.

Ismail, R. "Globalisation revisited." In *Language and Globalisation,* edited by H. Wong, S. Nair-Venugopal, N. Maarof, Z. Yahya and J. D'Cruz. Petaling Jaya: Pearson Educational, 2000.

Jesudasoon, J. "The syncretic state and the structure of opposition politics in Malaysia." In *Political Oppositions in the Industrialised Asia,* edited by R. Roden. London: Routledge, 1996.

Johnson, R. "What Is Cultural Studies Anyway?" Working paper, University of Birmingham: Centre for Contemporary Cultural Studies, 1983.

Kell, P. "Teaching in the fast lane: Fast capitalism, knowledge, labor and organisations in vocational education and training." *Education Links* Winter 55 (1997): 24–27.

———. *From Billabong to the Mainstream? A Teachers' Guide to Australian Training and Literacy Policy Developments from 1974–1998.* Brisbane: NLLIA, 1998.

———. "Working the market: Shifting boundaries and practices in VET." *Fine Print, A Journal of Adult Language Literacy and Education.* Summer Edition, (1999): 8–11.

———. *Good Sports: Australian Sport and the Myth of the Fair Go.* Sydney: Pluto Press, 2000.

Kell, P., J. Balatti, and S. Muspratt. "The private, public and open training markets: A study of private training providers in regional north Queensland." *Australian Educational Researcher* 24, 2 (1997): 43–59.

Kell, P., J. Balatti, S. Muspratt, and A. Hill. "Mapping Teachers Work Charting New Futures." Paper presented as part of the 5th International Literacy and Education Research Network Conference, Alice Springs, 24–26 September 1997.

Kementerian Pendidkan Malaysia. *Huraian Sukatan Pelajaran: Bahasa Inggeris.* Kuala Lumpur: Dewan Bahasa dan Pustaka, 1990.

———. *Huraian Sukatan Pelajaran: Bahasa Inggeris.* Kuala Lumpur: Dewan Bahasa dan Pustaka, 1991.

———. *Huraian Sukatan Pelajaran: Bahasa Inggeris.* Kuala Lumpur: Dewan Bahasa dan Pustaka, 1994.

———. *Huraian Sukatan Pelajaran: Bahasa Inggeris KBSM*, edisi Sekolah Bestari, Pusat Perkembangan Kurikulum. (Disember) 1998.

———. *Kurikulum Bersepadu Sekolah Menengah (KBSM)—Huraian Sukatan Pelajaran: Sastera Dalam Bahasa Inggeris—Tingkatan 6.* Kuala Lumpur: Dewan Bahasa dan Pustaka, 1999.

Kenway, J. "Reality bytes: Education, markets and the information superhighway." *Australian Education Researcher.* 22, 1 (1995): 35–65.

Kitley, P,, and W. Mules. "The Flor Contemplacion case as a media event." In *Foreign Devils and Other Journalists,* edited by D. Kingsbury, E. Loo and P. Payne, 77–94. Monash University: Monash Asia Institute, 2000.

"Klan takes hold in Australia," *The Star* 3rd June 1999.

Koh, E. K. *Education for Unity in Malaya.* Chicago, Illinois: National Sunday School Assn. Commission on Research in Christian Education, 1967.

Lankshear, C., I. Snyder and B. Green. *Teachers and Techno-literacy: Managing Literacy, Technology and Learning in Schools.* St. Leonards, NSW: Allen and Unwin, 2000.

Lee, M. "Corporatisation, privatisation and internationalisation of higher education in Malaysia." Paper presented as part of the The Role of Private Higher Education in the

21st Century conference, Boston College, MA, USA, 27–30 May, 1998.

———. *Private Higher Education in Malaysia.* Penang: Universiti Sains Malaysia, 1999.

Lepani, B. "Future Directions in VET: Implications for TAFE staff." Paper presented as part of the ATMA Conference, Coffs Harbour, September, 1996.

———. *Vocational Education and Training VET 2005: A Discussion Paper on the Roles and Competencies of the VET Teacher in the Year 2005.* University of Sydney, NSW: Report by ACIIC, Engineering Faculty, 1995.

The Lesser-Used Languages Software Developers' Association. 24th March 1998 (updated) http://www.egt.ie/lulsda/. 23rd March 2001 (visited).

Lo Bianco, J. "The big and future picture(s)." *Prospect* 11, 2 (1996): 5–14.

———."Hard option, soft co-option; Is that all there is to languages in schools." *Education Australia* 31 (1995): 9–12.

———. "Policy words: Talking bilingual education and ESL into English literacy." *Prospect* 14, 2 (1999): 40–51.

Lockard, J. "Babel machines and electronic universalism." In *Race in Cyberspace,* edited by B. Kolko, L. Nakamura and G. Rodman. New York: Routledge, 2000.

Loh Kok Wah. "Post NEP politics in Malaysia, Ferment and Fragmentation." Paper presented as part of the 2nd Australia Malaysia Conference, Australian National University, Canberra, May 2000.

Luke, A. "Getting our hands dirty: Provisional policies in postmodern conditions." In *After Postmodernism: Education, Politics and Identity,* edited by R. Smith and R. Wexler. London: Falmer Press, 1995.

MacDonald, J. "Sham students sent home after visa rort." *The Age,* February 2000, 17.

Macedo, D. "English only: The tongue-tying of America." *Journal of Education* 173, 2 (1991): 9–20.

———. "The colonialism of the English only movement." *Educational Researcher* 29, 3 (2000): 15–24.

Mahathir, M. *The Malay Dilemma.* Kuala Lumpur: Time Books, 1970.

———. "When the ugliness of capitalism reveals itself." *The Star* 30th September 1999, pp. 19, 21.

———. *The Australian* 17th May 2000, p. 1.

Malaya (Federation). *Report of the Education Committee, 1956 (The Razak Report).* Kuala Lumpur: Government Press, 1958.

Malaya (Federation). *The Report on The Barnes Report on Malay Education and Fenn-Wu Report on Chinese Vernacular Schools.* Kuala Lumpur: Government Press, 1951.

Malaysia. *Education Act 1995—all amendments up to March, 1996.* Kuala Lumpur: MDC, 1996.

Malaysia. *Higher Educational Institutional Act—all amendments up to October 1996.* Kuala Lumpur: International Law Book Services, 1996.

Malaysia. *The National Accreditation Board Act, 1996.* 14th December 1999 (updated). www2.moe.gov.my/-lan/ 29th January 2001 (visited).

Malaysia (Kementerian Pendidikan). *Report on the Implementation of the Recomendations of the Education Review Committee, 1960 (The Rahman Talib Report).* Kuala Lumpur: Dewan Bahasa Dan Pustaka, 1971.

Malaysian Government (Economic Planning Unit—Prime Minister's Department). *The*

Seventh Malaysia Plan 1996–2000. Kuala Lumpur: Percetakan Nasional Malaysia Berhad, 1996.

McArthur, T. *The English Languages*. Cambridge: Cambridge University Press, 1998.

McCarthy, C. *The Uses of Culture: Education and the Limits of Ethnic Affiliation.* New York: Routledge, 1998.

Mignalo, W. "Globalisation, civilisation processes and the relocation of languages and cultures." In *The Cultures of Globalisation,* edited by F. Jameson and M. Miyoshi. North Carolina: Duke University Press, 1998.

Mohamed Amin Embi. "Classroom based teacher research: Can it promote educational excellence?" *Journal Penyelidikan Pendidikan* 1 (1999): 29–39.

Moore, H. "Blurred vision: Linguistic pluralism or economic rationalism." *Education Australia* 31 (1995): 15.

Morley, D., and K. Robins. *Spaces of Identity*. London: Routledge, 1995.

The Most Clearing House on Linguistic Rights. 24th April 1998 (updated). (http://www.unesco.org/most/ln1.htm) 23rd March 2001 (visited).

"Moves to Prevent the Erosion of English," *The Straits Times* 29th October 1999, p. 1.

Nair-Venugopal, S. *Language Choice and Communication in Malaysian Business*. Bangi: Penerbit Universiti Kebangsaan Malaysia, 2000.

Nakamura, L. "Where do you want to go today? Cybernetic tourism, the Internet, and transnationality." In *Race in Cyberspace,* edited by B. Kolko, L. Nakamura and G. Rodman. New York: Routledge, 2000.

Nakata, M. "History, cultural diversity and English language teaching." In *Multiliteracies: Literacy Learning and the Design of Social Futures,* edited by B. Cope and M. Kalantzis. South Yarra (Vic): Macmillan Publishers Australia Pty Ltd, 2000.

Nathan, D. *Arabana to Yugambeh. Aboriginal Languages of Australia.* 11th March, 2001 (updated) www.dnathan.com/VL/austLang.htm. 23rd March 2001 (visited).

Nettle, D., and S. Romaine. *Vanishing Voices: The Extinction of the World's Languages.* Oxford: Oxford University Press, 2000.

Newbrook, M. "Which English? Institutionalised second-language varieties of English in Asia and the implications for educators: The cases of Singapore and Hong Kong." *Journal of Intercultural Studies* 14, 1 (1993): 1–17.

New Sunday Times 11th December 2000, p. 27.

Nicholls, C., and J. Nungarrayi. "The Little Red Hen and Her Friends: The Lajamanu School Bi Lingual Literacy Program." *Education Australia* 31 (1995): 9–20

Noonan,G. and A. Contractor. "The new import export trade" *The Age* 20th January 2001, p. 5.

Omar, A. *Language and Society in Malaysia.* Kuala Lumpur: Dewan Bahasa & Pustaka, 1982.

Osmond, W. "Downer toys with British Council idea." *Campus Review* 9, 8 (1999): 3.

Ow, J. "The revenge of the yellow-faced cyborg: The rape of digital geishas and the colonisation of cyber-coolies in 3D realms' Shadow Warrior." In *Race in Cyberspace,* edited by B. Kolko, L. Nakamura and G. Rodman. New York: Routledge, 2000.

Padilla, A. "English only vs. bilingual education: Ensuring a language-competent society." *Journal of Education* 173, 2 (1991): 38–51.

Pakir, A. "Linguistic alternants and code selection in Baba Malay." *World Englishes* 8, 3

(1989): 379–388.

Pandian A. *Global Literacy: Vision, Revisions and Vistas in Education*. Serdang Malaysia: Universiti Putra Malaysia Press, 1999.

Palfreeman, A. C. *The Administration of the White Australia Policy*. Melbourne: Melbourne University Press, 1967.

———. *Literasi Dalam Pendidikan: Perubahan & Cabaran*. Kuala Lumpur: CEDC, 1999b.

———. "K-English Teachers, K-Society and K-Economy." Paper presented at Malaysian International Conference on English Language Teaching (MICELT) organised by Universiti Putra Malaysia, Serdang on 15–17 May in Malacca, Malaysia. 2000.

Pennycook, A. *English and the Discourses of Colonialism*. London: Routledge, 1998.

———. *The Cultural Politics of English as an International Language*. London: Longman, 1994.

Phillipson, R. "Realities and myths of linguistic imperialism." *Journal of Multilingual and Multicultural Development* 18, 3 (1997): 238–247.

Phillipson, R. and T. Skutnabb-Kangas. "Englishisation: One dimension of globalisation." In *English in a Changing World*, edited by D. Graddol and U. Mienhof. Guildford (UK): Cathcline/AILA Review 13, 1999.

Platt, J., and M. L. Ho. "Discourse particles in Singaporean English—Substratum influence and universals." *World Englishes* 8, 2 (1989): 215–221.

Rachod, S. *Women's Net*. www.womensnet.org.za/ humanrights.

Readings, B. *The University in Ruins*. Cambridge: Harvard University Press, 1996.

Riddell, C. "University funding: Disastrous to our profession." *Literacy Links* April (2000): 3.

Ritzer, G. *The McDonaldisation of Society: An Investigation into the Changing Character of Contemporary Social Life* (rev. ed.). Thousand Oaks: Pine Forge Press, 1996.

Robertson, R. *Globalisation: Social Theory and Global Culture*. London: Sage, 1992.

Rudd, K. "Creating an Asian-literate Australia." In *Living with Dragons: Australia Confronts Its Asian Destiny*, edited by G. Sheridan. St. Leonards, NSW: Allen & Unwin, 1995.

Rushdie, S. *Imaginary Homelands: Essays and Criticism 1981–1991*. London: Granta, 1991.

Said, E. *Orientalism*. London: Penguin, 1978.

———. *Culture and Imperialism*. London: Chetto & Windus, 1993.

Schofield, A. "Malaysian national culture and foreign relations with Australia." In *Foreign Devils and Other Journalists*, edited by D. Kingsbury, E. Loo and P. Payne. 229–254. Monash University: Monash Asia Institute, 2000.

Sheil, P. "Broadcaster Minds Its ABC." *The Australian*, 11th May 2000, p. 8.

Singh, M. "Becoming socially critical: literacy, knowledge and counter-construction." Australian Journal of Reading 11, 3 (1988): 155–164.

———. "Internationalising educators' work." *Discourse* 19, 3 (1998a): 379–389.

———. "Globalism, cultural diversity and tertiary education." *Australian Universities' Review* 41, 2 (1998b): 12–17.

———. "Innovation in TESOL provision: Local responses and engagements in globalisation." *Education Australia Journal* 18, 1 (2000): 12–21.

———. "Multilingual applications and possibilities with digital technology." In *Creator to Consumer in a Digital Age: Australian Book Production in Transition,* edited by B. Cope and D. Mason. Seaholme (Vic.): Common Ground, 2001a. 223–248.

———. "Championing a cosmopolitan language policy: In *Literacy Matters: Issues for New Times,* edited by M. Kalantzis and A. Pandian. Sydney: Common Ground, 2001b.

Singh, M. and J. Greenlaw. "Postcolonial theory in the literature classroom: Contrapuntal readings." *Theory into Practice* 37, 3 (1998): 193–202.

Singh, M., B. Harreveld and N. Hunt. *Virtual Flexibility: Adult Literacy and New Technologies in Remote Communities.* Brisbane, Queensland: Adult English Language, Literacy and Numeracy Council, 1997.

Singh, M. and L. Singh. "Global/local Englishes: Building intercultural competence for global/local markets." In *Striving for the Third Space: Intercultural Competence through Language Education,* edited by J. Lo Bianco, A. Liddicoat, and C. Crozet. Melbourne: Language Australia, 1999.

Smart School Project Team. *Smart School Conceptual Blueprint.* Kuala Lumpur: Government of Malaysia, 1997.

Straits Settlements Committee. *Report of a Committee Apppointed to Enquire into the System of Vernacular Education in the Colony.* Paper prepared for the Legislative Council as requested by the Governor. 1894.

The Sun 21st December 2000, p. 7

The Sun, "'Critical thinking' questions should not be blamed for drop in English language passes." 22nd December 2000, p.4

Taylor, C. "The language of the Web." *Far Eastern Economic Review* 7th December (2000): 68–69.

Taylor, P. *The Texts of Paulo Freire.* Buckingham: Open University Press, 1993.

Thiong'o, N. "The language of African literature." In *Colonial Discourse and Post-colonial Theory,* edited by P. Williams and L. Chrisman. New York: Columbia University Press, 1994.

Turner, B. *Orientalism, Postmodernism and Globalism.* London: Routledge, 1994.

Viswanathan, G. "The beginnings of English literary study in British India." In *'Race,' Culture and Difference,* edited by J. Donald and A. Rattansi. London: Sage, 1992.

Wallraff, B. "What global language? Don't bet on the triumph of English." *The Atlantic Monthly,* 286, 5 (2000): 52–66.

Warschauer, W. *Electronic Literacies: Language, Culture, and Power in Online Education.* Mahwah, NJ: Lawrence Erlbaum, 1999.

Warschauer, M. "Language, identity and the Internet." In *Race in Cyberspace,* edited by B. Kolko, L. Nakamura and G. Rodman. New York: Routledge, 2000.

Waters, M. *Globalisation.* London: Routledge, 1995.

Williams, B. *Overseas Students in Australia, Policy and Practice.* Canberra: IDP, 1989.

Williams, R. *Toward 2000.* London: Chatto & Windus, 1983.

———. *The Long Revolution.* London: Pelican, 1965.

Williamson-Fien, J. "Constructing Asia: Foucauldian Explorations of Asian Studies in Australia." (Unpublished PhD thesis). St. Lucia (Qld): University of Queensland, 2000.

Wilmoth, P. "Speaking the Language of Chairman Stan", *The Age,* 20 March, 1999.

Winant, H. "Racial formation and hegemony: Global and local developments." In *Racism, Modernity & Identity,* edited by A. Rattansi and S. Westwood. Cambridge: Polity Press, 1994.

Woolcott, R. "A few notes shy of a symphony." *The Australian* 26th January 2000, p. 15.

Woolgar, S. "Virtual society? Beyond the hype?" (www.virtualsociety.org.uk) 1st July, 2000 (visited).

Yahya, Z. "National language and literature: Necessary boundaries in a globalised world", In *Language and Globalisation,* edited by H. Wong, S. Nair-Venugopal, N. Maarof, Z. Yahya and J. D'Cruz. Petaling Jaya: Pearson Educational, 2000.

Yardley, R. "CEO acumen multimedia, Melbourne." *The Sunday Age* 10th December 2000, p. 6.

Zhenhua, H. "The impact of globalisation on English in Chinese universities", In *English in a Changing World (The AILA Review 13),* edited by D. Graddol and U. Mienhof. Guildford (UK): Association Internationale de Linguistique Appliquee, 1999.

Index

J

K

L

M

new literacies ¶

AND DIGITAL EPISTEMOLOGIES

Colin Lankshear, Michele Knobel, Chris Bigum, & Michael Peters
General Editors

New literacies and new knowledges are being invented "in the streets" as people from all walks of life wrestle with new technologies, shifting values, changing institutions, and new structures of personality and temperament emerging in a global informational age. These new literacies and ways of knowing remain absent from classrooms. Many education administrators, teachers, teacher educators, and academics seem largely unaware of them. Others actively oppose them. Yet, they increasingly shape the engagements and worlds of young people in societies like our own. The *New Literacies and Digital Epistemologies* series will explore this terrain with a view to informing educational theory and practice in constructively critical ways.

For further information about the series and submitting manuscripts, please contact:

Dr. Colin Lankshear
"Papeleria Garabatos"
Av Universidad #1894, Local 1
Col. Oxtopulco Universidad
Mexico City, CP 04310 MEXICO
Fax 1-508-267 1287
c.lankshear@yahoo.com